Student Companion to

Edith
WHARTON

**Recent Titles in
Student Companions to Classic Writers**

Jane Austen *by Debra Teachman*

Charlotte and Emily Brontë *by Barbara Z. Thaden*

Charles Dickens *by Ruth Glancy*

F. Scott Fitzgerald *by Linda C. Pelzer*

Nathaniel Hawthorne *by Melissa McFarland Pennell*

Ernest Hemingway *by Lisa Tyler*

Zora Neale Hurston *by Josie P. Campbell*

Arthur Miller *by Susan C. W. Abbotson*

George Orwell *by Mitzi M. Brunsdale*

Edgar Allan Poe *by Tony Magistrale*

John Steinbeck *by Cynthia Burkhead*

Mark Twain *by David E. E. Sloane*

Tennessee Williams *by Nancy M. Tischler*

Richard Wright *by Robert Felgar*

Student Companion to
Edith
WHARTON

Melissa McFarland Pennell

Student Companions to Classic Writers

Greenwood Press
Westport, Connecticut • London

Library of Congress Cataloging-in-Publication Data

Pennell, Melissa McFarland.
  Student companion to Edith Wharton / Melissa McFarland Pennell.
    p. cm.—(Student companions to classic writers, ISSN 1522-7979)
  Includes bibliographical references (p.) and index.
  ISBN 0-313-31715-1 (alk. paper)
    1. Wharton, Edith, 1862-1937—Criticism and interpretation—Handbooks,
manuals, etc.   2. Women and literature—United States—History—20th
century—Handbooks, manuals, etc.   I. Title.   II. Series.
PS3545.H16 Z76 2003
813'.52—dc21   2002032076

British Library Cataloguing in Publication Data is available.

Library of Congress Catalog Card Number: 2002032076
ISBN: 0-313-31715-1
ISSN: 1522-7979

First published in 2003

Greenwood Press, 88 Post Road West, Westport, CT 06881
An imprint of Greenwood Publishing Group, Inc.
www.greenwood.com

Printed in the United States of America

The paper used in this book complies with the
Permanent Paper Standard issued by the National
Information Standards Organization (Z39.48-1984).

10 9 8 7 6 5 4 3 2 1

For my parents,
John and Rosalie McFarland

Contents

Series Foreword

This series has been designed to meet the needs of students and general readers for accessible literary criticism on the classic American and world writers most frequently studied and read in the secondary school, community college, and four-year college classroom. Unlike other works of literary criticism that are written for the specialist and graduate student, or that feature a variety of reprinted scholarly essays on sometimes obscure aspects of the writer's work, the Student Companions to Classic Writers series is carefully crafted to examine each writer's major works fully and in a systematic way, at the level of the nonspecialist and general reader. The objective is to enable the reader to gain a deeper understanding of the work and to apply critical thinking skills to the act of reading. The proven format for the volumes in this series was developed by an advisory board of teachers and librarians for a successful series published by Greenwood Press, Critical Companions to Popular Contemporary Writers. Responding to their request for easy to use, yet challenging literary criticism for students and adult library patrons, Greenwood Press developed a systematic format that is not intimidating but helps the reader to develop the ability to analyze literature.

How does this work? Each volume in the Student Companions to Classic Writers series is written by a subject specialist, an academic who understands students' needs for basic and yet challenging examination of the writer's canon. Each volume begins with a biographical chapter, drawn from published sources, biographies and autobiographies, which relates the writer's life to his or her work. The next chapter examines the writer's literary heritage, tracing the literary influences of other writers on that writer and explaining and discussing the literary genres into which the writer's work falls. Each of the following chapters examines a major work by the writer, those works most frequently read and studied by high school and college students. Depending on the writer's canon, generally between four and eight major works are examined, each in an individual chapter. The discussion of each work is organized into separate sections on plot development, character development, and major themes. Literary devices and style, narrative point of view, and historical setting are also discussed in turn if pertinent to the work. Each chapter concludes with an alternate critical perspective from which to read the work, such as a psychological or feminist criticism. The critical theory is defined briefly in easy, comprehensible language for the student. Looking at the literature from the point of view of a particular critical approach will help the reader to understand and apply critical theory to the act of reading and analyzing literature.

Of particular value in each volume is the bibliography, which includes a complete bibliography of the writer's work, a selected bibliography of biographical and critical works suitable for students, and lists of reviews of each work examined in the companion, both from the time the literature was originally published and from contemporary sources, all of which will be helpful to readers, teachers, and librarians who would like to consult additional sources.

As a source of literary criticism for the student or for the general reader, this series will help the reader to gain understanding of the writer's work and skill in critical reading.

Preface

As one of the most accomplished American writers in the early decades of the twentieth century, Edith Wharton achieved critical recognition and popular acclaim. The *Student Companion to Edith Wharton* provides an introduction to Wharton's fiction for readers who may know her best as the author of *Ethan Frome*, inviting them to consider the broader range of her work. Beginning with Wharton's life and career, the discussion places her within the context of her times, focusing on how Wharton was shaped by and reacted to the culture around her. The chapters on Wharton's fiction address short stories, novellas, and novels. The comments on the short stories focus on some of the best known and most frequently anthologized of Wharton's tales. The chapter on novellas looks closely at two works written during different periods of Wharton's career, *Madame de Treymes* (1907) and *The Old Maid* (1924). The chapters on the novels treat *The House of Mirth*, *Ethan Frome*, *Summer*, and *The Age of Innocence*.

Each chapter provides background material to assist the student and the general reader in understanding and interpreting Wharton's work. The biographical chapter provides an overview of Wharton's life, from her childhood in New York City to her final years in France. The chapter on her career traces Wharton's development as an author, her contributions to travel writing as well as to the short story and the novel, and her influence on contemporary and later writers. In examining the fiction itself, the chapters that follow feature close readings of texts that include analysis of setting, plot development, character development, and themes. Discussions of point of view, symbolism, and allusions appear where appropriate. The chapters on the novellas and novels also feature alternative readings that introduce critical approaches to fiction, including feminist criticism, new historicism, and cultural studies. These alternative readings demonstrate how varied approaches reveal greater complexity in Wharton's work. Lastly, the bibliography provides information on Wharton's published works, biographies, contemporary reviews, and recent critical studies.

Acknowledgments

I wish to acknowledge the University of Massachusetts, Lowell, for support of my research. I thank my colleagues, especially Mary Kramer and Todd Avery, for their generous assistance. Thanks, also, to the students in my courses, whose questions and insights helped to shape this volume, especially Rena DiLando and Niamh Brady. My heartfelt appreciation goes, as always, to my husband, Steve, for his countless gestures of support and encouragement that make all things possible.

The Life of Edith Wharton

Tradition, heritage, and exclusivity—these defined Old New York society in the mid-nineteenth century. Into this world of privilege and decorum, Edith Newbold Jones was born on January 24, 1862. The youngest of three children and only daughter of George Frederic and Lucretia Rhinelander Jones, Edith enjoyed the benefits of her family's station in life but chafed against the restrictions it placed upon her. From her childhood on, literature became for her, both as a reader and a writer, a means of escaping these limitations.

Edith's parents were descendents of old New York and New England families, tracing their lineage to early English and Dutch settlers. George Frederic Jones was a gentleman of leisure whose inherited real estate holdings in Manhattan and Brooklyn generated the income upon which his family lived. Lucretia Rhinelander Jones, whose family had suffered financial distress after her father's death, enjoyed the pleasures of clothing, jewelry, and travel that her husband's income provided. During Edith's childhood, her parents lived by a code of decorous reserve, but Edith was fascinated by tales of her parents' courtship. One story in particular made a strong impression upon her, that of George Jones's creation of an improvised sailboat that enabled him to meet Lucretia near her family's home. Edith later used this episode to create a scene in her novella *False Dawn* (1924). Part of the episode's appeal for her may have been the inventiveness and spontaneity that seemed absent from her parents' marriage.

Like others in their social circle, the Jones family visited Europe, often living there for extended periods when economic conditions in the United States made Europe a more affordable choice. Such was the case in 1866 when real estate values fell after the Civil War. George Frederic Jones leased his homes in New York and Newport and moved his family first to Rome, then Paris. Edith spent much of her childhood absorbing the atmosphere of Italy, France, and, later, Germany. This early exposure to Europe fostered what became an abiding interest in travel in Edith's adulthood.

A bright and inquisitive child, Edith began making up stories at an early age, indulging her gift of imagination and her early facility with language. While her family lived in Paris, Edith's father taught her to read, opening the world of books to her. From an early age she was an avid reader, drawn to works such as Tennyson's *Idylls of the King,* as well as Lewis Carroll's *Alice's Adventures in Wonderland.* Unlike her brothers, who had received a formal education, Edith studied under the guidance of governesses. She preferred to read from her father's library, beginning what became a life-long habit of intellectual self-cultivation. This habit was held in check when her family returned from Europe in 1872. Her parents, especially her mother, intended that Edith should develop those attributes that would make her a success in their social world. Mrs. Jones discouraged her daughter's reading and writing, at one point dismissing Edith's earliest literary efforts with a rebuke (Lewis 30). Her mother's lack of enthusiasm heightened Edith's anxieties about the quality of her work and the appropriateness of her desire to write.

Despite this lack of maternal encouragement, at the age of fourteen Edith began her first sustained effort in fiction, a novella she entitled *Fast and Loose.* The manuscript included fabricated critical reviews, suggesting that she took her art seriously from the beginning. She shared this manuscript with her close friend Emelyn Washburn, but concealed its existence from her family. During this time Edith was also writing poems, an activity that her mother apparently found more acceptable as an appropriate feminine interest. With her mother's financial support, she had *Verses* (1878) privately printed in Newport. Family friends passed the volume along to Henry Wadsworth Longfellow, who sent it to William Dean Howells, then editor of the *Atlantic Monthly.* Howells selected a poem from the volume for publication in 1879.

While these early literary endeavors were important to her, Edith also followed the course expected of young women of her social status. She made her social debut at the end of 1879. Viewed as a significant moment in a young woman's life, this event for Edith was "a long cold agony of shyness" (Lewis 33). Entering society introduced Edith to the rituals of courtship and marriage that defined life for young women of her social circle. It also exposed her to the pressures of making a good match and to the power of gossip. While her own circumstances were quite different from those of Lily Bart in *The House of Mirth,* Edith's experience provided her with insights into the dilemmas that someone like Lily might face, adding to the realism and poignancy of the novel.

Courted by Henry Stevens of New York, a young man who enjoyed sports and social activity, Edith experienced her first sustained relationship. Her father's failing health caused the family to return to Europe in 1880, but Edith continued to see Henry, who visited the family in Venice in 1881 and stayed with them through George Frederic Jones's last illness in Cannes. Edith's father, after suffering paralysis, died in the spring of 1882, and the Jones family returned to America. Later that summer, Edith's engagement to Henry Stevens was announced in Newport. The engagement was broken, however, in October of that year, because Henry's mother did not approve of the match. Presumably Mrs. Stevens, a socially ambitious woman, believed her son could make a more advantageous union.

A broken engagement created socially awkward moments for Edith, but by early 1883 she was again attending events of the New York season. As she had in summers prior to her father's illness, Edith went with her family to Bar Harbor, Maine, another resort for the elite. There in 1883 she met Walter van Rensselaer Berry. Drawn to his intellectual ease and his aesthetic sense, Edith enjoyed being in his company. Their mutual attraction resulted in no engagement, however, and Berry's departure marked the start of his fourteen-year absence from Edith's life. This brief summer encounter laid the foundation for what was to become a significant friendship for both later in life.

During the remaining summer season of 1883 in Bar Harbor, Edith was visited by Edward (Teddy) Robbins Wharton, a friend of her brother Henry's and twelve years her senior. A sports and outdoor enthusiast, Teddy Wharton had little interest in the literary and intellectual questions that intrigued Edith, but he, like Henry Stevens, enjoyed the social life and activities of Newport and Bar Harbor. Teddy and Edith were married at Trinity Chapel in New York City on April 29, 1885. They promptly moved into Pencraig Cottage, a small house on the Jones estate in Newport, keeping Edith within the social sphere of her family. Initially the two seemed to enjoy a companionable marriage, if not a passionate one. Their failure to establish sexual intimacy, the result of Edith's ignorance and Teddy's inexperience, created a gulf between them that would become more significant over the years. This lack of intimacy may have spurred Wharton to seek intellectual companionship from men who formed parts of her social circle, while Teddy became her devoted traveling companion.

During the 1880s, Wharton turned her attention away from writing, as her personal life and the social duties that shaped it demanded her energies and time. A few in her circle of friends, especially Egerton Winthrop, encouraged her to read widely, not only in literature and in history but in the natural and social sciences. Winthrop introduced her to the works of Darwin, Huxley, and Spencer, natural and social scientists whose ideas provided the foundation for aspects of the naturalism that later influenced her fiction. Winthrop also encouraged her to develop a systematic approach to analyze what she read. He did not serve as a conventional literary mentor for Wharton, but he provided her with a plan for regular study absent from her earlier education.

In 1888 the Whartons spent nearly a year's income to take a three-month cruise among the islands of the Aegean sea, an expenditure their families thought foolish. The travels were invaluable for Wharton, who saw the trip as an extension of her critical study of European culture. Upon their return, Wharton learned that she had inherited, unexpectedly, a substantial legacy from a cousin, Joshua Jones. The money gave her a sense of independence from her family that she had not before enjoyed, enabling her and Teddy to buy their own home in New York as well as Land's End in Newport.

The year 1889 marked the return of Wharton's literary activity. She had poems accepted for publication by *Harper's, Scribner's,* and *Century* magazines and in 1890 had her short story "Mrs. Manstey's View" published in *Scribner's.* These successes inspired Wharton's continued efforts. By the end of 1893, she published the stories "That Good May Come," "The Fullness of Life," and "The Lamp of Pysche" in *Scribner's* and began work on additional pieces to form a collection. Following her visit to Italy in 1894, she also published an article in *Scribner's* on Italian art and landscape, the first of her many contributions to travel literature and cultural analysis. Wharton's appreciation of the visual arts and design influenced much of her writing. In 1896–97, she worked with Ogden Codman, an architect from Boston, to produce *The Decoration of Houses* (1897), a historical study of the relationship between interior design and architecture. Wharton was committed to the completion of this volume, but her partnership with Codman did not always function smoothly. Her renewed acquaintance with Walter Berry at this time proved an invaluable resource to her, as much for his encouragement as for any advice he gave her.

These accomplishments indicate the range of Wharton's interests and her desire to express herself in writing, but the 1890s proved a difficult decade. In 1890 Wharton began to suffer bouts of melancholy and nausea that often interfered with her work, culminating in a breakdown in 1898. She sought treatment for her condition in Philadelphia, where the physician S. Weir Mitchell had put into practice a regimen called the "rest cure" that entailed substantial meals, massage, and little physical or intellectual activity. Although Wharton did not receive formal treatment from Mitchell, aspects of her stay at the Stenton Hotel reflected his influence. She did, however, continue to read and write while undergoing the cure, something out of the ordinary for the Mitchell program. Wharton recovered but continued to have bouts of illness throughout her life.

For Wharton and her husband, travel often provided an outlet for their nervous energies and an escape from the pressures Wharton experienced over the publication of her work. Through her frequent travels in Europe, Wharton found a means of constructing a literary and artistic network that remained important to her until her death. Her early European circle included Violet Paget (an English author who published under the name Vernon Lee) and Paul Bourget (a French novelist Wharton had entertained in Newport) but quickly expanded to include Henry James. Through Bourget and James, Wharton entered the intellectual and literary circles of Paris and London. Many of the friends she made in Europe contributed to Wharton's continuing intellectual inquiries, often by introducing her to work by writers and philosophers, such as Friedrich Nietzsche, who would have a profound effect upon her thinking.

Although she spent increasing portions of each year overseas, Edith Wharton periodically returned to America. Hoping to find an environment in New England that would prove more healthful and invigorating than Newport, Wharton began to spend time in the Berkshires, primarily in Lenox, Massachusetts. In 1901 she purchased property there and had a house built for her, which she named The Mount. The Mount served as a social center for Wharton where she entertained members of the literary and intellectual circles important to her. During the decade that she owned the house, her guests included Brooks Adams, Walter Berry, Henry James, Howard Sturgis, Moncure Robinson, and Robert Grant, among others. Unfortunately, the Berkshires did not prove a healthful retreat for Teddy, who suffered his first nervous collapse in the fall of 1902, foreshadowing the long deterioration from mental illness that plagued the remaining twenty-six years of his life.

Fully immersed in the social facets of her life, Wharton was constantly at work on her writing as well. In 1899, *Scribner's* published Wharton's first short story collection, *The Greater Inclination,* which was well received. The following year, they published her novella *The Touchstone.* This marked the beginning of a remarkably productive period for Wharton. In 1901 she published another collection of stories, *Crucial Instances,* followed by her historical novel set in eighteenth-century Italy, *The Valley of Decision* (1902). In 1903 and 1904, Wharton published travel articles in *Century,* the novella *Sanctuary* in *Scribner's*, and another collection of stories, *The Descent of Man.* The appearance of her first New York novel, *The House of Mirth,* in 1905, established Wharton as a significant voice in American fiction. Buoyed by the critical and popular success of *The House of Mirth,* Wharton began work on her next major novel, *The Fruit of the Tree* (1907). This novel reflected Wharton's ambitions to chronicle the wider aspects of American life as she turned her attention to industrial production and labor reform. Following the publication of *The Fruit of the Tree,* Wharton began work on *The Custom of the Country* (1913), a novel that took her five years to complete. A complex narrative, this novel explores how its main character, Undine Spragg, uses multiple marriages to advance herself in the social hierarchy.

As her writing reflected greater complexity of subject and story, Wharton's personal life also became increasingly complicated. In 1907 she met a friend of Henry James, Morton Fullerton, then working as a journalist and correspondent in Paris. During October, Fullerton visited at The Mount and Wharton found herself passionately attracted to him. She returned to Europe earlier than planned to be near him. Over the next few months their relationship intensified, but Wharton, always aware of decorum and propriety, did all that she could to conceal the nature of their relationship from others. Troubled by self-doubts and by Fullerton's at times inexplicable silences, Wharton experienced both intense desire and disappointment with him. They became lovers in early summer of 1909, and their affair ended that autumn (Benstock, *No Gifts* 213–215). For all the difficulties this relationship entailed, it brought Wharton a sense of personal fulfillment that she had not found in her marriage. Through her own experiences, Wharton recognized the primal role that sexuality plays in an individual's sense of identity and explored its implications in much of her fiction.

While Wharton had been preoccupied with her own emotional turmoil in her relationship with Fullerton, Teddy again suffered from physical and mental illness. Though he was no longer central to her life, Wharton felt a duty to her husband and was concerned about his well-being. The seriousness of his problems became more evident in the early winter of 1909 when he admitted that he had gambled in the stock market using resources embezzled from his wife's accounts. Further complications ensued when Teddy revealed that he had been living with a mistress in Boston. He regretted what he had done, but his instability continued. His physicians recommended that he enter a sanatorium for treatment because he showed increasing signs of mental illness. His family initially rejected this course, but in 1910 he began treatment in Switzerland. Unfortunately, it did him little good and he deteriorated further, eventually becoming incapacitated by manic depression and psychosis. His sister and brother refused to acknowledge the severity of his condition, and he continued to engage is various destructive acts, including spreading rumors of his wife's mistreatment of him. Wharton sued him for divorce on the grounds of adultery in 1913; her petition was granted in Paris.

Even though dealing with Teddy's illness demanded much of her energy and concentration, Wharton continued to write. In the midst of her marital problems, she published *Ethan Frome* (1911), perhaps her best-known work. Once freed from some of the anxiety over Teddy's condition, Wharton spent time traveling in Italy and Germany following her divorce. Other plans that Wharton had made in 1914 were soon altered when World War I erupted. She chose to return to France, working first for the benefit of refugees, later for wounded soldiers. One of Wharton's chief contributions to these efforts was fundraising, but she also made personal visits to hospitals and to the front, determining what supplies and support were needed. She also wrote of what she witnessed, publishing articles in *Scribner's* that later appeared as *Fighting France* (1915). As a fundraising project to support relief causes, she edited *The Book of the Homeless,* published by Scribner's in 1916. It contained contributions from many well-known writers and artists, including Henry James, Thomas Hardy, William Butler Yeats, Joseph Conrad, Anna De Noailles, Jean Cocteau, and Claude Monet. The war brought Wharton great responsibility through her outreach to those in need and broadened her sympathies for those who came from circumstances different from her own. The government of France recognized her contributions by awarding her the Legion of Honor in 1916. The war years, however, also marked a time of personal losses. Her secretary, Anna Bahlmann, at one time Wharton's governess, died in 1915; Henry James, friend, critic, and advisor, died early in 1916; and Egerton Winthrop died later that year.

When the war ended, Wharton moved to a house in St. Brice, a village outside Paris. She also resumed travel in Europe and the Mediterranean. Even during the demanding war years, Wharton continued to write fiction, publishing *Xingu and Other Stories* in 1916, followed by a novel, *Summer,* in 1917. The years following the war proved to be another highly productive period for Wharton. In 1920 she published *The Age of Innocence,* a novel of Old New York for which she received the Pulitzer Prize in 1921. Never one to ignore the contemporary scene, Wharton focused her attention on a modern couple of the 1920s in her next novel, *Glimpses of the Moon* (1922). This was followed by another juxtaposition of past and present with the publication of *Old New York* (1924) and *The Mother's Recompense* (1925). During this period, she also began to receive numerous awards for her contributions and achievements as a writer. Yale University bestowed an honorary Doctor of Letters in 1923, and in 1924 she received the Gold Medal from the National Institute of Arts and Letters.

Wharton appreciated the recognition she received but was not satisfied to rest on her achievements of the past. From her early years, she had taken seriously the work of being a writer and believed that good fiction was more than just a source of entertainment. She expressed her views and offered advice to aspiring writers in *The Writing of Fiction* (1925). Wharton was also pleased by the regard paid and guidance sought by younger writers. F. Scott Fitzgerald was to become the best known of those she influenced, but Wharton was generous with her time and insights in assisting a number of writers.

Remembering the benefit of Winthrop's guidance, Wharton often rec-ommended a course of regular study and critical reading. At the end of the decade, her accomplishments were again acknowledged when she was awarded the Gold Medal by the American Academy of Arts and Letters and elected a member in 1930.

In 1934 she published her autobiography, *A Backward Glance,* in which she presented an appraisal of her life and the various influences that had shaped her sensibilities. Her work appealed to modern au-diences, and the dramatizations of *The Old Maid* and *Ethan Frome,* as well as film versions of many of her novels, brought Wharton sub-stantial financial rewards. In June 1937, Edith Wharton suffered a stroke at her home in St. Brice. She died on August 11 of that year and was buried in the Cimetiere des Gonards, at Versailles, France. Her life had been rich and complex, challenging and fulfilling. Until her last days she never lost the joy she had discovered as a child of making up plots and scenes: She sent her literary agent a final story, "All Souls'," in February of her last year.

2

Wharton's Career and Contributions to American Literature

Edith Wharton's literary career spanned forty-six years, from the publication of her first short story, "Mrs. Manstey's View," in 1891 to the completion of her last, "All Souls'," in 1937. During this time she witnessed profound changes in American culture brought about by diverse factors, including the expansion of industry and the fortunes made by the robber barons, the increase in labor conflicts and political unrest, and the continuing evolution of the roles of women in public life. In her fiction, Wharton responded to what she perceived happening around her, treating some topics directly while presenting others as subtexts in her narratives.

WHARTON'S CAREER

Beginning in childhood, Edith Wharton enjoyed exercising her imagination by inventing stories to entertain herself. This interest continued into her teenage years, and by the age of fourteen she knew she wanted to be a writer, despite the lack of encouragement from her family. Her family and her peers expected Wharton to lead an active social life, allowing little time for a literary career, but Wharton never relinquished her ambition. Even though she did not pursue an active career until she was twenty-seven years old, her love of literature and her extensive reading sustained her until opportunities arose for her to commit time to her own work.

Although she published a few poems in 1889, Wharton's principal focus became fiction. Her sustained venture into the literary marketplace began in 1891 with the publication of her short stories in *Scribner's Magazine,* a monthly produced by Charles Scribner's publishing firm. Her success in placing stories with *Scribner's* proved fortunate for Wharton, establishing a steady business relationship with the house that lasted for nearly thirty years. The editor of *Scribner's Magazine,* Edward L. Burlingame, became an important guide and resource for Wharton, advising her on the selection of stories for her collections and on revisions of individual tales. Early on, Wharton relied on Burlingame's advice, but as she became a more experienced author, she began to question his recommendations. She also sought counsel from William C. Brownell, the editor of the book division and literary advisor at Charles Scribner's Sons publishers, but did not hesitate to voice her opinion to him as their relationship continued. From the beginning, Wharton took charge of her own career, despite her insecurities and bouts of ill-health. Over the years, she proved to be not only a successful author but also an astute businesswoman.

While she continued to work on her fiction, Wharton agreed to co-author, with Ogden Codman, a volume on architecture and decor, *The Decoration of Houses* (1897). In preparation for this volume, Wharton traveled extensively in Europe, taking notes and photographs of French and Italian villas, analyzing the architectural designs and furnishings that gave these houses their proportion and coherence. Wharton believed that principles of good design and congruence between architectural style and interior decor transcended a particular time and place, that the techniques and ideas from the past had much to offer the present. Publication of the volume proved a challenge. First accepted by Macmillan, who later withdrew the contract over financial concerns, *Decoration* was published by Scribner's, a move rewarded when the first run of the American edition sold out. Not only did *Decoration* provide Wharton with valuable experience for other nonfiction volumes she would produce, it also enhanced her eye for detail, evident in the descriptions of interior spaces and landscapes throughout her fiction.

With the completion of *Decoration,* Wharton returned to fiction, writing four new stories to be included in her first collection, *The Greater Inclination* (1899). *Scribner's Magazine* continued to be the main vehicle for serial publication of Wharton's work, where her no-vella *The Touchstone* appeared in 1900. In *The Touchstone,* Wharton treated the ethical issues involved in the sale for publication of love letters by a famous woman author to her younger lover. After the death of the author Mrs. Aubyn, her younger lover, Glennard, decides to sell her letters to him to obtain funds to marry his new love. This decision later haunts Glennard and creates tension between him and his wife, until his wife finds a redeeming element in what has occurred. Own-ership of letters and their use was an issue that Wharton raised in a number of her works, including *The House of Mirth*; it became an issue of personal concern later in her life, prompting her to request the return of letters from various correspondents.

As her productivity increased, Wharton began to publish her short fiction in *Harper's Magazine* and *Collier's,* publications that com-peted with *Scribner's,* but her collection *Crucial Instances* was pub-lished by Scribner's in 1901. While making decisions about the stories to include in collections, Wharton made her first foray into writing a novel. Drawing upon her love for Italy and her understanding of its history, she wrote *The Valley of Decision* (1902), a two-volume work set in late eighteenth-century "Pianura," a fictionalized dukedom blending attributes of Parma and Mantua. The period in which Whar-ton set her novel was marked by social and political upheaval as the old principalities of Italy were beginning to crumble. She wanted to capture the conflict between the customs and tradition of this old world and the ideas that were beginning to undermine them. Her central character, Odo Valsecca, whose exposure to Enlightenment philosophy affects his ideas on the church, government, and freedom, finds himself at the center of conflict. Valsecca attempts to implement some of his enlightened ideas about self-government, but finds that his good intentions fail when the common people are not receptive to his reforms. Reviews of the novel were generally positive, but some felt that the history of the era dominated the narrative and inhibited the development of its characters.

In commenting upon *Valley,* Henry James encouraged Wharton to focus instead on American material that she knew well, to "Do New York!" (Benstock, *No Gifts* 125). James's remark forecast the setting of Wharton's work over the next several years. Wharton, however, remained wary of being linked too closely to James. Early critics had noted the resemblance between her work and his, a comparison that she did not always appreciate. This comparison also influenced academic appraisals of Wharton's work well into the twentieth century, casting her unfairly in James's shadow.

Before embarking on another novel, Wharton published additional travel pieces; another novella, *Sanctuary* (1903); and another collection, *The Descent of Man and Other Stories* (1904). Gaining confidence in her abilities and attaining greater control over technique, Wharton began work in 1903 on what would become *The House of Mirth* (1905). Her first major success and one of the pivotal works of her career, *The House of Mirth* traces the experiences of Lily Bart as she tries to negotiate her way through the complicated world of elite society in early twentieth-century New York. A popular and critical success, the novel strengthened Wharton's position with Scribner's, allowing her to negotiate better contractual terms for her ensuing work, especially in light of interest being expressed by other publishers.

As her career developed, Wharton chose to distance herself from most of the women writers who had preceded her and from her female contemporaries. She used the term "authoress" in references to them, not only observing the feminine suffix, but hinting that it implied the diminutive as well. Wharton set high standards for her work and applied them in judging the work of others. She was especially critical of Louisa May Alcott, whose stylistic flaws she lambasted as "the laxities of the great Louisa" (*A Backward Glance* 822). She also found the careers of some women writers limited by a reading public that expected them to address pleasant and predictable subjects. In her memoir, *A Backward Glance,* she identified what she saw as the essential difference between her vision and that of New England regionalists such as Sarah Orne Jewett and Mary Wilkins Freeman, who saw through "rose-coloured spectacles" (1002), denying the harsh realities of New England villages. These comments reflected Wharton's desire to claim authority for her voice and a larger scope for her fiction than she felt women novelists were usually granted.

Her next novel, *The Fruit of the Tree* (1907), reflected Wharton's interest in addressing issues at the heart of American culture, particularly the implications of the industrial-capital economy and the relationship between workers and owners. Creating a triangular relationship among her central characters, John Amherst, Justine Brent, and Bessy Westmore, Wharton explored tensions related to class, reform, and philanthropy. She also explored, as she had in *The House of Mirth,* the ways in which women are shaped and limited by the culture that surrounds them. Early responses to the novel were critical of Wharton's depiction of textile manufacturing, but again she had done research, visiting the Plunkett Mills in North Adams, Massachusetts, to observe industrial production firsthand.

As the first decade of the twentieth century came to a close, Wharton continued to publish short stories. She produced two collections, *The Hermit and the Wild Woman and Other Stories* (1908) and *Tales of Men and Ghosts* (1910), the latter reflecting her growing interest in the Gothic and the supernatural. Between the publication of these two volumes, Wharton also published a collection of verse, *Artemis to Actaeon* (1909). Although never the dominant focus of her creative efforts, poetry appealed to Wharton as a vehicle for expressing deep emotion within disciplined forms. *Artemis to Actaeon* contained numerous love poems, including a sonnet series, "The Mortal Lease," inspired by her relationship with Morton Fullerton.

The early years of the next decade proved a prolific period for Wharton. Her novella *Ethan Frome* appeared in 1911, provoking mixed responses from critics, who appreciated its stylistic achievements but found its treatment of rural life harsh. Wharton's novel *The Reef* appeared in 1912, published by D. Appleton and Company, who would become the major outlet for her work after 1920. *The Reef* explores the dilemmas faced by Anna Leath, a reserved and proper woman who struggles with conflicting emotions of love and jealousy. She discovers that George Darrow, the man she hopes to marry, has had an affair with the young Sophy Viner. As she attempts to understand herself and the nature of sexual attraction, Anna must make decisions that will affect the futures of all three.

In 1913, Wharton published *The Custom of the Country,* a novel she had begun five years earlier. It presents a study of American consumerism and the drive for upward mobility by those born outside the elite. In striking contrast to the refined Anna Leath of *The Reef,* Undine Spragg, the protagonist of *The Custom of the Country,* emerges as one of Wharton's most assertive and crass characters. The novel traces Undine's so-called career as she uses serial marriage to achieve social prestige and material comfort. She studies the social codes and mannerisms of each level of society, ready to alter her image as she aspires to new heights in the social hierarchy. Her quest ultimately brings her full circle as she remarries her first husband, Elmer Moffat, who has during the course of the novel made his fortune. Undine, however, can never fully satisfy her desire for admiration and status; even in the last chapters of the novel, she considers the possibility of yet another divorce and remarriage.

In 1914, the eruption of World War I affected how Edith Wharton spent her energies. She dedicated herself to relief work but throughout the war continued to write. From 1914 to 1918 she published *Xingu and Other Stories* (1916), *Summer* (1917), and *The Marne* (1918), as well as essays about the war in France. While some of the stories collected in *Xingu and Other Stories* had been published before the war, Wharton's creative energies seemed inexhaustible, despite the anxieties caused by war and the demands placed upon her by her charitable work. Her writings about the war, especially her short novel *The Marne,* attracted the interest of readers at the war's end. The critical reputations of both *The Marne* and her later novel, *A Son at the Front* (1923), suffered, however, when compared to treatment of the war in novels by emerging authors such as *Three Soldiers* (1921) by John Dos Passos.

Following the war, Wharton turned her attention once again to Old New York, the focus of her Pulitzer Prize–winning novel *The Age of Innocence* (1920). In the novel, Wharton explored the conflict between individual desires and cultural expectations through the experiences of her protagonist Newland Archer and his love for two different women, May Welland and Ellen Olenska. Wharton's next novel, *The Glimpses of the Moon* (1922), also treated questions of love, marriage, and social expectations, but in the context of the 1920s. Her central characters, Susy and Nick Lansing, find themselves torn between their love for each other and their need for financial resources to maintain their place in an elite social circle. Their lifestyle and the choices they make, including their agreement to divorce after a year if either of them finds a wealthy partner, reveal the changing values and mores of the 1920s. Both *The Age of Innocence* and *The Glimpses of the Moon* were published by D. Appleton and Company, as Wharton shifted her allegiance from Scribner's. As she had with earlier editors, Wharton developed an important business and literary relationship with Rutger B. Jewett, the editor at Appleton, who actively promoted Wharton's work and her reputation.

In *Old New York* (1924), Wharton presented four novellas, each set in a different decade from the 1840s to the 1870s. Two of these, *False Dawn (The 'Forties)* and *The Spark (The 'Sixties),* present contrived situations, but *The Old Maid (The 'Fifties)* and *New Year's Day (The 'Seventies)* present interesting studies of character as well as the social moment.

Wharton again followed her treatment of the past with a novel set in the present. In *The Mother's Recompense* (1925), she explores how a mother's past has the power to affect her daughter's future and happiness. Kate Clephane, who has lived abroad for years since her divorce, discovers upon her return to New York that her daughter Anne plans to marry Chris Fenno, the man with whom Kate has had a passionate affair. Kate, who still has feelings for Fenno, must decide whether to tell Anne the truth about her own relationship with Fenno or keep silent and withdraw from her daughter's life. The subjects that Wharton had begun to treat openly in her fiction, including unwed motherhood and extramarital relationships, created difficulties for the serial publication of her work. Magazine editors shied away from material that might offend their readers, but Wharton refused to alter her work, instead pressing her publishers to find other outlets for it.

Drawing on more than thirty years experience as an author, Wharton presented her views on the nature of prose fiction and the elements necessary to its success in *The Writing of Fiction* (1925). She praised the work of many English and Continental authors, emphasizing the importance of tradition and what she saw as the writer's eye for the vital truth of human experience. Although she was often critical of the experimentation that characterized the emergence of literary modernism, Wharton's last chapter in *The Writing of Fiction* offered an appreciation and appraisal of Marcel Proust's accomplishments in his series of novels *Remembrance of Things Past* (1913–27). Proust had developed a dense narrative style that represented the inner musings of his characters, an exploration of consciousness that appealed to early modernists, but Wharton also praised his work for its "exquisite delicacy of touch, a solicitous passion for detail" (*Writing* 166).

Her own commitment to writing fiction continued during the last decade of her career, her output remaining as prolific as ever. Wharton produced a story collection *Here and Beyond* in 1926, followed by the novel *Twilight Sleep* in 1927. Her novel *The Children* appeared in 1928, followed by another collection of stories, *Certain People,* in 1930. In both *Twilight Sleep* and *The Children,* Wharton focused on American values and behaviors in the 1920s, revealing that the social frameworks that had regulated personal behavior in the past no longer held sway. She produced two more novels, *Hudson River Bracketed* in 1929 and its sequel *The Gods Arrive* in 1932, shaped around the life and career of a writer, Vance Weston. Wharton's novels written after 1925 fared less well in critical reviews, some critics claiming that Wharton was writing too quickly or attempting to appeal to popular tastes rather than maintaining the standards of high art.

In 1933, Wharton began work on her final novel, *The Buccaneers,* in which she returned to the 1870s and the social world she had satirized in much of her earlier fiction. The main characters, five young women who are the buccaneers of the title, see themselves as American adventurers who will use the rituals of courtship and marriage to conquer London society. Left unfinished at the time of Wharton's death, the novel was published with outlines for the remaining chapters in 1938; a version completed by Marian Mainwaring appeared in 1993. The energy and appealing freshness of the main characters inspired a television adaptation of *The Buccaneers* in 1995.

In 1934, Edith Wharton published a memoir entitled *A Backward Glance,* offering a picture of her development as a writer and touching briefly on many of the relationships that were important to her. Unlike the confessional autobiographies often written today, Wharton's account of her life maintained a personal reserve throughout, creating the image that she wanted the reading public to have. She offered critical insights into her own work and that of other writers but avoided commenting on many of the private matters that have intrigued biographers. In her last years, Wharton assembled three collections of stories, *Human Nature* (1933), *The World Over* (1936), and *Ghosts* (published posthumously in 1937), bringing to a close a productive and successful career.

WHARTON'S CONTRIBUTIONS TO TRAVEL AND CULTURAL WRITING

Edith Wharton saw America as a young nation without a long or deeply embedded sense of history and tradition. She felt that newness and innovation defined America, in contrast to the history and continuity she associated with Europe. She was fascinated by the contrasts between American and European sensibilities, a topic she addressed in works such as *Madame de Treymes* (1907), and believed that Americans could gain greater perspective by developing an awareness and understanding of European culture. Her interest in what defined a culture and its traditions influenced many of her nonfiction works, including *Italian Villas and Their Gardens* (1904), *Italian Backgrounds* (1905), *A Motor-Flight Through France* (1908), *Fighting*

France (1915), *French Ways and Their Meaning* (1919), and *In Morocco* (1920). All of these volumes reflect Wharton's habits of careful observation and disciplined study as she explores how traditions, values, and beliefs influence behavior and are embedded in ideas of taste and design. These works have enjoyed renewed interest from Wharton scholars and critics, who see in them expressions of Wharton's complex views on nationalism, imperialism, and race.

WHARTON'S CONTRIBUTIONS TO THE SHORT STORY

The short story appealed to American writers who experimented with the genre throughout the nineteenth century. Washington Irving and Nathaniel Hawthorne used the form to explore America's colonial past and its myths. Edgar Allan Poe used Gothic elements and the supernatural to further the rise of the horror story. Later in the century, regionalist writers, including Sarah Orne Jewett, Mary Wilkins Freeman, and Kate Chopin, revealed through their stories the potent connection between character and place. While Edith Wharton appreciated these contributions to the short story, she looked to the work of Europeans as models of success. She claimed that in the work of French and Russian authors, the reader encountered "great closeness of texture" and "a shaft driven straight to the heart of human experience" (*Writing* 36). In her own stories, Wharton blended the richness of social context favored by European writers with the concern for individual realization that shaped much American fiction.

Over the course of her career, Wharton developed definite opinions about the nature of the short story. She felt that a short-story writer needed a clear idea of what he or she wished to tell and why it was worth telling. She believed that the short story achieved its greatest effect through the "dramatic rendering of a situation" presented through the careful ordering of event and detail (*Writing* 47). In *The Writing of Fiction,* she argued that to achieve verisimilitude or the illusion of reality, a writer must confine the events of the plot to a brief period of time and must report them from a consistent angle or point of view. For Wharton, the opening of a tale often governed its success or failure. If the reader was immediately drawn into the situation, finding it probable and compelling, the story had every chance of succeeding. If not, the chance was lost.

Although Wharton claims that character is not the major element of the short story, she often shapes her stories around moments of conflict that reveal the inner natures of her characters and the psychological tensions that govern situations. Many of her stories focus on the nature of competition between women, the expectations and misunderstandings that characterize relationships between women and men, and the ways events from the past have a controlling influence in the present. At times, Wharton invites the reader into a sympathetic understanding of one or more of the characters, as she does in "Souls Belated" (1899) or "Autre Temps" (1911). In some instances, however, she uses satire and irony to maintain a critical distance from characters in order to reveal their foibles and failings, as she does in "Xingu" (1911). Building on the contributions of her predecessors, Wharton reveals the way communities continue to shape individuals, relying on the careful selection of detail to create the social contexts within which her characters act. She explores the continuing interaction between the individual and his or her social world, demonstrating that the underlying tensions that define this interaction remain, even when social contexts have changed over time.

WHARTON AND THE NOVEL OF MANNERS

During the early decades of the nineteenth century, American authors felt that America lacked the complex social structure and traditions that provided English and European writers the materials necessary to create novels. To compensate, American authors, including Sedgwick, Child, Cooper, Hawthorne, and Melville, wrote prose narratives classified as romances, in which they explored America's colonial past or adventures set in remote places. The term "romance" describes prose fiction that is the product of imagination rather than observation and presents events and situations that are unlikely or improbable. Early American romances often incorporated elements of the mythic or supernatural to enlarge the action or characters beyond the everyday. In sentimental romances, also popular during the era, authors focused on characters' emotional responses to events and conditions in their lives, attempting to stimulate the readers' emotional responses as well. In writing romances, authors felt they could explore human experience without confining themselves to the limited social arena that constituted the American scene.

In the mid-nineteenth century, American authors began to embrace literary realism, with its emphasis on the believability of characters, details drawn from direct observation, and plausibility of action. A number of women writers who produced what have been labeled domestic novels, including Harriet Beecher Stowe, Susan Warner, and Louisa May Alcott, paved the way for this transition by emphasizing the details of family relationships and daily life within the households they depicted. For authors drawn to realism, such as William Dean Howells and Henry James, the novel offered opportunities to explore the nature of human experience within the social contexts that contained it. During the course of the nineteenth century, America had evolved into a more complex and hierarchical social order compared to that of the early 1800s, one in which the elite and the middle class differentiated themselves from the lower classes through their notions of etiquette and decorum. Americans also traveled more widely, making the American encounter with European culture another topic that invited treatment in the realist novel. These changes spurred interest in creating the American novel of manners.

The nature of individual experience lay at the heart of Wharton's novels, a form that allowed for the "gradual unfolding of the inner life of its characters" (*Writing* 42). For Wharton, this unfolding of the inner life always occurred within a social context and not without complications. Wharton was drawn to the novel of manners as a narrative form that allowed her to explore the conflict between the individual and his or her social world. The term "manners" encompasses the codes of speech, dress, behavior, and decor that embody and express the values and mores of a particular culture or social class. In the novel of manners, the novelist uses the details that convey these codes as more than just background for the characters and actions of the narrative. Manners and the values they represent serve as operative forces in the lives of the characters, providing security and a sense of identity but at times inhibiting self-realization or thwarting the fulfillment of personal desires. The protagonist of a novel of manners often reflects the influence of Romantic ideals, especially the belief in the uniqueness of individual perception and the value of the individual over the social group. In many of Wharton's novels, including *The House of Mirth* and *The Age of Innocence,* her protagonists find themselves torn between embracing the culture, its manners, and the identity it provides and rejecting these in favor of an alternative, idealistic or Romantic vision. Such characters often elicit the sympathy of the reader but are defeated by the rigid social order that surrounds them.

In the novel of manners, determinism, the belief that human beings do not direct their own lives but instead are subject to the working of outside forces, plays a part in shaping the events of the plot and the development of character. These outside forces, usually the social conventions and expectations that define a character's place in the world, limit the degree of freedom with which a character can act. In a number of her novels, Wharton alludes to determinism through her references to the Fates, figures from classical mythology who were thought to control the length and direction of each human life.

In some novels, Wharton also incorporates aspects of determinism associated with literary naturalism. For literary naturalists, the scientific discoveries of the nineteenth century profoundly influenced ideas about human experience and the natural world. Charles Darwin's work on evolution contributed to the concept that individuals are controlled by biological determinism, by their heredity and their ability to adapt to the environment. Wharton blends this type of determinism into her narratives, never using it as an exclusive governing force but suggesting that it too plays a part in the entrapment of her characters. Her treatment of Charity Royall in *Summer* foregrounds the issue of heredity as a factor that influences Charity's behavior and understanding of herself. Wharton often raises questions about the nature of maternal legacies, especially to daughters, suggesting a relationship between biological origins and personal character.

The novel of manners not only provides a means through which an author can explore the nature of an individual's experience in his or her world but also critique the social world in which characters exist. Frequently writers develop this critique through the use of satire, a form of humor that points out the foibles of individuals and the failings of human institutions. In many of her novels that treat New York's social milieu, Wharton shows how the emphasis on good form and propriety conceals a multitude of flaws, cultural as well as personal. The majority of individuals who inhabit Wharton's social environments are blind to the problems or limitations of their cultural world and cannot understand the alienation or frustration of the individuals who do perceive them. Wharton often uses irony, the discrepancy between appearances and reality, or between the apparent and intended meaning of an individual's words, to create satire. Irony can highlight the smug complacency of a Lawrence Lefferts in *The Age of Innocence* or the deceit of a Lucius Harney in *Summer.*

WHARTON'S USE OF THE GOTHIC

The Gothic tradition in fiction emerged in the eighteenth century through the work of writers such as Horace Walpole, "Monk" Lewis, and Ann Radcliffe. The term "gothic" was applied to their fictions because they were set during the medieval era. The focus of their novels was not historical romance but the creation of a plot and atmosphere that would inspire terror on the part of readers. These novels often included encounters with the supernatural, innocent maidens in distress, and devilish villains. Early Gothic novels marked a rebellion against the emphasis on rationality and order that dominated the Age of Reason, exploiting the irrational and inexplicable, suggesting that there was more to human experience than could be determined by empirical evidence. By the nineteenth century, the term "gothic" was applied to fiction that inspires terror or horror even though not set during the middle ages. These narratives drew upon the supernatural or irrational, suspense, a sense of foreboding, and an atmosphere of gloom.

Edith Wharton saw elements of the Gothic tradition as devices that allowed her to explore the psychological or emotional states of characters. In some of her ghost stories, she uses castles or remote country houses to evoke the atmosphere of the traditional Gothic tale, as she does in "Kerfol." In some stories, such as "Afterward" or "The Eyes," she creates suspense through the use of spectral images, while in others she creates anxiousness and suspense for the central character and the reader through the mysterious absence of other living beings, as in "All Souls'." Wharton cautioned, however, that any of the elements or devices associated with the Gothic tradition should not be used indiscriminately or with a heavy hand; she encouraged writers to practice "the economy of horror" to stimulate more profound fear in the reader (*Writing* 40).

Wharton introduced Gothic elements in works other than her ghost tales to convey the unsettled mental state of her characters. In *Ethan Frome,* Ethan believes his wife Zeena exercises supernatural powers to control his life, associating her with a witch. When Charity Royall arrives on the Mountain after her mother's death in *Summer,* Wharton describes the burial scene in terms that evoke the gothic to underscore the horror of the situation for Charity. Often Wharton introduces these elements to highlight the powerlessness of her characters against the forces that shape their lives.

WHARTON'S INFLUENCE

During her own career, Edith Wharton never enjoyed a conventional mentoring relationship with an established author who guided her through the early stages of her literary development. She did receive advice from editors and various friends, but she often had to rely on her own instincts, both artistic and financial, when making decisions that would affect her career. After her own career was well established, however, Wharton proved to be a friend to younger writers, offering praise and encouragement where she felt it due. She often used her contacts with editors to assist in the publication process and recommended the work she appreciated to other writers. She also gave advice, both in *The Writing of Fiction* and in the personal letters she wrote. She encouraged the development of disciplined work habits and the pursuit of critical reading, echoing Egerton Winthrop's recommendation to her years earlier. Wharton did not believe in offering false praise or encouraging continued work where there appeared to be no potential, as her letter to Victor Solberg reveals (Killoran, "Meeting" 124-25).

Among the younger generation of writers who sought connections with Wharton, F. Scott Fitzgerald was probably the most direct. Supposedly their first encounter took place in the offices of Scribner's in 1923, when Fitzgerald barged into a meeting to see her (Benstock, *No Gifts* 382). In a 1925 letter to Fitzgerald, Wharton praised his accomplishments in *The Great Gatsby,* and later invited him to tea at her home, Pavilion Colombe. This visit proved disastrous, although accounts differ as to what precipitated its failure. Their meeting ruled out the possibility of a lasting personal relationship, but their work was frequently compared in reviews.

As did Wharton, Fitzgerald wrote of America's leisure class and the changing mores of American culture; for Fitzgerald, marked changes occurred in the post–World War I years that gave rise to the period Fitzgerald dubbed the Jazz Age. Fitzgerald's early work reflected his familiarity with Wharton's fiction and the techniques she used to convey the social environment of her characters. In an early story like "Bernice Bobs Her Hair" (1920), Fitzgerald draws upon the details of clothing, speech mannerisms, and decor to express the values and expectations of the young country-club set among whom Bernice finds herself when she visits her cousin Marjorie. Fitzgerald uses satire to expose the competition and jealousy that emerges between Marjorie and Bernice after Bernice begins to enjoy social success, echoing the subject of many Wharton stories. In the ironic closure of the tale, Bernice, who has been humiliated by her cousin's friends for having bobbed her hair, exacts her revenge on Marjorie by cutting off Marjorie's braids while she sleeps, giving Marjorie a bob of her own. Like Wharton, Fitzgerald recognized the power of irony to intensify the dramatic moment. In his later works, such as *The Great Gatsby* (1925) and *Tender is the Night* (1934), Fitzgerald experimented with narrative techniques not common in Wharton's work, but he continued to address topics that were important to her, including how the male gaze defined women and how the inability to communicate affected relationships between men and women.

Unlike Fitzgerald's brief acquaintance with Wharton, Sinclair Lewis enjoyed a long personal friendship with her. Lewis, whose novels of manners explored the sensibilities of the middle class and Middle West, saw Wharton's work as among the most important produced in the first decades of the twentieth century. As did Wharton, Lewis viewed the social world that he depicted with a critical eye. He noted the stifling power Midwestern provincialism held over characters that paralleled the limitations imposed by Society in Wharton's New York. In *Main Street* (1920), Lewis traces the experiences of Carol Milford Kennicott as she attempts to find direction and purpose in her life, chafing against the restrictions imposed on her by Gopher Prairie and by her marriage. Lewis also draws upon the details of manner and dress, as well as the activities of the Gopher Prairie Dramatic Association, to satirize small town pretensions.

Lesser-known writers also sought Wharton's guidance or responses to their work, among them Zona Gale, Howard Sturgis, Percy Lubbock, Katherine Fullerton Gerould, and Vivienne de Wattville. Similarities or parallels between Wharton's work and that of Dorothy Parker, Theodore Dreiser, Kay Boyle, and Nella Larsen have been noted by Wharton scholars as well. These relationships suggest the importance of Wharton's contributions, but during the last decade of her life and for a period of time after her death, Wharton's reputation was eclipsed by that of writers engaged in the narrative experimentation that defined modernism. Wharton herself was conscious of this trend, commenting in a letter to Sinclair Lewis that she was afraid the younger generation saw her "as the—say the Mrs. Humphry Ward of the Western Hemisphere; though at times I wondered why" (*Letters* 445). Her reference to a popular woman author of the nineteenth century whose works had been deemed outdated and moralistic by twentieth-century readers revealed Wharton's concern about what her own legacy might be.

The presence of *Ethan Frome* on required reading lists has ensured that new generations of readers encounter Wharton's fiction. More recently, the work of feminist scholars has focused attention on the range of Wharton's achievements, distinguishing her work from that of her male contemporaries, especially Henry James. Wharton also continues to exercise influence on creative writers, evident in the many novels of manners being written today, especially those of John Updike and Anita Shreve. Both Updike and Shreve explore themes and topics that Wharton addressed, including passion, jealousy, betrayal, divorce, and adultery. They often treat the experiences of middle-class characters and provide a richly detailed social context within which their characters function. In their novels, characters often face conflicts that force them to confront either the morality of their decisions or the limits that social expectations impose on their freedom.

In his comments on Wharton, John Updike acknowledges the success of some of her best-known works, especially *Ethan Frome* and *The Age of Innocence,* about which he says, "there has never been much doubt; their perfection and power were immediately apparent" (198). He values her careful use of language and of the detail that shapes the power of her narrative. Updike admires the consistency of her vision, that she will not create an artificial happy ending that undermines the truth as she sees it, but he claims that "she denies her characters the liberation she herself found" (212). He considers Wharton's treatment of sexuality reserved by today's standards but admits that in her own day, she tested boundaries. Updike has also tested boundaries with his work; his novel *Couples* (1968), a frank exploration of sexual freedom within the framework of a novel of manners, created a stir when published.

For Updike, the power of Wharton's fiction derives from the entrapment that her characters suffer, the inescapability of their context. Also recognized as a chronicler of the American social scene, John Updike records the life of middle America, especially the suburban existence that has defined middle-class experience since World War II. He uses the details of settings, mannerisms, and gestures as a means of conveying the context of his characters' lives, the context against which they often rebel. As does Wharton, Updike emphasizes the feeling of entrapment that engulfs his characters, particularly Harry (Rabbit) Angstrom in *Rabbit, Run* (1960). Rabbit typifies the small town high school athlete who lacks direction after his sports career has ended. He finds himself overwhelmed and frustrated by what appear to be dead-end jobs and a stifling marriage. He attempts to escape his situation first through an affair and then by literally running away. In the three successive volumes that follow his development over a thirty-year period, Rabbit struggles against the social conditions and personal failings that leave him dissatisfied and disillusioned, including the materialism and consumerism that shape his and his family's life.

Inspired by her first encounter with Edith Wharton's work, Anita Shreve claims, "Each writer has a particular book that unlocked the desire to write. For me, I think *Ethan Frome* was that book. I read it when I was a junior in high school. I consider it a nearly perfect novel" (Papinchak 28–29). The power of that first impression on Shreve is evident in her work. Not only does she allude to *Ethan Frome* in her novels *Eden Close* (1989) and *Strange Fits of Passion* (1991), she also focuses on the ways that houses and communities affect the characters who inhabit them and shape the narratives of their lives. Some of her novels, including *Where or When* (1993) and *The Pilot's Wife* (1998), contain elements of the novel of manners tradition, while others, including *The Weight of Water* (1997) and *The Last Time They Met* (2001), reveal experimental narrative techniques that alternate events and points of view from the past and the present.

In writing her novels, Shreve emphasizes the details that create the sense of time and place for her characters. Whether the setting is the 1870s of *The Weight of Water,* the 1940s of *Resistance,* or the 1990s of *The Pilot's Wife,* the details work to create the interconnection between characters and their worlds, anchoring them in a reality that is crucial to the themes Shreve explores. In her novels, Shreve treats the complications of passion, its energy, and its demands. She explores various patterns of deception and betrayal, including adultery, often as a means of underscoring the moral or ethical dilemmas her characters face, dilemmas always rooted in questions of trust. Frequently her characters, like those of Edith Wharton, find themselves attempting to read gestures and verbal nuances because forthright communication, especially between men and women, falters. For some of her characters who struggle to connect, as do Charles Callahan and Siân Richards of *Where or When,* fate is as cruel as in any of Wharton's novels. Shreve creates compelling narratives by eliciting sympathy for her characters and initiating the reader's desire to know the outcome of their struggles with love and loss, employing the same "delicate thread of literary suspense" (Papinchak 29) that Shreve finds in *Ethan Frome.*

3

Short Stories

Edith Wharton wrote short stories throughout her career, beginning with "Mrs. Manstey's View," published in 1891. She produced eighty-five stories, seventy-two of which were gathered into eleven collections. Her appreciation of the form and her understanding of the techniques necessary to produce a good story influenced her comments in *The Writing of Fiction* (1925). There, Wharton defined important aspects of the short story, especially its emphasis on situation rather than sustained character development. She, like Edgar Allan Poe, stressed the need for each detail to contribute to the meaning and effect of the tale. She also argued that the "germ of the whole" should be contained in the first page of the story.

The stories discussed in this chapter are those considered among Wharton's best and are frequently anthologized. In these stories, she presents situations that allow her to address a number of themes, including the entrapment of women by social conventions, the competition that defines relationships between women, and the impact a mother's past has upon her daughter. Wharton was also intrigued by the possibilities of exploring human psychology through use of Gothic elements and the supernatural, drawing upon them in her numerous ghost stories.

"SOULS BELATED" (1899)

In this early short story first published in *The Greater Inclination,* Wharton presents a situation that reveals a woman's feelings of entrapment and her realization that freedom remains elusive. The protagonist, Lydia Tillotson, has left her first husband in search of the opportunity to lead the life she desires. As the story progresses, Lydia discovers that she cannot separate herself from the world that has defined her. Her relationship with Ralph Gannet, her lover, forces her to confront the ironic reality of her situation: Her romantic flight has brought her back to the social conventions she hoped to escape.

POINT OF VIEW

The first four sections of this story are narrated in a voice sympathetic to Lydia's point of view and privy to her inner thoughts. This allows Wharton to reveal Lydia's doubts and insecurities, her inner debate over what her future holds. It also presents Gannet from Lydia's perspective as she attempts to read his gestures and expressions for clues to his true feelings. In the last section of the tale, the point of view shifts to Gannett's. This change creates the ambiguity that surrounds Lydia's decision, for the reader does not learn whether love or resignation determines her choice to turn back. It does, however, reveal the power of the male gaze, implying that Gannett will be the one to define Lydia, as she has feared. Wharton returns to this question of a man's authority to define a woman's life at the end of *The House of Mirth.*

SETTING AND PLOT

In the first section of "Souls Belated," Wharton offers extended exposition to create the context for her characters' situation in time present and to reveal how the past affects it. The story opens on a train traveling north from Bologna, Italy, as Lydia Tillotson and Ralph Gannet continue their journey. Empty but for them, the train car in which they ride seems to suspend them briefly between past and future, between the social world they have known and the new world Lydia hopes to find. The references to their continuing travels underscore the restlessness that has defined their relationship. They have reached a point of transition, for as the newness of their life together has faded, their actions and conversations are becoming routine. The arrival of Lydia's divorce decree has also made possible this transition, but Lydia fears the onset of the boredom that she associates with routine. Her first marriage had been characterized by dullness and predictability, the Tillotson household governed by prudence and regularity. To escape this stifling atmosphere, Lydia had taken flight with Gannett. Now that "new topics were at a premium" between them (96), Lydia worries that she and Gannett are drifting toward their own predictability, symbolized for her by the social rehabilitation their marriage will provide.

The train journey ends in the northern Italian lake district where Lydia and Gannett retreat to the Hotel Bellosguardo, an inn frequented by an Anglo-American clientele. Although Italy is often associated with romantic love and the heat of sexual passion, Lydia and Gannett adopt a sedate, reserved manner at the inn. Lydia finds herself comfortable resuming the patterns of social interaction she has known, and Gannett believes he can return to writing, which he has not done since they departed New York. The surface regularity of their life conforms to the expectations of the inn's other guests, articulated by Miss Pinsent and embodied by Lady Susan Condit. These women place a premium on respectability and the morality that underpins it, judging others by the degree to which they conform to the rules of propriety. Miss Pinsent informs Lydia that she and Gannett have been approved by Lady Susan. During their conversation, Miss Pinsent introduces the topic of the Lintons, a couple Lady Susan deems unacceptable and to whom she has given the cold shoulder. The juxtaposition of the "Gannetts" and the "Lintons" in the conversation presents an irony for Lydia, given that she and Gannett are not married.

Her own social deception generates Lydia's crisis during her encounter with Mrs. Linton in the third section of the tale. Mrs. Linton reveals her true identity, that she is Mrs. Cope traveling incognito with her lover, Lord Trevenna. They are awaiting Mrs. Cope's divorce decree so that they can marry and legitimize their relationship. Mrs. Cope confesses because she hopes to obtain from Lydia the knowledge of what has passed between Lord Trevenna and Gannett. In the course of this conversation, Mrs. Cope appears to be a social-climbing, manipulative woman, who fears she is losing control over Trevenna as his family attempts to end their relationship. Lydia finds Mrs. Cope an unpleasant figure and attempts to distance herself. When Lydia excuses herself from their conversation with a degree of self-righteousness, Mrs. Cope calls her on it. Mrs. Cope tells Lydia that she knows Lydia only poses as Gannett's wife. To gain the information she desires, Mrs. Cope attempts to blackmail Lydia, threatening to reveal Lydia's secret to Lady Susan and her circle. Lydia knows this will expose her and Gannett to the social ostracism that "the Lintons" have experienced.

Following this encounter, Lydia takes a walk alone in the mountains, separating herself from her social world to contemplate her own history and situation. She admits to herself how easy it has been to slip back into familiar patterns of social behavior. She also knows that she and Gannett have been avoiding the discussion about their future. When she tells Gannett what has occurred, he informs Lydia that she has been spared the need to act, for Mrs. Cope's divorce decree arrived and "the Lintons" departed the inn. Lydia, however, does not find relief in this information. During her walk, she has recognized her own conventionality, her own willingness to engage in masquerade to avoid social difficulties. She tells Gannett that even being married to him will necessitate some degree of performance, of falsehood. Lydia believes that to prevent this and be true to herself, she must leave him. In his anger and surprise, Gannett asks, "Where would you go if you left me?" (119), a question that forces Lydia to consider the limited options for a woman alone. They part company on a note of frustration and cooled feeling.

In the last section of the story, Gannett hears a noise from Lydia's room that attracts his attention. He listens for her movements and watches as she leaves the hotel, heading toward the ferry dock. After he watches Lydia purchase a ticket and sit down to wait for the boat, Gannett thinks about her and about their relationship. He pities her and believes that he has overlooked her "feminine cast of mind" (120) that allows emotion to dominate reason. He sees Lydia as a social being, believing that isolation and a lack of friends will be her undoing should she attempt life on her own. Gannett observes the ferry's arrival and Lydia's hesitation to board. She descends the gangplank halfway and then turns back, eventually walking toward the hotel. Upon seeing this, Gannett believes she has returned to him, and reaches for his Bradshaw, a volume of railway timetables, to book their trip to Paris, where he promised they would wed. The ending, especially the references to Lydia's slow progress toward the hotel and her furtive look toward Gannett's window as she returns, suggests that resignation rather than passion has influenced her decision, despite Gannett's interpretation.

CHARACTERS

Lydia Tillotson, who grew up in a small town and entered New York society through her marriage, discovered that in addition to her husband, she had married his wealth, his views, and his family's way of life. After years of accepting this situation, Lydia found herself attracted to Ralph Gannett, to the newness and adventure he represented. Lydia anticipated that life with him would be exciting and fulfilling in ways that her marriage was not. She believed that she was strong enough to defy social conventions, and that escape with Gannett would give her access to a world where she might define herself. Her initial desire to please Gannett, to function on his intellectual level to maintain his interest in her, belies her own lack of self-confidence. After the novelty of her situation has faded, Lydia recognizes how little her life has actually changed and how deeply she has internalized the rules of convention that have defined her. She wants to be free to live life on her own terms, but as the story progresses, she confronts various barriers that prevent that from happening, including her love for Gannett.

Ralph Gannett, a writer who has the financial means to enjoy an extended period of leisure, thinks of himself as a rational man. His travels with Lydia have brought some change to his life, evident in his failure to write anything since their departure, but he seems less affected by what has happened. He believes he sees the wider picture of life and the ways that Lydia needs social interaction, but he too feels more himself once he can enjoy the company of Lord Trevenna at the hotel. Gannett accepts that it will be his responsibility to define Lydia's place in the world, that he will do the right thing by marrying her and giving her a new identity. He cannot understand why Lydia sees this option as no better than the situation she has left, an indication of his own acceptance of social conventions and expectations.

The other characters who surround Lydia and Gannett at the Hotel Bellosguardo convey the power and pervasiveness of social conventions. Lady Susan Condit and the circle of women who see her as their leader assert the superiority of the British Empire and those values that support its existence. The "Lintons," Mrs. Cope and Lord Trevenna, are especially troubling to Lady Susan because their actions undermine the image of British aristocracy she strives to maintain. If a peer of the realm fails to uphold standards, the power of empire and the control it implies stand at risk in her eyes. The "Lintons" also serve as a mirror of Lydia's situation with Gannett, reflecting how they will fare should their truth be known.

THEMES

The entrapment of women by the network of gender expectations and social conventions that define their world appears in much of Wharton's fiction. Through Lydia's situation in "Souls Belated," Wharton reveals both the impossibility of escaping this entrapment and the levels of deception and self-deception in which women engage to avoid facing the truth. She also demonstrates how gender roles give men power to define women, both through public social relations and through private reflections. Gannett's role as a writer links this power to the authority that men assume in writing, authority that women must struggle to find.

"THE OTHER TWO" (1904, 1904)

The issue of divorce and remarriage influences the situation Wharton presents in "The Other Two," first published in *Collier's,* then collected in *The Descent of Man.* Alice Waythorn has used serial marriage as a means of advancing herself on the social ladder. At each level she attains, she adapts to new expectations, refining the mask she presents to those around her. As Mrs. Waythorn, Alice has reached the pinnacle of her social success. After the novelty of their marriage and the afterglow of their honeymoon diminishes, Waythorn reaches a degree of familiarity with his wife and her actions that redefine her for him. Waythorn perceives that she is not the woman he believed he married, but he comes to accept the woman that she is.

POINT OF VIEW

As in "Souls Belated," point of view plays an important role in "The Other Two." Although the story is told in the third person, the narrative presents the situation from Waythorn's perspective, providing his observations of Alice and her former husbands. Through this perspective, Wharton also reveals Waythorn's sense of himself and his changing view of Alice and his marriage as the story progresses. Wharton makes use of numerous ironies that Waythorn perceives in his situation, adding to his discomfort but allowing him to reach a new understanding of himself as well as his wife.

SETTING AND PLOT

Set in New York City in the late nineteenth century, "The Other Two" takes place in the locations that have shaped Waythorn's identity. Much of the action occurs in his home, except for a few scenes that take place in his office, on public transportation, or at social events. Although Alice serves as the focal point of Waythorn's thoughts, the plot unfolds along his pattern of action and interaction.

Having just returned from his honeymoon and still enjoying the contentment of his newly married state, Waythorn contemplates his wife Alice while he sits near his "drawing-room hearth" (433), a position that evokes domestic contentment. Pleased by her responsiveness to her daughter Lily Haskett's illness, Waythorn admires Alice's composure and envies the comfort her presence must bring. He reflects on the grayness of his own life and his hopes that Alice's freshness and gaiety can enliven his existence. He believes his knowledge of Alice's character and her past sufficient to allow him to "discount" the unpleasant things said about her by some in his social circle. He believes that his own social status and reputation will redefine Alice's position in their world. When she joins him in the drawing room, Alice informs Waythorn that Haskett, her first husband and Lily's father, has contacted her through his lawyers, asking to visit Lily during her illness. This request upsets Waythorn, who sees it as an intrusion of his wife's unhappy past into their present happiness. He acquiesces upon seeing Alice's distress and seems pleased that she can so quickly dismiss it from her thoughts.

The thought of Haskett's visit makes Waythorn feel dispossessed in his own house, so he leaves earlier than usual for work. On his way to the office, he encounters Gus Varick, his wife's second husband. Sensing the irony of the situation, Waythorn perceives that he cannot escape his wife's past. As luck would have it, he also sees Varick at lunch, although Varick does not see him. Waythorn takes the opportunity to observe Varick surreptitiously, noticing his mannerisms and silently evaluating him. When he returns home, Waythorn's attitude toward his wife has begun to change, evident in the fact that "a day earlier [her appearance] would have charmed him" (439). Instead, he scrutinizes her as he asks about Haskett's visit, noting her hesitation to respond but feeling reassured when she says she did not see him. While they are relaxing after dinner, Waythorn again values Alice as a creature "all compact of harmonies" (440), until she pours his coffee. Before passing it to him, Alice adds a shot of brandy to it, as Waythorn had seen Varick do at lunch. When he tells Alice of her mistake, both she and Waythorn are unsettled by it. The error also suggests that beneath her calm surface, Alice has felt greater anxiousness over her husband's questions about her possible encounter with Haskett.

Circumstances continue to place Waythorn into contact with his wife's ex-husbands. At work, a senior partner asks Waythorn to handle Varick's account during the partner's absence. Waythorn finds the encounter with Varick less unpleasant than he had expected, but he learns more about Varick's circumstances that may have affected Alice's second marriage than he wishes to know. A few weeks later, Waythorn returns home from the office to find Haskett waiting in the library, the room Waythorn considers his personal retreat. Startled, he escapes to his room, where he puzzles over why Haskett disturbs him so much. He realizes that Haskett offers a key to Alice's past. He envisions her middle-class life with Haskett and what she has done to shed all traces of that life. Waythorn perceives that his assumptions about Alice being "brutalized" (445) by her first husband are probably not true, and worse, that she may have been the one to inflict pain. Waythorn considers the word *duplicity* in relation to Alice, a word that means deliberate deceptiveness in behavior or speech, and can imply a double life or dual identity. Waythorn begins to wonder which Alice is the woman he married, troubled by what he perceives as Alice's alter ego.

A short time later, Waythorn again encounters Haskett. This time, however, Haskett intends to see him. Haskett voices his concerns about Lily's tutor, attributing to the tutor's negative influence Lily's increasing desire to please and tendency to lie to do so. In the course of the conversation, Haskett reveals that he has already raised the issue with Mrs. Waythorn. Upon hearing this, Waythorn realizes that Alice has deceived him but tries to excuse her actions. Haskett's devotion to his daughter and willingness to assert himself on her behalf increase his standing in Waythorn's opinion. Waythorn's greater knowledge of Alice forces him to acknowledge "unpleasant contingencies" (447) about her past, but when he confronts her with his questions, he finds himself irritated that "she expected him to regard her as a victim" (447). At a social event, Waythorn discovers Alice chatting with Varick, and this, too, bothers him. He reflects that "her pliancy was beginning to sicken him" (448) and derogatorily compares her to an old shoe, suggesting that she has been an easy fit for too many men. His thoughts reflect his growing awareness that he does not have sole "ownership" of Alice, that each man to whom she has been married has defined her in some way.

As Waythorn discovers more about his wife, he also discovers how his marriage to her has redefined him. He compares himself to "a member of a syndicate," an association of people authorized to transact business or carry out an enterprise. Through this image, Waythorn considers how each of Alice's husbands have invested in her, have in effect made her what she is. The conclusion of the tale brings the three men together in Waythorn's home. Having gathered in the library, they stand awkwardly before Alice when she enters the room. She, however, "swept aside their embarrassment with a charming gesture" (453) as she turns to pour tea. She hands cups to Haskett and Varick, then to Waythorn, who "took the third cup with a laugh" (453), as he realizes that she has become exactly what he wanted, a woman whose social grace and composure bring ease to his life. He sees that his own life is interwoven with that of his wife, so that he too cannot escape her past.

CHARACTERS

Known only by his surname, Waythorn serves as the central consciousness of the story and shapes how the reader sees him and his situation. Although he thinks he wants Alice to add sparkle and excitement to his dull life, Waythorn likes his routines and prefers to be in control. Conscious of what others think and expect, Waythorn deceives himself when he believes he can ignore the implications of Alice's past. He remains attuned to other's reactions to him and looks for signs of their affirmation or disapproval. He compares himself to the two men who have previously defined Alice's life, hoping to see himself in the most favorable light. When he discovers that neither of his predecessors is what he thought, Waythorn can no longer see himself as the man who has rescued a victimized Alice. Waythorn wants to believe that he is the sole "owner" of Alice and her affections, but over the course of the story discovers that she cannot shed her past and that he must accept her entire package.

The other two of the title, Alice's ex-husbands, are as different from each other as they are from Waythorn. Haskett embodies a number of middle-class virtues, including honesty and forthrightness. Quietly assertive rather than the brute Waythorn expected, Haskett acts out of concern for his daughter, for whom he has sacrificed everything that once defined his life. After meeting Haskett, Waythorn suspects that he was as devoted to Alice, and that she may have been the party who did wrong. In contrast to Haskett, Gus Varick has an appetite for the sensual pleasures of life. Of greater social standing than Haskett, Varick has a moderate degree of wealth and a business acumen that Waythorn admires. When Varick admits that he wished he made greater profits from his investments earlier, Waythorn begins to suspect that Varick, too, was not at fault for the end of his marriage, that Alice was looking for a man with greater means and social connections.

Although she does not change outwardly, Alice undergoes a series of transformations in Waythorn's eyes. Initially he appreciates her girl-ish attributes, qualities that also make him feel younger. He believes that in both her divorce suits, she had been the wronged party, that she had good cause to leave each of her marriages. In the story's opening, he sees Alice through the eyes of a lover who recognizes only the positive; but by its end, he sees her faults as well. At first troubled by them and what he believes has been the false image she projected, Waythorn comes to see that Alice is a mixed being just as he is, that she is a product of her social world, a product he desired. Because her self is her only resource, Alice functions as a commodity who ultimately goes to the highest bidder.

THEMES

Through Waythorn's point of view, Wharton reveals how the male gaze defines woman as object, something to be desired, owned, and defined. She also reveals how men depend upon women to ease their social interactions, to provide the civilizing touch that at least tem-porarily quiets their competitive instinct. Through Alice's past, Whar-ton delineates how women who have no access to public careers see marriage as the only means by which they can advance their financial and social standing. Alice's career as the wife of successively wealthier and more prestigious men only becomes possible after the wider ac-ceptance of divorce in the late nineteenth century. Wharton returns to the question of social advancement through a series of marriages in her novel *The Custom of the Country* (1913), in which the more aggressive and calculating Undine Spragg manipulates men to get what she desires.

"THE EYES" (1910, 1910)

Describing the qualities of an effective ghost story, Wharton explained, "once the preliminary horror [is] posited, it is the harping on the same string—the same nerve—that does the trick. Quiet iteration is far more racking than diversified assaults" (*Writing of Fiction* 40). In "The Eyes," Wharton uses a single spectral image as a source of terror for its witness and of suspense for the reader. She treats the supernatural and the uncanny as devices for exploring the psychological states and moral sensibilities of the three central characters in the tale. She also makes use of a frame story, a technique she employs to strong effect in *Ethan Frome* (see Plot and Structure, Chapter 6). Here, the frame story allows Wharton to create a mood of expectation and suspense, as the narrator discusses the pleasure of telling ghost stories among a circle of friends. First appearing in *Scribner's Magazine,* "The Eyes" was included in *Tales of Men and Ghosts.*

SETTING AND PLOT

The frame story takes place within Culwin's library, the atmosphere created by the haze of cigar smoke and the "drowsy gleam of a coal fire" (810). A group of friends have gathered there after dinner and taken turns telling ghost stories, which they have all enjoyed. Of the eight men present, only the host, Andrew Culwin, has not contributed a tale. Members of the group depart, leaving behind the narrator and Phil Frenham, a young protégé of Culwin. An exchange between Frenham and Culwin ensues, during which Frenham questions whether Culwin has seen a ghost. Wharton draws the reader into the story within a story through the posture of Frenham, who "leaned forward with his listening smile . . . " (813).

Culwin's tale begins in the Hudson Valley of New York, where he has taken up residence in the home of an elderly aunt after spending time abroad. He alludes to the local fascination with the supernatural through his mention of Washington Irving, author of "The Legend of Sleepy Hollow" and "Rip van Winkle." Culwin was contemplating writing a book, so his aunt "gave up to [him] her Gothic library" (814), his use of the term Gothic referring to architectural style, but also alluding to the literary tradition of supernatural tales.

To assist in his literary efforts, Culwin's aunt had "lent [him] a cousin to copy [his] manuscript" (814). The copyist, a young woman named Alice Nowell, appears happy with herself and her life. Culwin decides to probe her nature to discover "the secret of her content" (814), much as a Hawthornean or Jamesian protagonist might do. This situation also indirectly alludes to the story of Faust's desire for secret knowledge and ultimate contentment (see "Allusions" section in Chapter 8). Alice's romantic feelings for Culwin unsettle him. He contemplates leaving for Europe to escape her, but when she kisses him, he feels drawn to her, more out of curiosity than genuine feeling. Her kiss elicits the gift of his ring and the promise that she will travel with him, even though the picture of domestic contentment that he imagines makes him uneasy.

This encounter with his cousin creates the context for the first appearance of the supernatural. When Culwin retires to his chamber and lies in bed, he sees "a vague glimmer at the foot of the bed [that] turned into two eyes staring back at me" (816). Startled by what he sees, Culwin cannot look away. He describes the eyes as being "the very worst I've ever seen: . . . The orbits were sunk, and the thick, red-lined lids hung over the eyeballs like blinds. . . . One lid drooped a little lower than the other, with the effect of a crooked leer" (816). He believes they are the eyes of a man who "had done a lot of harm in his life, . . . not the eyes of a coward, but of someone much too clever to take risks" (817). Haunted through the night by this vision, Culwin fearfully departs the next day, leaving no word for Alice to explain his actions. He excuses what he has done, stating that his time abroad made him see that marriage to Alice Nowell would have been a terrible mistake.

Freed for a time from his ghost, Culwin settles in Rome to write a book on Italian art. While there he receives a visit from an attractive young man, Gilbert Noyes, bearing a one-line letter of introduction from Alice. Her letter asks that Culwin befriend young Noyes, who believes he has talent and also wishes to write. Culwin sees this as an opportunity to compensate Alice for his earlier behavior, so takes on the role of mentor to Noyes. Culwin reveals that Noyes had little talent, and that his desire for a literary career was in truth the desire to avoid family responsibilities and life behind a desk, the same life Culwin had escaped. Noyes was good company and visually appealing, however, so for a period of time Culwin refrains from telling Noyes the truth about his work. Having decided to confront him, Culwin loses his nerve, telling Noyes that his work has potential. That evening, Culwin finds himself once again haunted by the eyes, which have grown worse in their appearance since he saw them last.

With the reappearance of the eyes, Wharton breaks the narrative thread of Culwin's story, bringing the reader back into the narrator's time present. This adds to the tension of the tale by prolonging suspense, for Culwin's narrative has not reached its conclusion. During this interruption, the narrator describes the actions of Phil Frenham, whom Culwin has compared to Noyes during the course of his tale. Having bumped a table mirror, Frenham readjusts its angle and then resumes his listening pose. This pause invites the reader to recall the current relationship between Culwin and Frenham in light of what Culwin has just revealed.

Following this break, Culwin resumes his tale. He admits to having a confrontation with Noyes, blaming all that happens on Noyes's blindness and obstinacy. He raises the expectation of a tragic outcome when he admits that he left Noyes alone in Rome, but then says, "Oh, nothing tragic happened—the episode never rose to *that!*" (827). Culwin admits that Noyes decided to return to America, leaving a note of explanation for his departure, a sign that he behaves more responsibly than Culwin had in similar circumstances.

The narrative again returns to time present in which the real horror of the story emerges. At first it seems that the horror will relate to Noyes when the narrator asks Culwin about him. Culwin responds that he "vegetated in an office" and "married drearily" (827), failures compounded by Noyes's having lost his youthful attractiveness, and, as rumor had it, taken to drink. Culwin blames all of this on Noyes's individual failings. Having finished his recitation, Culwin approaches Phil Frenham, who appears both spellbound and distressed. Their eyes meet, after which Frenham buries his head in his arms, a gesture of shock and despair. The eyes that have haunted Culwin are the spectral image of Culwin's own, perceived first by Frenham and then by the narrator and Culwin who see them reflected in the mirror. As Culwin experiences the shock of recognition, he glares at his reflection with hatred: He is the figure he had described earlier as a man "who had done a lot of harm in his life" (817). The moment of insight and revelation forces him to confront who and what he is. It also frightens Frenham, who not only recognizes the truth about a man he has admired but sees what his imitation of Culwin might make of him.

CHARACTERS

Of the group of men who surround Culwin, only the narrator and Frenham emerge as distinctive characters. The narrator includes himself among those who avoid the "habit of sending our souls into the invisible" (810), emphasizing his rationality. He describes Frenham, an intelligent young man who has been recruited to their circle by Culwin. In joining them, Frenham has escaped the "fog of family dulness" (812), his nature enlarged through Culwin's influence. Frenham still believes in romantic ideals, what the narrator labels sacred stupidities, that form the basis of Frenham's admiration of Culwin.

The narrator uses much of the frame story to describe Culwin's character, presenting a man of epicurean tastes and sensibilities. He sees him as a "detached observer of the immense muddled variety show of life" (810), a man who enjoys gathering about him other men who will stimulate his thoughts and appetites. Another guest, Fred Murchard, claims that in admitting new members to their circle, Culwin "liked 'em juicy" (811), suggesting that Culwin consumes those he mentors. This remark and the allusion to Antinous, a beautiful youth who was the companion of the Roman emperor Hadrian, introduces a subtext of homosexuality into the tale. Culwin's efforts to distance himself from women, who are "necessary only because someone had to do the cooking" (811), reinforces the homosexual subtext and invites the reader to view more critically the relationship between Culwin and Noyes.

As he narrates his ghostly tale, Culwin reveals his alter ego or "shadow self" (Dyman 58). In the two instances that precede the appearance of the eyes, Culwin acts in exploitative and deceptive ways, unable to recognize the humanity of others. His fear of commitment with Alice Nowell hints at his homosexual inclinations as well as his fear of an ordinary life. His decision to deceive Noyes provides him with a companion whose charm with women provides cover for Culwin's homosexual interest. Each time he admits to a choice or action that appears questionable, Culwin excuses himself, refusing to accept responsibility for his actions. When he describes the spectral eyes that he has seen, he recognizes that they belong to an individual who has acted out of base and self-protective motives, but he fails to see the link between himself and these eyes until the end of the tale.

THEME

In this story, Wharton explores the theme of self-discovery, especially the recognition of dark aspects of the self that have been denied or repressed. Culwin has denied many truths about himself and his behavior, truths that are painful to acknowledge. He has used others to gratify his own desires, exploiting both men and women for selfish ends. Given the time in which the story was written, Culwin has also repressed public acknowledgment of his homosexuality. This creates an internal struggle that results in self-distrust, manifested in his mistreatment of others, allowing him to sever ties to anyone who has become too close to him.

SYMBOLS

The eyes and the mirror serve as multifaceted symbols in this tale. Eyes, sometimes referred to as mirrors of the soul, are thought to reveal deep truths about an individual, truths usually shielded from exposure. The spectral eyes that confront Culwin serve as "a representation of the repressed knowledge" that Culwin has of himself (Dyman 54). The mirror that appears in the middle and again at the end of the tale suggests a number of meanings. The mirror symbolizes the way that Culwin's narrative itself functions as a reflective surface, offering him a picture of his true self. Frenham's adjustment of the mirror's angle suggests that he is beginning to see Culwin from a new perspective, one that shows him a different man than he has seen before. It also suggests the way that Culwin's narrative functions like a looking glass for Frenham, revealing one vision of his own future.

"XINGU" (1911, 1916)

An amusing story that satirizes intellectual and social pretensions, "Xingu" addresses a topic of renewed interest, the book discussion group. In Wharton's treatment of the Lunch Club, she depicts six middle-class women who consume culture as they would any other commodity that in their eyes advances their social standing. The members of the club have little understanding of the books they read or the topics they discuss, but are convinced that their actions reflect their roles as cultural leaders of Hillbridge. Their intense competition and their fear of appearing in the wrong with their opinions keep all but Mrs. Roby from experiencing life or art. The title story of *Xingu and Other Stories,* it first appeared in *Scribner's Magazine.*

SETTING AND PLOT

"Xingu" takes place in suburban Hillbridge, a town without cultural distinction. Sensitive to the possibility of living in a cultural backwater, the members of the Lunch Club attempt to present themselves as in the know regarding cultural and intellectual trends. They treat culture as they do fashion, avoiding anything they fear is outdated or unsophisticated. Limited to six members to accommodate the size of Miss Van Vluyck's dining room, the club sees itself as upholding standards of high-brow taste and status, unconscious of the ways they display middle-brow preferences and attitudes.

The opening section of the story presents the club's anxieties over their decision to invite best-selling author Osric Dane to one of their meetings. Through their conversations with each other, Wharton reveals the insecurities and presumptions of each member. She highlights the nature of their competition, characterizing them like school girls vying to be head of the class. Mrs. Plinth's overbearing assertiveness and Mrs. Leveret's timid insecurities establish the parameters within which the club members vie for position. Only Mrs. Roby, viewed with distrust and disdain by the other group members, has enjoyed a life that has taken her beyond the small confines of Hillbridge. She cares little for what the other club members think of her, a trait that explains why someone like Professor Foreland might call her "agreeable" (2). When questioned as to why she has not read Osric Dane's work in preparation for the meeting, Mrs. Roby admits that her copy of one of the books had been tossed into the river while she was traveling in Brazil, a remark that confirms the club's opinion of her unsuitableness as a member.

When Osric Dane arrives, the general anxiety of the club members increases. Dane, clearly bored by having to make such appearances to promote her work, exhibits an air of superiority that unsettles the membership and leaves them speechless. She hopes by doing so to cut her appearance short, escaping the tedium of a conversation with fawning women. Mrs. Roby, who identifies Dane as a "brute" (9) when she enters, saves the club from Dane's merciless condescension by introducing the topic of Xingu. The other club members are as ignorant about Xingu as is Osric Dane, but they quickly chime in with remarks that imply knowledge without being specific, just as they have talked about every subject they have addressed. Dane, who feels her control of the situation slipping away, tries to determine what Xingu might be so that she can regain her authority. Meanwhile, Mrs. Roby drops vague hints through her remarks, manipulating language to keep all of her listeners guessing. Tiring of Mrs. Roby's dominance over the conversation, the club president brings the conversation back to Osric Dane's books. At this juncture, Mrs. Roby excuses herself, pleading lack of preparation and a prior engagement to play bridge. Seeing her opportunity for escape, Osric Dane, feigning great interest in Xingu, accompanies Mrs. Roby out the door.

Left to their own devices, the other members of the club rehash what has occurred. They display all their customary habits and eccentricities, eventually claiming victory over Osric Dane's snobbishness and diminishing any credit Mrs. Roby might deserve. Eventually they try to decipher just what Mrs. Roby meant by Xingu, looking up the word in an encyclopedia where they discover that it's the name of a river in Brazil. As they piece together what has been said, they discover that Mrs. Roby has simply been retelling her experience of the boat ride during which she lost her copy of Dane's novel. Incensed by what they now perceive as Mrs. Roby's betrayal, the members, led by Mrs. Plinth, demand that the president ask Mrs. Roby to resign from the club, or tender her own resignation to compensate for their embarrassment.

CHARACTERS

The members of the Lunch Club have distinctive qualities, but each serves as a representative type, rather than a rounded character. Mrs. Plinth's resistance to questioning, Mrs. Leveret's hesitations, Miss Van Vluyck's preference for statistics over fiction, Miss Glyde's skating over the surface of subjects, and Mrs. Ballinger's pride in offering the thought of the day govern the ways in which the women converse. None has a real desire to do the work of genuine study necessary to comprehend many of the topics they choose to address. They all, however, pretend to knowledge.

Mrs. Roby follows her own inclinations, seeing through the other members' pretensions and unwilling to adopt their views of life. Her firsthand experience of travel and her honesty give her credibility that the others lack. When she meets Osric Dane, Mrs. Roby perceives a figure as unpleasant and pretentious as the members of the club. She uses her discussion of Xingu to deflate both Dane and the club members, knowing that none of them will admit to their ignorance and ask her a direct question. Her announcement that she has not prepared for the book discussion and intends to leave to keep a bridge date reveals Mrs. Roby's lack of reverence for Hillbridge's pseudo-cultural pretensions. Her wit and ability with language indicate that she has creative talents, unlike any of the others.

Osric Dane, the haughty and condescending "lady author," provokes the club's anxieties, using her barbed comments to conceal her own shallowness. Her behavior signifies her boredom with the routines of an author's book tour because she shows little interest in cultivating this audience for her work. Faced with the possibility of an entire afternoon of platitudes and vague remarks, Dane seizes her chance to escape when Mrs. Roby announces her departure. She has no real interest in Xingu, but it provides her with an excuse to accompany Mrs. Roby out the door.

THEMES

In satirizing the intellectual and cultural pretensions of the Lunch Club, Wharton comments on the difference between genuine knowledge and acquisition of superficial bits of information. She treats the women of the club as consumers, as ready to select subjects from a varied menu of current topics as if they are merchandise from a department store counter. They want their knowledge, like their clothing and their homes, to be fashionable. Wharton suggests that in the capitalist marketplace of America, literary culture has become one more accessory. Through the behavior of the club, Wharton addresses the stultifying aspects of women's roles that generate their petty competitions and meaningless rivalries. Because they have no meaningful outlets for their energies, they engage in a performance meant to invoke cultural meaning, one for which each player has memorized her part.

ALLUSIONS

The allusions that appear in the story convey the pedestrian sensibilities of the book club as well as their pretensions toward knowledge of literature and art. When the group compares the significance of Osric Dane's work to the importance of *Robert Elsmere,* a novel by Mrs. Humphrey (Mary Augusta) Ward, they reveal their lack of discrimination. Ward, a popular British novelist of the late nineteenth century, wrote bestsellers that convey earnestness and high moral purpose, but lack the literary qualities of first-rate fiction. The references to "Prince Rupert" and to "Apelles" are attempts to claim an appreciation of art history, but serve little purpose in adding clarity to the conversation. The irony of the club's love of allusions emerges in Mrs.

Leveret's need to carry her copy of a volume entitled *Appropriate Allusions.* She has never been able to use the only allusion she can remember—a verse from Job.

"AUTRE TEMPS" (1911, 1916)

In "Autre Temps," Wharton explores whether Mrs. Lidcote, a divorcée, will experience social rehabilitation upon her return to America following years of exile in Europe. She had violated a taboo of her culture by divorcing her husband to marry another man and believes she still pays the social price for that decision. Her own daughter Leila has also divorced her first husband to marry another, without suffering the ostracism and condemnation that Mrs. Lidcote experienced. Mrs. Lidcote wonders whether the passage of time and changing social codes will allow her to resume a life in society and to enjoy a romantic relationship with an old friend, Franklin Ide. Individuals close to her keep repeating that times have changed, but Mrs. Lidcote questions the truth of this maxim that influences the story's title. A selection in *Xingu and Other Stories,* "Autre Temps" first appeared in *Scribner's Magazine.*

SETTING AND PLOT

The story opens as a steamship approaches New York, whose skyline to Mrs. Lidcote appears as a "huge, menacing mass" (59). The source of Mrs. Lidcote's "unreasoning terror" (59) lies not in the city itself, but in the social world it symbolizes to her. During her journey, thoughts of the past have weighed heavily on Mrs. Lidcote and she wonders how she will be received. The society that matters to her had excluded her years earlier in the aftermath of her divorce, an action it viewed as a transgression of the social code. For eighteen years she has lived abroad, returning only for brief visits with her daughter. She has remained sensitive to any sign of reproach from others, such as the cold shoulder or cut she perceives as coming from Mrs. Boulger.

Mrs. Lidcote finds it hard to read the social world to which she returns, with its "fluid state of manners" that leaves her feeling as though she still operates within "old-fashioned categories" (61). In some respects, she hopes change has occurred, both for herself and her daughter, Leila. Leila has divorced Horace Pursh to be able to marry Wilbour Barkley, causing Mrs. Lidcote to fear that people will think "like mother, like daughter." While on shipboard, her encounter with Franklin Ide gives Mrs. Lidcote hope that "things are different now" (63). His obvious romantic interest makes Mrs. Lidcote think that a new life may begin for her.

When she arrives in New York, Mrs. Lidcote finds a cousin, Suzy Suffern, waiting for her. Miss Suffern explains Leila's absence and seems to accept the turn Leila's life has taken. Mrs. Lidcote remarks on Suzy's outlook, that she no longer harbors the conservative sensibility and censorious ways of Old New York, another sign of hope for Mrs. Lidcote. Before she travels to join her daughter, Mrs. Lidcote visits with Franklin Ide, confessing to him that she now wonders what her role will be in Leila's life. While her daughter was unhappily married, Mrs. Lidcote served as a sympathetic mainstay, but Mrs. Lidcote fears that Leila's new marriage will create distance between them.

Leila has suggested that her mother remain with Miss Suffern through the weekend while Leila and her husband Wilbour entertain other guests at their summer home. Mrs. Lidcote, however, decides to travel directly to Lenox (site of Wharton's summer home in the Berkshire Hills of Massachusetts). During their journey, Miss Suffern provides additional details about Leila's situation and about her ex-husband Horace's plans to remarry as well. This information makes Mrs. Lidcote wonder "since her daughter had no penalty to pay, was not she herself released by the same stroke?" (71). In her daughter's warm embrace, Mrs. Lidcote finds further assurance that all will be well, but once alone in her room, she senses "the deepest feeling of security for Leila and the strongest sense of apprehension for herself" (72). She begins to resent her years of exile and the toll social ostracism took on the man she loved. She wonders whether her own divorce simply occurred at the wrong time and begins to feel a degree of envy over her daughter's opportunity to find happiness without paying so great a price.

Having begged off afternoon activity in light of fatigue, Mrs. Lidcote awaits a private conversation with her daughter. To her dismay, the conversation lasts only an hour before Leila is called away. When Mrs. Lidcote proposes going down to tea, Miss Suffern dissuades her as the housemaid enters with a laden tea tray. Mrs. Lidcote questions Leila's "excess of solicitude" (74) and suspects that Miss Suffern has been asked to keep her out of sight until the other guests depart. During their tea, Miss Suffern lists who will attend the dinner being given for Mrs. Boulger that evening. She explains that Leila's husband Wilbour hopes to receive a foreign service appointment to Rome, where Mrs. Boulger's husband serves as consul. Upon learning of this, Mrs. Lidcote wonders whether Leila has hidden her away to avoid conflict. She decides to go down to dinner to determine the truth.

Before dinner, Leila again visits her mother, commenting on her need for more rest. When Mrs. Lidcote asks whether the other guests will find it awkward to encounter her at dinner, Leila says nothing, but blushes "to her very temples" (80) in embarrassment over the truth. Not wanting to put her daughter through the kind of torments she herself has faced or to be a source of contention between Leila and her husband, Mrs. Lidcote excuses herself from dinner. Her fear that her daughter's new marriage will create distance between them is not without merit.

Perceiving the truth through what has transpired, Mrs. Lidcote decides to return to Italy, informing Leila after the other guests have departed. Knowing that Franklin Ide hopes to visit her when she returns to New York, Mrs. Lidcote resolves not to see him. He arrives at her hotel room and attempts to convince her that she has been mistaken in her interpretation of events. He assumes that she had attended the dinner given by Wilbour and Leila and cannot understand why she thinks women like Mrs. Wynn, a former friend, cut her. When she explains what occurred in Lenox, and how one former friend visited her surreptitiously "at the eleventh hour" (84), Ide accuses her of imagining that slights were intended. Because his own happiness hinges on her acceptance of his proposal, Ide does everything in his power to persuade Mrs. Lidcote that the past has been forgotten.

Ide asks her why she did not put her "preconceived theories" (86) to the test by joining her old friends at dinner. Mrs. Lidcote appreciates his kindness, but cannot overlook his "unreality" (87). She puts Ide's convictions to the test instead, suggesting they go together to call on Margaret Wynn. Ide invents a series of excuses to avoid doing so; then blushes, much as Leila did, when Mrs. Lidcote sees through his prevarications. Knowing that life for her has not changed, that "the veil of painted gauze was torn in tatters and that she was moving again among the grim edges of reality" (88), Mrs. Lidcote prepares to resume her exile, knowing that she must do so alone.

CHARACTERS

Similar to Lydia Tillotson of "Souls Belated," Mrs. Lidcote left her husband to be with a man she loved. Through her experience, Mrs. Lidcote discovered that love "is worth so much and no more" (73), something the man she loved had realized first, eventually ending their relationship. Mrs. Lidcote has been alone for most of the eighteen years since she departed New York. During her exile she has felt the past weigh heavily upon her, defining who she is and controlling the way former friends treat her. She believes that she has never been forgiven for what she has done, even though over the years society has become more tolerant of divorce and remarriage. Throughout her exile she has maintained a relationship with her daughter, which has provided some meaning and purpose in her life. When she returns to America to see her daughter, Mrs. Lidcote feels torn between two possibilities: She hopes that she can find freedom and a new life in the world that has evolved since her departure, but she fears that times have not changed, that judgments of her have been cast in stone.

Suzy Suffern, Leila Barkley, and Franklin Ide are all secure in their social positions, but none can guarantee Mrs. Lidcote's social redemption. All three attempt to convince her that the social scene has changed, that her own situation will improve under the new views held by society. At the same time, they all prevent Mrs. Lidcote from encountering members of her former circle whose reactions will reveal the truth. Miss Suffern colludes with Leila to keep Mrs. Lidcote confined to her room at the Lenox house. Miss Suffern wishes to protect Mrs. Lidcote from rejection, while Leila hopes to avoid the social awkwardness and possible damage to Wilbour's career that her mother's presence threatens. Franklin Ide, who believes his feelings for Mrs. Lidcote are strong enough that he can endure exile with her, tries to convince Mrs. Lidcote that she is mistaken about how people see her. His own actions at the end of the story, however, betray his lack of confidence. His convictions, like Leila's, fail when put to the test.

THEMES

As does Hawthorne, Wharton suggests that the past is inescapable, regardless of the social changes that have occurred in a given era. Part of the American myth offers the possibility of constructing a new self when the old one no longer suits, allowing an individual to walk away from the past. Mrs. Lidcote confronts the illusion of this myth, what she refers to as the "painted gauze" (88), when she encounters deep resistance as she tries to reenter her social world. Her former acquaintances have long memories, associating her forever with the rule she has broken.

"ROMAN FEVER" (1934, 1936)

Late in her career, Wharton wrote "Roman Fever," a story now considered a masterpiece in the genre. Published in the magazine *Liberty,* it was included in the collection *The World Over.* In "Roman Fever," Wharton captures the intensity of competition between two women, who, like Delia Ralston and Charlotte Lovell of *The Old Maid,* experience a lifelong rivalry rooted in their love of the same man. In the story, the situation in the present seems rather placid, as two widows, Mrs. Slade and Mrs. Ansley, sit on a terrace overlooking the Roman Forum. When they begin to talk about the past, however, the true nature of their relationship and feelings about each other emerge. Like gladiators in the Coliseum, they contend until only one is left standing.

SETTING AND PLOT

Set in Rome in the years following World War I, "Roman Fever" evokes the weight of the past through references to the Roman Forum and Coliseum, relics of an era of empire and conquest. The two central characters, Alida Slade and Grace Ansley, survey the scene from a restaurant terrace after lunch, enjoying the leisurely pace of the afternoon. They hear their daughters depart for an afternoon's adventure, reflecting on the way times have changed as their daughters go out unchaperoned. When Mrs. Slade poses the question, "Do you remember?" Mrs. Ansley says, "Oh, yes, I remember" (750), establishing the importance of memory and the past in both their lives. Mrs. Slade and Mrs. Ansley pass the afternoon in conversation, each revealing her impressions of the other and her view of their common past.

As their conversation continues, each woman realizes how little she actually knows of the other, and the narrator comments that each views the other "through the wrong end of her telescope" (753). After a period of silent reflection, Mrs. Slade remarks that Rome has meant different things to each generation, comparing the views of their grandmothers, mothers, and themselves. She recalls how their mothers struggled to ensure their propriety by restricting their movements, unlike the freedom given to daughters Barbara Ansley and Jenny Slade. Eventually their conversation turns to the last time they were both in Rome, when they were young.

Mrs. Slade instigates the beginning of their verbal contest by asking how Horace and Grace Ansley had ever produced a child as attractive and socially successful as Barbara. Mrs. Slade feels a degree of disappointment in her own daughter, Jenny, whom she feels lacks the dash that will make her a social success. Mrs. Ansley hesitates to respond, and Mrs. Slade feels guilty about her envy, but she presses on. She recalls a story of Mrs. Ansley's aunt who had sent her own sister into the Forum at night hoping her sister would contract an illness to eliminate her as a rival for a man's love. Again, Grace Ansley diminishes the importance of the story, trying to ignore these references to the past. Mrs. Slade finally reaches the issue she has wanted to discuss, the rivalry between the two women over Delphin Slade and the ruse Mrs. Slade staged to get Mrs. Ansley out of her way. So pleased is she by what she had done that Mrs. Slade goes into detail about the note she sent arranging a rendezvous in the Coliseum between Delphin and Grace. Mrs. Slade admits that she hated Mrs. Ansley for attracting Delphin Slade's attention and wanted to punish her. Her sense of superiority asserts itself again in their conversation, as Mrs. Slade "continued to look down on" Mrs. Ansley (760).

Just as Mrs. Slade reaches her moment of triumph and begins to excuse her actions as a nasty joke, Mrs. Ansley interrupts her. Mrs. Ansley confesses that she did meet Delphin at the Coliseum. She had answered the note that Mrs. Slade had written, assuming it was from Delphin, and he "had arranged everything" (761). In telling her that she feels sorry for her, Mrs. Ansley rekindles Mrs. Slade's pride and mettle. Mrs. Slade asserts that she has been the victor because Grace Ansley had Delphin for one night, whereas Alida Slade had him for twenty-five years. With a single line, Mrs. Ansley deflates Mrs. Slade's pretensions to victory when she states, "I had Barbara" (762) and walks away.

CHARACTERS

When they first appear in the story, Mrs. Slade and Mrs. Ansley seem indistinguishable, "two American ladies of ripe but well cared for middle age" (749). Mrs. Slade, of richer and darker coloring, seems robust

and full of self-confidence, while Mrs. Ansley, "smaller and paler" initially seems modest and retiring, the opposite of her companion. As
the tale progresses, their distinct personalities emerge and govern
their interaction.

Mrs. Slade believes her life has been one of great social import as
the wife of the successful Delphin Slade. Now that her husband has
died, Mrs. Slade has little role to play and fears that she will be forgotten in circles that matter. To measure her own success, she has
compared herself to Mrs. Ansley throughout their adult lives, always
perceiving herself to be the better, happier woman. She pities Mrs.
Ansley for the quietness of her life and believes that she has missed
out on the exciting opportunities Mrs. Slade has enjoyed. The one
point of comparison that fails to bring Mrs. Slade satisfaction is the
consideration of their daughters. Mrs. Slade clearly wants to see the
competition with Mrs. Ansley continue into the next generation, but
she feels frustrated that her own Jenny is no match for Mrs. Ansley's
Barbara.

Mrs. Ansley, on the other hand, appears reserved and retiring, not
one to seek the limelight or public notice. She seems to have thought
little about Mrs. Slade, even though for years they lived across the
street from each other. She has a quiet confidence about her and an
appreciation of her daughter that suggests that Barbara's social ease
derives from her mother's affirmation. The narrative reveals that what
has sustained Mrs. Ansley through the years is the secret she has kept,
the truth about her meeting with Delphin Slade and Barbara's pater-
nity. Free of the anxieties that plague Mrs. Slade, Mrs. Ansley has never
felt the need to use her knowledge to score a point in their competition. Not until pressed to her limit does Mrs. Ansley land the blow
that ends the contest.

THEMES

In this story, Wharton raises questions about the effects of the past
on the present. She considers how individuals construct their identities based on their interpretations of the past and the meaning of their
actions. Both Mrs. Slade and Mrs. Ansley have kept secrets that have
given them a sense of security through the years, shaping how each
has responded to the circumstances in her life. Through their relationship, Wharton explores the destructive aspects of female rivalry
and the covert actions that women pursue to achieve their ends. She

also considers how mothers influence their daughters, both through heredity and socialization, an issue that makes more pointed the defeat suffered by Mrs. Slade.

Wharton explores the complex nature of relationships between men and women in many of her stories, including "The Dilettante" (1903, 1904) and "The Twilight of the God" (1904). She presents women as authors or public speakers in "April Showers" (1900), "Copy" (1900, 1901), and "The Pelican" (1898, 1899) as well as "Xingu." Other examples of Wharton's ghost stories, such as "Afterward" (1910, 1910), "The Lady's Maid's Bell" (1902, 1904), and "Pomegranate Seed" (1931, 1936) have attracted the interest of readers and critics alike.

4

Two Novellas: *Madame de Treymes* (1907) and *The Old Maid* (1924)

One of Edith Wharton's first sustained efforts in fiction was the novella *Fast and Loose,* written in 1876, but not published until 1977. Wharton returned to this form throughout her writing career. Sometimes referred as a novelette, the novella is a prose narrative longer than a short story, but shorter than a novel. It usually contains greater development of character and motive than does the short story, but fewer characters and more limited action than the novel. In writing novellas, Wharton often employed a longer time span than she felt the short story could support, using the effects of the passage of time to heighten the psychological tensions between her characters. In addition to *Madame de Treymes* (1907) and *The Old Maid* (1924), other examples of Wharton's use of this form include *The Touchstone* (1900), *Sanctuary* (1903), and *Bunner Sisters* (1916).

Seventeen years separate the composition of *Madame de Treymes* (1907) and *The Old Maid* (1924). Although they differ in setting and plot, the underlying issues that generate dramatic tension in *Madame de Treymes* resonate in *The Old Maid.* In both novellas, Wharton explores the exercise of family power that controls the future of those subject to it. She also reveals the gender expectations that govern women's places and limit their options. In both novellas, maternal attachments to children further limit the options women see for themselves, especially when the threat of losing a child looms. This dilemma arises through different plot lines in each novella, but through each Wharton introduces the theme of renunciation, which she identifies as one of the earliest sources of fiction in *The Writing of Fiction.*

MADAME DE TREYMES (1907)

As did Henry James in much of his fiction, Wharton examines the difficulties Americans have interpreting European culture in her novella *Madame de Treymes.* She uses the word *read* to describe how American characters attempt to decipher the linguistic and behavioral codes that convey European values and expectations. She identifies the source of characters' difficulty as the American emphasis on individual conscience that makes problematic the European loyalty to family and tradition. She further suggests that Americans approach conflict in a straightforward manner that makes them easy to deceive. The American John Durham does not perceive Madame de Treymes' signals that indicate he must look more deeply into the question of Fanny de Malrive's divorce.

SETTING

Set in Paris at the turn of the twentieth century, *Madame de Treymes* presents a variety of contrasts that establish the context for the characters and their situation. The city is seen through the eyes of John Durham, who admits that it may be "the most beautiful city in the world," especially when compared to the "unenlightened ugliness" of New York (3). He concedes, however, that his perceptions of the city are governed by his mood: If he succeeds in winning Fanny de Malrive, Paris will retain its beauty and reputation as city of romance.

In addition to the physical setting of Paris, Wharton emphasizes the cultural setting, especially the concepts of tradition, heritage, and family that govern how Parisians see themselves and the world. When John Durham goes to the Hôtel de Malrive, he sees the family portraits, the "great gilt consoles" and the "monumental gateway" (24) as signs not only of the family's past, but also its connections to the history of France. Wharton uses the figures who appear at the Marquise de Malrive's to represent this historic legacy and the attitudes that preserve it. The older women dressed in somber black and purple, present "in [their] remoteness and solidarity . . . [Durham's] first glimpse of the social force of which Fanny de Malrive had spoken" and he realizes "as he observed them, that he had never before known what 'society' meant" (25). Their uniformity of appearance and attitude reflect the barriers that Durham knows he must surmount to achieve his goal.

In this novella, Wharton also uses metaphors associated with the cycle of the seasons to foreshadow the outcome of Durham and Fanny's relationship, a technique she employs again in *Summer.* The opening chapters take place in spring, evoking the possibilities of new life and a fresh start, especially for Fanny de Malrive. Traditionally, spring also connotes youth and the opportunities for romance. The negotiations between the lawyers for Madame de Malrive and her husband take place in summer, a time associated with optimism and fruitfulness. Durham's return to Paris in the early autumn, however, foreshadows diminished hopes. Associated with the story of Adam and Eve's expulsion from Eden, fall evokes sober reflection and a recognition of the consequences of one's actions. By the end of his conversations with Madame de Treymes, Durham realizes that his own hopes of an untroubled union with Fanny de Malrive have been dashed.

PLOT AND STRUCTURE

A focused narrative, *Madame de Treymes* traces John Durham's efforts to free Fanny de Malrive from her unhappy marriage so that they might marry. Wharton organizes the plot in stages, first presenting Durham's attempt to learn the lay of the land, then examining his strategy to approach Madame de Treymes, and finally, through their cryptic conversations, revealing his thwarted dream. Wharton describes the encounters between Durham and Madame de Treymes through the metaphor of a fencing match. Fencing depends as much on mental discipline as on physical strength, more on position and grace of movement than on brute force. John Durham assumes that the duel will be a direct confrontation, unaware of the feints and distractions that Madame de Treymes and her family will use to gain their point.

Durham's need to survey his situation begins with his relationship with Fanny de Malrive. As the novella opens, Durham presents himself as a careful observer, a man who notices details and nuances. He attempts to read Fanny's behavior for signals that will tell him where he stands with her. He also appreciates the changes that have occurred in her as she has been molded by European culture. Attracted to her greater refinement, Durham notices her increased depth of character and her social ease. He feels fairly confident in interpreting her signals, but also engages her in conversation to determine exactly what barriers prevent their marriage.

In these conversations, Fanny reveals her need to remain near her son. She does not want her son reared under the same conditions and social system that corrupted his father. She fears that her son will be detained if she leaves France, and cannot contemplate the possibility of surrendering him to her husband's family. Further, she assumes that her husband will contest any divorce action, making it impossible for her to remarry in France. She implies that her husband's family is not to be trusted, that they will engage in devious means to prevent her from dissolving her marriage. Durham pledges his efforts to remove the barriers that prohibit their union, agreeing to forego life in America to forward his suit. He decides to approach Fanny's sister-in-law, Madame de Treymes, for assistance. She seems the only member of the Malrive family sympathetic to Fanny.

Upon making this decision, Durham again surveys his situation. He observes Madame de Treymes during their first encounter, noting that she projects an "*aura* of grace" (18) that makes her handsome, if not conventionally beautiful. He notices that she too perceives the nuances of motion, gesture, and expression; despite their stilted conversation, she has gained much insight and information. Durham realizes that Madame de Treymes will not be easy to persuade, so before approaching her directly, he seeks more background about her from his cousins the Boykins. What he learns reveals that Christiane de Treymes has a complex history, replete with extramarital relationships that compensate for her own unhappy marriage. Durham hopes that her personal background will make Madame de Treymes more receptive to his appeal.

After Durham learns what he can about Madame de Treymes, he pursues the opportunity to meet and to explain his request. Spending lavishly at a charity function hosted by members of Madame de Treymes' circle, Durham receives an invitation to an afternoon at the Hôtel de Malrive. Accustomed to the openness of American conversation, Durham feels as though he moves in darkness when speaking to Madame de Treymes, finding it hard to get his bearings. During their conversation, she listens attentively as Durham asks her to intercede. Even in this conversation she tells him that "family considerations are paramount" (28), but Durham believes he has gained some ground in persuading Madame de Treymes to help him. He invites her to attend a dinner at the Boykins' where they can continue their discussion.

In their conversation following dinner, Madame de Treymes presents her own dilemma to Durham, explaining that she has used money that was not her own to support the gambling of her current love, the Prince d'Armillac. She explains that she will be more inclined to help Durham if he will compensate her for her assistance. Shocked by this request that invites him to "buy the right to marry Fanny de Malrive" (35), Durham recoils from Madame de Treymes' proposition. When he sees Fanny the next day, Durham tells her that he has not succeeded in his quest, that they will receive no assistance from Madame de Treymes. He does not tell her of the monetary terms raised by Madame de Treymes, for he does not wish to owe his happiness or Fanny's to a bribe. They part company "on a note of renunciation" (38), assuming that they have no hope of being together. Both are surprised when Fanny receives news that her husband has decided not to contest the divorce, and she believes that Durham has been successful after all.

To maintain the propriety of their relationship, Durham agrees to leave Paris for the summer while the negotiations for the divorce proceed. He does so with a degree of uneasiness, believing that things are not entirely as they appear, but gives in to Fanny's optimism. Before he leaves, he has another conversation with Madame de Treymes, whose own situation with the Prince d'Armillac has come to grief. Durham attempts to thank her and apologize for his refusal to assist her earlier. She responds by telling him that she has taken something as compensation for her pains to assist him, but does not explain. She smiles at him "elusively, ambiguously" (46), as her words foreshadow the unpleasant truth that awaits Durham, a truth he does not anticipate.

When he returns to Paris in early autumn, Durham agrees that he cannot visit Fanny because her divorce decree has not been finalized. He accepts her request that he visit instead with Madame de Treymes. In the conversation that ensues, Madame de Treymes tells Durham that she knows he is a man of principle because he did not tell Fanny of the financial proposal. In light of this, she says she must tell him the true situation: The family has agreed to the divorce because under French law they can reclaim Madame de Malrive's son. Madame de

Treymes reminds Durham that family takes precedence and that her family's sole object was to get the boy, whatever the cost. Seeing Durham's pained reaction, she tells him that she may be lying once again, that he should not trust her. Durham knows, however, that Fanny will never agree to a divorce if it means surrendering her son. He cannot deceive her to be able to marry her. His own principled nature and his genuine love for Fanny create his dilemma. He calls Madame de Treymes a "poor, good woman" (59), believing that she has fore-warned him and given him the opportunity to make the decision about his future. She sees in him a man who will sacrifice his own happiness for the happiness of a woman he loves, and calls him in turn a "poor, good man" (59).

CHARACTERS

In the novella, the action revolves around three main characters—John Durham, Fanny de Malrive, and Christiane de Treymes. Durham's character develops through his interactions with others because the third-person narration follows his perspective. Through his observations and evaluations, the reader gains insights into the appearances and traits of both Fanny de Malrive and Christiane de Treymes.

A middle-aged American, John Durham believes that in Fanny de Malrive he has found the woman he wishes to marry. Willing to do whatever necessary to make their marriage possible, he accepts the challenge of persuading Madame de Treymes to intercede for Fanny. At times he thinks of this as a mission or a quest he has undertaken to free the captive Fanny, but Durham does not see himself as a traditional romantic hero. His rational approach to life and the questions before him anchor him in a world of reality. A man of principles, he cannot violate them to find an easy way out of his problems. When he refuses Madame de Treymes' request for money and later decides to sacrifice his own happiness with Fanny, Durham believes he must do the right thing.

When known as Fanny Frisbee in New York, little distinguished Fanny de Malrive from the other young women in her set. She had then been "bold," had "dash," and the "showiest national attributes, tempered only by a native grace of softness" (16). Fanny Frisbee drew no special interest from John Durham, but he is drawn to the Madame de Malrive who has absorbed the refinements of culture and has matured in her understanding of life. Fanny still holds a positive view of

American freedom and individualism. She calls Americans "good, sweet, simple" (5), a sentiment echoed in *The Age of Innocence* by Ellen Olenska, who also tries to leave an unhappy European marriage.

Fanny de Malrive has separated from her husband, a French aristocrat, but retains custody of their son, whom she hopes to raise with an American sensibility. Her own struggles with the entrenched power of the family have made her wary of attempting to negotiate with her husband for a divorce. She believes that her husband and his family will either openly oppose the divorce suit or will engage in subterfuge to keep the divorce decree from being granted. Fanny wants to believe in Durham's ability to make their future possible. When she thinks he has succeeded, her own optimism carries her through the summer and she does not question her husband's decision.

A more complex character than Fanny de Malrive, Christiane de Treymes intrigues and troubles John Durham. He sees her as the product of her culture, for good and ill. Durham admires Madame de Treymes' way of carrying herself, her perceptive attention to detail, and her penetrating gaze. Through conversations with his cousins, he learns that Madame de Treymes has an unhappy marriage. Denied an opportunity to seek divorce due to religious teachings and family expectations, she engages in extramarital affairs. While his cousins express disdain toward Christiane de Treymes and object to her behavior, Durham feels a degree of sympathy for her. He does, however, find frustrating her ability to say two things at once, to imply an undercurrent of meaning in her words. Durham hesitates to trust her, especially after she raises the issue of monetary compensation, but sees no other recourse.

During their first substantive conversation, Madame de Treymes tells Durham that family considerations outweigh all else. She hints from the beginning that Durham must look beyond surface issues, to consider French attitudes and legal history. He assumes that all of her references are to divorce, but she means child custody. In their final conversation, she claims that her own suffering has allowed her to understand both Durham and Fanny de Malrive. She admits that in their previous conversations she spoke an "old language" that both foreshadowed and concealed the misery in store for Durham. She rebukes Durham for his trust and faith, but then plays upon it one last time when she tells him what may be the truth. She knows that whether she speaks the truth or not, Durham will not risk bringing lifelong unhappiness to Fanny. Durham's assessment of her is that she has acted out of right feeling, that despite her loyalty to family and tradition, she is at heart a good woman.

MINOR CHARACTERS

The minor characters in the novella, including John Durham's mother and sisters as well as his cousins the Boykins, provide additional insight and commentary on the main characters. They also reflect American views of Europe, expressing the chauvinism of those who see American national identity as superior.

John Durham's mother represents the very simplicity and sweetness that Fanny de Malrive associates with America. Mrs. Durham hopes to see her son happy, even though she wishes he had picked a Fanny Frisbee for his future wife rather than Fanny de Malrive. Mrs. Durham fears that the complications of Fanny's life will bring additional burdens to her son, but she is willing to do whatever she can to support them. Less concerned with their brother's situation, Durham's sisters Nannie and Katy reflect both the naiveté and chauvinism of young Americans. They are impressed by and judgmental toward what they encounter in Paris, suggesting the narrowness of their previous experiences.

Elmer and Bessy Boykin reinforce this narrowness of view. They have lived in Paris for twenty-five years, leaving America because it did not offer the standard of decorum by which they wished to live. Through the Boykins, Wharton satirizes a number of American presumptions and expectations. The Boykins have retained their American sensibility, in part because they seldom mix with the French. They view French aristocrats with suspicion, believing that invitations they receive are only to solicit contributions for charities. They thrive on the gossip that they hear about these same aristocrats, hoping to be perceived as having inside knowledge. They envy the French aristocrats as well, sensing that their own life in Paris leaves something to be desired. The Boykins believe that they are above social climbing, but are quite flattered when Madame de Treymes agrees to attend a dinner in their home.

THEMES

In *Madame de Treymes,* Wharton treats a number of themes that recur in later works, including the ways that families influence and control the lives of individuals. Madame de Treymes tries to explain to Durham that family sensibility and cultural expectations are one in the same in her world. To say that the culture does not accept something means that the family will not condone it either. This attitude creates a foundation for social stability, for it honors the concept of unity and tradition, thus preserving the status quo.

Wharton also explores the ways in which an individual consciously attempts to resist the power of the culture in which he or she exists. For Fanny de Malrive, this occurs both through her desire to reclaim her own American sensibility and to protect her son from a culture she sees as destructive. Fanny believes that the control exerted by family, church, and tradition stifles individual development and freedom. She wants her son to enjoy possibilities of self-realization that aristocratic French culture will not permit. Only by keeping him close to her and overseeing his upbringing and education will she ensure his freedom, even if she cannot have her own.

The problem of language forms another significant theme in the novella. Rather than focus on the differences between English and French, Wharton explores the ways that words in any language can signify more than one meaning, depending on how they are manipulated by the speaker and interpreted by the listener. For John Durham, the words used by Madame de Treymes create as many questions as they answer, but he feels unsure at times about which questions to ask. Madame de Treymes perceives the limits of Durham's outlook on the problem before him, so she knows that when she makes certain statements, he will interpret them in ways that serve her plans. Language thus functions as a means of conveying and concealing information and ideas.

THE OLD MAID (1924)

Published in 1924 as part of a series of novellas collected under the title *Old New York, The Old Maid* juxtaposes the proper, married Delia Ralston to the frustrated spinster, Charlotte Lovell. Delia appears to have everything that Charlotte does not: a secure marriage, healthy children, and a happy household. As the narrative develops, the reader discovers that Charlotte has enjoyed one thing for which Delia envies her, a love affair with the artist Clement Spender. This union produced the child known as Tina Lovell, whose daughterly devotion both women hope to win. The rivalry between the two women drives the plot, a situation Wharton also employs in "Roman Fever." In 1935, Zoe Akins, an American playwright, wrote a dramatization of *The Old Maid* that won a Pulitzer Prize. In 1939, her dramatization was made into a film starring Bette Davis in the title role.

SETTING

The Old Maid is subtitled "The Fifties," a reference to the 1850s, during which Part II of the novella takes place. The opening chapters are set in the 1840s, and Wharton uses the details of the physical and social setting to create a context for her characters. She emphasizes that in the New York of this era, a few families ruled society in a world defined by simplicity and affluence. Wharton provides many details about interior settings and meals to evoke the atmosphere of a bygone era for her readers. These details also reaffirm Delia Ralston's sense of identity as she views her surroundings. She sees in them a reflection of the values and mores that have shaped her life.

In the opening chapter, Wharton outlines the mindset of the Ralston family and uses them as the conservative epitome of this social world. To the Ralstons, the most important aspects of life are the preservation of family vigor and family fortunes. Spouses are chosen not only for their social status, but also for their good health and sturdiness, their ability to add children to the family line. The Ralstons are cautious in their investments, avoiding needless risk and preferring steady returns, a "3% investment," from things sanctioned by their financial and social peers. In fact, the family watchwords, *soundness, safeness,* and *suitability,* have echoed through the choices Delia, a Ralston by marriage, has made.

PLOT AND STRUCTURE

The narrative of *The Old Maid* is divided into two parts, each focusing on a crisis that will affect the future for the central characters. The crises occur approximately fourteen years apart, but the nature of the second crisis hinges on the outcome of the first. In each instance, Delia Ralston takes it upon herself to manage the situation. In each she acts to preserve her own interests as much as to protect the well-being of those she has promised to help.

The first crisis occurs in the mid 1840s, in the early years of Delia Ralston's marriage. Her cousin, Charlotte Lovell, with whom Delia has had a close but competitive relationship, seeks Delia's help. Charlotte, engaged to marry Joe Ralston, has been told by him that upon their marriage she must give up the day-nursery she maintains for indigent children. He fears that her work with such children will expose Charlotte and later their children to some incurable contagion. His anxieties reflect the upper-class view that the working poor are a source of contamination and a threat to the elite's well-being. Delia sympathizes with Charlotte's feelings toward the children, but in light of her social position and her own two children, appreciates Joe's concern. In the course of their conversation, Charlotte reveals the reason she has maintained the nursery: One of the children is her own daughter. She asks Delia's assistance in making arrangements that will allow Charlotte to continue to watch over this child, even though she cannot acknowledge the girl.

Shocked by this revelation that undermines her assumptions about Charlotte, Delia presses her to reveal the name of the father. In reconfiguring her image of Charlotte, Delia tries to cast her in the role of victim of an unscrupulous seducer. After making some broad hints that prepare Delia for the truth, Charlotte states that the father is Clement Spender. An artist that Delia had given up for the safety of a socially approved, financially secure marriage, Clem Spender remains the secret love of Delia's life. Charlotte's revelation ignites jealousy that Delia cannot admit, but deeply feels. Her own marriage, based on friendly affection and mutual respect, has not brought Delia the passion and fulfillment she believes would have been hers with Clem. After she has visited the nursery and seen the resemblance between Tina and Clem, Delia resolves that she must do something to save Clem's child. She also hopes to punish Charlotte, whom she sees as a usurper.

Delia believes that she cannot countenance a lie to Joe Ralston, keeping Tina's existence a secret and allowing Charlotte's marriage to occur. When she sees blood coughed up on Charlotte's handkerchief, Delia seizes on this to prevent the union, knowing Joe Ralston will not marry a woman too sickly to provide him with children. Delia does not tell Charlotte what she plans, but Charlotte intuits that to save her child she will have to sacrifice her upcoming marriage and the happiness it may afford her.

As she has promised, Delia manages the situation and reveals that she is a consummate strategist. To ensure that her husband, Jim Ralston, will be receptive to her plan, Delia draws upon her skills in the domestic arts to set the stage. She sees to it that her husband and Joe, his unexpected dinner guest, enjoy a substantial meal in pleasant surroundings. Her ability to do this confirms Jim's opinion of her as an excellent manager and a competent wife for a successful man. She listens to Joe's explanation of his feelings about Charlotte and the day-nursery, expressing her understanding of his concerns as well as her valuing of Charlotte's maternal instincts. Delia also reveals the return of Charlotte's illness, approaching the issue in a calm and rational way, just as a Ralston would. Her husband admires her compassion and reason, seeing in her an affirmation of his own good judgment. When Joe leaves, Jim reaches out to his wife with amorous intentions, but Delia initially demurs. She tells him of her desire to provide support for the foundling child most dear to Charlotte. To make Jim feel that theirs is a joint decision, she literally manipulates the moment by extending her hands to him. Moved by the sentimental power of Delia's maternal image, Jim agrees to her proposal, embracing her while she invokes the vision of their children sleeping upstairs.

While Delia finds managing Jim a simple exercise, she finds it harder initially to control Charlotte. When she tells Charlotte to "give up follies" (402), she not only implies that Charlotte's dreams of having both a marriage and Tina are foolish, but also rebukes her for her actions in the past. She warns Charlotte that if Charlotte's resolve weakens and she attempts to pursue marriage to Joe Ralston, Delia will do nothing for her. Delia has determined that Charlotte must also renounce something, as Delia had once done, to compensate for the help and secrecy Delia offers her.

The actions surrounding the first crisis of the novella occur during two days in the 1840s. Part II of the novella, which takes place during the 1850s, begins with a brief account of how the intervening years have passed, including the death of Jim Ralston. Following Jim's death, Charlotte and Tina move into the Ralston home. The second crisis develops when Tina Lovell, who has been cared for by Charlotte and Delia, reaches a marriageable age. Over the years, Tina has become the focal point of their rivalry. Each woman believes she knows Tina best and knows what is right for her future. The crisis emerges through a series of confrontations between the two women, their final battle waged the night before Tina's wedding. Although she does not use the metaphor of the fencing match as she had in *Madame de Treymes,* Wharton structures the confrontations between the two women around a pattern of thrust and parry.

Delia has seen her own two children married off "safely and suitably" into "New York alliances" (409) that mirror her own marriage.

Freed from obligations to her children, who are Ralstons through and through, she can direct her energies toward a stronger connection to Tina. Her interest in Tina stems not only from the girl's appealing nature, but also from Delia's desire to reclaim her own youth. She sees her early self reflected in Tina, the self that existed before her marriage, when she was free to love Clem Spender.

For Charlotte, the passing years have underscored her dependence on Delia, not only for housing, but also to maintain the secret of her past. Over the years, this secret has become increasingly important to Charlotte and keeping it provides the only means by which she feels safe with her daughter. There are costs for Charlotte, conveyed by the way in which she has evolved into the stereotype of the "old maid," a gray, rigid, quiet figure who seems to have little vitality. Like Delia's performance as the model of sentimental motherhood in Part I, the "old maid" becomes the performance Charlotte must enact throughout Part II. Only in her private confrontations with Delia does the true Charlotte emerge, a figure whose independence and anger simmer beneath her surface.

Confrontations between the two women erupt as Tina enters the transition from girlhood to womanhood. Delia assumes that Tina is, as Delia herself was, a "nice girl in the nicest set" (376), whose innocence will be preserved until she makes a proper marriage. Charlotte, who has taken on the realistic sensibilities Delia had urged on her, sees danger for Tina in her relationship with Lanning Halsey. Charlotte knows, much to Delia's surprise, that Lanning has told Tina that he cannot marry her, that he cannot afford it on his small allowance and lack of a profession. Hearing this, Delia thinks of her own situation with Clem Spender and assumes that Tina will forego the relationship with Lanning. The pitch of the argument intensifies when Charlotte raises the issue of Tina's sexuality, that in continuing to see Lanning, Tina may give way to her desire, just as Charlotte had with Clem. Delia's response, "No decent girl—" (417), reveals not only her assumptions about Tina, but her judgment of Charlotte as well. Charlotte, accepting the jibe, presses her point, forcing Delia to face the "dark destinies coiled under the surface of life" (417).

Charlotte sees in Tina's situation the problem that will continually arise: Given the mystery of her origins, Tina has no prospects for a suitable marriage within the upper class. Charlotte proposes leaving New York to live in more modest circumstances where Tina will have better prospects for a stable marriage. Delia objects to this plan, as much out of fear of the loss of Tina's company as out of her concern for Tina's happiness. Delia thinks that such a move will induce a revolt from Tina and produce a greater fall, the stock events from melodrama providing Delia with images that her own experience cannot.

The issue of usurpation resurfaces, this time from Charlotte's point of view, as Delia attempts to assert maternal authority. Delia urges Charlotte to trust Tina, but Charlotte relies on her own instinct to choose her course of action. When she confronts Tina and Lanning, who have entered what they assumed would be a slumbering household, Charlotte interrupts the scene she has anticipated. Having retreated to her bedroom, Delia watches from her window as the couple approaches the house. She imagines the scene that occurs as they enter and when Lanning departs a few minutes later, she cedes a temporary victory to Charlotte. Not one to accept defeat easily, Delia formulates a new plan to manage the situation and regain control of Tina's future. She decides to adopt Tina legally, giving her the Ralston name and a small financial legacy, which will enable her to marry Lanning, if she wishes. When Delia consults Dr. Lanskell about the soundness of her plan, he informs her that Jim knew the truth about Tina's origins and had admired Delia for what she had done. This, along with Dr. Lanskell's opinion that Delia's actions will limit the burden of the past, strengthens Delia's resolve.

To present her plan to Charlotte, Delia again sets the stage for her encounter as she had done with Jim in Part I. She asks Charlotte to come to her room and guides her away from the chintz lounge where Charlotte had wept over her child's fate. Delia wants to present her plan as a rational, reasonable one, and does not want Charlotte to associate the current situation with the emotional scene of fourteen years earlier. She also does not want Charlotte to think that once again she must submit to Delia's will or lose everything. Initially, Charlotte rejects the plan, seeing in it Delia's victory. Delia prevails, however, when she accuses Charlotte of sacrificing Tina to satisfy her own desire for mastery.

The last chapter presents what appears to be a conventional happy ending in the upcoming wedding of Tina Ralston. Before the conflict resolves, however, a final confrontation occurs between Delia and Charlotte. They argue over who will have the "mother's talk" with Tina on her wedding eve. In this last confrontation, Charlotte accuses Delia of having done everything for Clement Spender, a truth that unsettles Delia. Charlotte further startles Delia by confessing that she,

Charlotte, has managed from the beginning, consciously using Delia and her feelings for Clem. Stunned by this, Delia concedes that Charlotte should talk with Tina, surrendering her claim. Charlotte recognizes the impossibility of her situation, for she cannot maintain her role as "the old maid" and enjoy the one mother's right she has claimed for herself. Part of the "mother's talk" includes discussion of sexual relations, no matter how obliquely conveyed, about which an "old maid" cannot know. While Charlotte struggles with her decision, Delia perceives that neither Clem nor his child ever really belonged to Charlotte. She understands why Charlotte has resented her interventions, however intended, and can see Charlotte through the lens of sympathy rather than pity. When Delia does speak to Tina, she asks that before leaving the wedding celebration, Tina bestow her final kiss upon Charlotte, a sign of gratitude and benediction to the woman who has embodied maternal self-sacrifice.

CHARACTERS

In appearance, personality, and personal history, Delia Ralston and Charlotte Lovell stand in sharp contrast. Beneath the surface, however, they have attributes in common, including their strong wills, their profound attachment to Tina, and their early love for Clement Spender. Each woman has played a role created for her by family obligations and social values. For each, this role has entailed the denial of aspects of self. Out of these shared traits and experiences, as well as the general rivalry they feel, emerge the tensions that define their lives.

When Delia Ralston first appears, she is a married woman, settled but restless. Already a young matron, she is plump according to the fashion of the time, but still fresh, her movements still "as quick as a girl's" (376). Her blond hair and rosy complexion highlight her vitality and associate her with the heroine of romantic fiction. She surveys her surroundings with a degree of satisfaction and even complacency. Proud of her abilities to manage her household, her husband, and life's situations, Delia senses that she has missed out on something, that marriage and even children have not brought her the fulfillment she expected. Periodically she takes a critical look at her life, but quickly brushes aside her doubts. Delia has followed a conservative course in the decisions she has made, conforming to the expectations of the Ralston family and her social world.

Over the course of years, Delia finds that she is aging, fearing that the future will bring "accumulating infirmities" (422). Of greater import, however, is her "deep central indifference" that "had gradually made her regard herself as a third person" (420). Delia feels alienated from herself. When she decides to act for the second time, she acknowledges that she does so "for her own sake" (421). She hopes, through her relationship to Tina, to experience vicariously the love and desire she has missed. She hopes, too, that this will slow the inevitable process of decline. She has a need to assert control over life, to feel that she can still have some effect on her destiny.

In contrast to her cousin Delia, Charlotte Lovell had been more striking in appearance when she entered society. Not a conventional beauty, she had bright red hair, pale brown eyes, a slim waist, and vivacious personality that attracted male admiration. Even after her bout with lung fever and her secret pregnancy, she retains a distinctive look with a transparent complexion and redder hair. Her wardrobe, never extensive, is even plainer when she returns from Georgia, emphasizing the quieter life she has chosen to follow. She devotes herself to the day-nursery she has opened, and her work there allows her to engage in nurturing acts for all the children, so that her attention to Tina does not attract attention.

Although Delia uses Charlotte's illness to prevent her marriage, Charlotte recovers her health and succeeds in caring for Tina. Charlotte's family has assumed that she is destined to be an "old maid," and she silently fulfills their expectation. Over the years she cultivates all the stereotypical attributes of a spinster. Her plain appearance and stiff posture convey a rigid adherence to decorum. She effects these mannerisms as a form of disguise, a means of concealing the truth about her past and her own passionate nature. Only in conversations with Delia does the real Charlotte speak. During these encounters she reveals the temper, anger, and strength of will that have enabled her to persevere in the path she has chosen. Similar to Delia, Charlotte sees in Tina a reflection of her own inner self and hopes that in controlling Tina's future she can correct the mistakes of the past.

MINOR CHARACTERS

Two of the minor characters, Tina Lovell and Dr. Lanskell, play important roles within the novella. The others, including Jim Ralston and his cousin Joe, Delia's children, and Sillerton Jackson, serve as vehicles through which the cultural expectations of the era are expressed, especially those of the upper class.

Tina Lovell, known for a time as the "hundred dollar baby," arrives in New York as a foundling, a hundred dollar bill pinned to her blanket. Her appearance initially excites curiosity, but her origins remain shrouded in mystery. The truth of her background is kept from her, in part to shield Tina from the disgrace and social stigma that will befall her if the truth be known. As a child unburdened by the past, Tina grows up freer and livelier than those around her. She identifies with Delia, whom she sees as the model of a fulfilled woman, rather than Charlotte, whom she assumes cannot understand her. Tina accepts the surface images of both women, unable to perceive their true beings. Tina's freer nature places her in the danger that Charlotte fears, but also generates the vitality that Delia envies. When Delia adopts Tina and changes her name from Lovell to Ralston, she wants to put safeguards around that zest for life that makes Tina vulnerable to her passions.

In the small, circumscribed world of Old New York, Dr. Lanskell serves not only as physician but as father-confessor. A man of probity and reason, he is consulted for moral as well as medical advice. He debunks some of the social taboos that influence the mindset of his circle. He encourages Delia to take risks and enables her to do what she thinks is right by revealing that Jim Ralston was a man of greater understanding and compassion than she had realized. Dr. Lanskell has also sheltered Charlotte by keeping her secret over the years, and believes that her mistakes do not have to be paid for by her child.

THEMES

In *The Old Maid,* Wharton explores a number of themes related to individual identity. She reveals how familial and social expectations govern the ways in which Delia and Charlotte express themselves and envision their futures. She explores how fear and the need for security drive characters to conform to social expectations. In her treatment of these two women, Wharton also demonstrates the negative consequences of the competition among women to succeed in the marriage market.

For both Delia and Charlotte, the need for security comes with significant costs. For Delia, it has entailed sacrificing love and what she believes her life might have been. For Charlotte, it means relinquishing her maternal role. Both women also react out of fear. Initially Delia fears social disapproval when she contemplates married life with Clement Spender. In Part II her fears have changed, so that what she dreads is the process of aging and all the signs that she has passed her prime without experiencing a great passion. Charlotte, on the other hand, fears both social disapproval and the loss of her daughter at the outset. Later in life she fears the exposure of her past and how it will affect her relationship with Tina.

Wharton examines the nature of the rivalry between Delia and Charlotte. She reveals how jealousy and spite affect the lives of women who are measured solely by their success in the marriage market and their ability to produce children. This rivalry is seldom acknowledged openly, but is a source of tension whenever Clement Spender is the subject of conversation. Both Delia and Charlotte must ultimately overcome this destructive competition to break the hold that the past has over the present.

SYMBOLS

A wedding gift from Delia's aunt, the Parisian clock symbolizes the passage of time and the inability of human beings to control its progress. Its design presents the image of a romantic pastoral, depicting a shepherd stealing a kiss from an unsuspecting shepherdess. This design introduces the theme of *carpe diem,* or "seize the day." This theme, often expressed in love poems, encourages the surrender to passionate desires while one is youthful enough to enjoy them. Delia's aunt sent her the clock by way of Clem Spender, who delivered it just after Delia's wedding, highlighting the missed opportunity for Clem and Delia. For Delia, who keeps the clock in her bedroom rather than on public display, it symbolizes her secret love for Clem and her feeling of having failed to seize the day in her youth.

ALTERNATIVE READING: JUNGIAN CRITICISM

In *The Old Maid,* Wharton traces the parallel lives of two women who are connected through their past and the shared knowledge of Tina's origins. This pairing of characters lends itself to a reading influenced by Jungian criticism. Carl Jung, a psychoanalyst, was a student of Sigmund Freud, but he devised a different method for describing the nature of the individual. Instead of focusing on the ego, id, and super ego as Freud had done, Jung discussed the conscious ego and its persona along with the unconscious psyche that includes the shadow and anima or animus. In Jungian terms, the persona or mask is the face one shows to the world, while the shadow (the dark side of the self) is often denied or repressed. Each individual also possesses the anima, the female or feminine principle that complements consciousness in all males, or the animus, the masculine principle, that does so in all females. Jung theorized that these various aspects of the self must be recognized and accepted before an individual can achieve wholeness. Wharton's own interest in early modern anthropology and psychology may have influenced her treatment of the characters within this narrative.

The persona or mask reflects an individual's perceptions of what society expects him or her to be. In *The Old Maid,* Delia Ralston is particularly aware of her need to present a face to the world that it finds acceptable. She has shaped her life according to the dictates of her social sphere. She appears content in the life she leads, but she frequently reflects on the past and what she sees as the sacrifice of a love that expressed her true self. Delia finds these reflections uncomfortable and clings to ideals of goodness and the value of being a so-called nice girl who follows the rules. Even when she deceives herself about her true motives, Delia believes that she acts in accordance with her public image and reputation.

Charlotte Lovell also constructs a persona or mask to feel safe and accepted. As an "old maid," she presents a self that makes her non-threatening to her social world. Her manifestation of all the traits and behaviors associated with this role is so convincing that no one ever questions her past. Delia, however, knows the truth of that past, and because Charlotte has violated the norms that define a good girl in their world, Delia associates her with traits that must be repressed. Charlotte's constant presence reminds Delia of sexual desire, an aspect of the self that Delia believes must be controlled and even denied to suit the needs of the public self. In this respect, Charlotte serves as a representation of Delia's shadow, embodying those dark aspects of self and sexuality that Delia finds disquieting.

In Jungian psychology, a woman's feminine principle must be complemented by the presence of the animus, or masculine principle, for her to achieve balance. The animus, connected to rationality and objective reality, prompts reflection and evaluation. This aspect of self clearly predominates in Delia Ralston, who is tied to concepts of law and duty. She engages in judgment of herself and others, always measuring individuals against the standards she has internalized. In fact, she senses that her life is out of balance, that in repressing her passions and her related feminine principle, she has denied herself a full life. She attempts to blame this on the Ralstons and their love of conformity and predictability, but she must look to herself as the source of her vexation.

Charlotte Lovell also appears to be dominated by the animus in her public persona, but in private moments with Delia, she reveals the presence of a powerful feminine principle as well. Jung associated this principle with a "chaotic urge to life" and a "secret knowledge or hidden wisdom" (315). Charlotte's past links her to secret (sexual) knowledge and she demonstrates a wider understanding of human nature, good and bad. Her acceptance of these traits within herself also allows her to perceive their existence in Tina and to anticipate Tina's behavior with Lanning Halsey. Charlotte knows the consequences of allowing these traits to predominate, so she hopes to create a more balanced situation for her daughter.

In addition to his analysis of the "personal unconscious," Jung also explored the theory of what he termed the "collective unconscious," a repository of images and patterns that exists as a kind of primordial memory. Jung referred to these images and patterns as archetypes. Archetypes and archetypal stories often reflect attempts to explain natural processes and universal human experiences to which an individual responds with a sense of profound recognition and familiarity. Some literary critics have discounted the notion of a "collective unconscious," but use the term "archetype" to identify recurrent patterns of action, images, and character types that appear in a wide variety of literary forms and myths across cultures.

In *The Old Maid,* Wharton considers the archetypal pattern evoked by the phrase "the sins of the fathers." Dr. Lanskell specifically refers to this pattern in his conversation with Delia when he alludes to Exodus 20.5, "for I the Lord your God am a jealous God, visiting the iniquity of the fathers upon the children to the third and fourth generation." This archetypal pattern, articulated in various Biblical verses, also appears in numerous classical myths and dramas. It attempts to explain the misfortunes and suffering of those who may appear to be undeserving of punishment. This pattern also suggests that children inherit the tendencies of their parents, whether for good or ill, indicating that the past always exerts influence over the present. In the

conflict between Delia and Charlotte, the past has been a controlling factor, embodied by Tina's presence in their lives. Each woman hopes to prevent the mistakes of the past from affecting Tina's future, but neither can do so until she acknowledges how her own actions have made that past powerful.

5

The House of Mirth (1905)

Having gained recognition for her short stories and her first novel *The Valley of Decision* (1902), Edith Wharton felt ready to address a contemporary problem in her next major work. She turned her attention to the social world of New York, a familiar terrain she viewed with a critical eye. She began work on *The House of Mirth* in 1903 and agreed to its serial publication by Scribner's in 1905, before the manuscript was complete. The novel was well received by critics and readers, but for different reasons. Critics praised the novel for its realism and satire, while readers were drawn to the love story between Lily Bart and Lawrence Selden (Hoeller, *Dialogue* 96–102). Terence Davies' film adaptation of the novel released in 2000 foregrounds the love story between Lily and Selden, allowing the audience's preference for romance to overshadow the more troubling questions raised by the novel.

Wharton's original title for the novel, "A Moment's Ornament," captures the decorative role that a beautiful, wealthy woman played in Lily Bart's era as well as the brevity of her reign. Through the experiences of Lily, Wharton reveals the fleeting power that beauty enjoys, especially when it depends upon the appreciative gaze of others. Wharton took the title of the published novel from a Biblical verse, "The heart of the wise is in the house of mourning; but the heart of fools is in the house of mirth" (Ecclesiastes 7:4). This verse, one of a series of admonitions, calls attention to the moral folly of seeking only pleasure and entertainment. In calling the novel *The House of Mirth,* Wharton underscores Lily's inner debate over a life governed by principle versus one wasted in leisure.

SETTING

In *The House of Mirth,* Wharton develops three main settings for her characters: New York City, the Trenors' country home Bellomont, and the Mediterranean coastal resort of Monte Carlo. Wharton uses physical details of the settings, especially the interiors of houses and apartments, to convey the values, tastes, and personal attributes of her characters. In each of these locales, Wharton explores the dynamics of social interaction, the manners and gestures of characters that reveal the values that shape upper-class New York society at the turn of the twentieth century.

New York City functions as the center of capital, where men gain power through successful commercial ventures. Wealth, however, is not the only criterion for admission into the upper crust of New York. One's family name and origins, one's history and source of prosperity, all affect how one is received by this tightly knit social circle. For those who have recently attained wealth, admission to this echelon is seen as the final emblem of success and power. Those who already belong see themselves as guardians of its standards, charged to exclude those who might lessen this circle's exclusivity. This social circle feels pressure to change, to become more open to new people with new money, but their conservative impulses urge them to resist such pressure, to be judicious in selecting those for whom the gates will be opened.

This upper-class culture places great emphasis on appearances, not only physical attractiveness but also good form, what is done and not done according to the social code. Knowing how to decipher that code draws a line between insiders and outsiders; people such as the Brys and the Gormers look to willing insiders to provide the means of entree and the clues necessary to interpret the code. Because one aspect of good form entails avoiding direct statement of fact or open statement of feeling, gossip and innuendo hold powerful sway in this world. Affecting reputations, gossip allows those who seem powerless to manipulate information to gain a desired outcome. Gossip also has the power to undermine those such as Lily who do not recognize its potency.

The social codes and the manners that convey them affect not only the relationships between men and women, but also those that women have with each other. Because the women in this society have so few outlets for their abilities and energies, their rivalries assume even greater importance. In a world where a woman's value is measured by the wealth of the man she marries, women's competition in the social sphere is intense. Lily envies the power exercised by those like Judy Trenor and Bertha Dorset who enjoy the benefits of having secured wealthy, if boring, husbands. She dismisses as harmless those women who are already deemed spinsters, such as Grace Stepney and Gerty Farish.

While New York City presents the combined business and social interests of the elite, country retreats such as Bellomont represent the world of leisure. Wharton develops the environment and atmosphere of Bellomont over the course of five chapters in Book I, highlighting its spacious grounds, "a landscape tutored to the last degree of rural elegance" (50). In this setting, Wharton reveals the paradox of the country estate, for it symbolizes escape from the competitive world of the city, yet is governed by the codes and expectations that rule city life. The country setting enhances Lily's desire for freedom, but all around her she encounters reminders of the limitations she faces. The world of the country retreat reflects women's social influence; here women such as Judy Trenor exercise power through the invitations they extend and the hospitality they provide. Lily acknowledges her dependent status at Bellomont: She must pay her way by assisting her hostess in the tedious, behind-the-scenes duties of entertaining. The pressure to play the games of leisure also affects Lily more intensely at Bellomont, where she gambles at bridge, incurring debts beyond her resources.

In Monte Carlo, Wharton reveals how New Yorkers who travel do not grow beyond their New York mindset. Carry Fisher, who accompanies the Wellington Brys on their tour, despairs because Mrs. Bry "had not progressed beyond the point of weighing her social alternatives in public" (195), while Mrs. Jack Stepney anticipates Lord Hubert's telling them "who all the awful people are at the other place" (193), revealing the perpetual thirst for gossip. The travelers believe they are encountering foreign cultures, but they only socialize with those whose values and behavior reflect their own.

To measure the distance of Lily's fall from the elite sphere, Wharton reveals different aspects of New York City in the last chapters of the novel. When she finds herself homeless and disinherited but for a small legacy, Lily must find new quarters. Although her travels with the Gormers and her work for Mrs. Hatch allow her to postpone her fate, Lily takes up residence in a boarding house, where "she was beginning to feel acutely the ugliness of her surroundings . . . her narrow room, with its blotched wall-paper and shabby paint" (302–03). Lily's room, symbolizing her last attempt to retain some independence, stands in sharp contrast to Selden's comfortable bachelor quarters. Wharton uses this contrast to measure not only the distance down the social ladder that Lily has traveled, but also the different circumstances that govern the outcomes for men and women in Lily's world.

PLOT AND STRUCTURE

The narrative of *The House of Mirth* is divided into two books. In Book I, Wharton introduces all of the major characters and establishes the patterns of conflict that govern Lily Bart's life. The toll these conflicts take on Lily, both socially and psychologically, unfold through the action of Book II, for Wharton reveals that every action and choice has its cost. One might say that Book I records the process by which Lily Bart accumulates debts, while Book II reveals how she attempts to settle accounts to regain her self-respect, if not the esteem of others.

Through the opening episode between Lily Bart and Lawrence Selden, Wharton introduces a number of issues that drive the plot. In the course of their conversation in Selden's apartment, the narrative reveals Lily's interest in Selden, but his lack of money prohibits their marriage. Lily admires Selden's ability to express his critical insights on the world she inhabits and envies his freedom to do so. She believes Selden speaks to that side of her character that values the possibilities of self-realization. She knows, however, that her desire for the luxuries that wealth affords holds strong sway over her. Thinking she has enjoyed a brief interlude of independence in Selden's company, Lily confronts the pervasiveness and power of the social codes when she encounters Simon Rosedale. His comments on seeing her before the Benedick, which houses Selden's apartment, cause Lily to reflect that "a girl must pay so dearly for her least escape from routine"(16). Wharton indicates that the codes of behavior and those who understand their power will exert constant pressure upon Lily Bart, demanding her conformity or forcing her exile.

Following Lily's encounters with Selden and Rosedale, Wharton presents Lily's initial attempts to gain Percy Gryce's favor. Lily contemplates an engagement to Percy Gryce, thereby assuring herself financial well-being and a safe, if predictable, marriage. Their encounters on the train and at Bellomont establish an important pattern of behavior that Lily will follow in Books I and II. The narrative describes the work Lily does in her attempts to secure her future, but then reveals her failure to follow through. Wharton describes Lily as "studying her prey" and organizing her "method of attack" before approaching Gryce (18). She draws Gryce into conversation about his favorite topic, Americana, feigning interest in it. At Bellomont, Lily projects the image of a reserved and dignified woman, a churchgoer who hopes to have Gryce's company at Sunday services. Having created the right impression and gained suitable attention from Gryce, Lily undermines her own efforts by abandoning Gryce when Selden arrives at Bellomont.

During the train ride to Bellomont, Wharton introduces a second pattern that also shapes the plot. Just as Lily approaches a moment of success with Gryce, Bertha Dorset appears. She asks Lily for a cigarette, knowing that Gryce disapproves of smoking, forcing Lily to dissemble. In this scene, Bertha unsettles Lily merely for sport, but when she perceives Lily as a genuine rival for Selden's affections, her actions become more calculated. Bertha undermines Lily at every opportunity, contributing to Lily's social demise, if not her actual death.

Selden's arrival at Bellomont causes Lily once again to question membership in the social circle to which she aspires. Under his influence, she sees that circle as a "great gilt cage" (56) that confines her. When she spends an afternoon exploring the grounds of Bellomont with Selden, Lily considers her feelings for him. The natural setting suggests a world apart from that which Lily and Selden usually inhabit, a more genuine place where they can be honest. Lily thinks she may love Selden, but cannot risk doing so. Selden considers his feelings for Lily and what role he may play in Lily's "career" (71–2). Attracted by her beauty, he remains troubled by what he deems her artificiality.

While her rivalry with Bertha Dorset and her growing interest in Selden play major parts in shaping her fate, Lily also interacts with others who have profound effects on her well-being. Wharton creates scenes between Lily and these characters to reveal how all of Lily's relationships form a web that entangles her. These scenes allow Wharton to expose more fully the values that govern the world in which

Lily lives and that will determine Lily's options and outcome. They also reveal the covert actions of certain characters that strengthen the power of this web.

Both Gus Trenor's and Sim Rosedale's encounters with Lily reveal more about the rules and expectations that define relationships between men and women. Gus Trenor agrees to help when Lily speaks of her need for financial guidance. Lily engages in flirtatious behavior to engage his sympathies, but believes she can "hold him by his vanity" (89), avoiding sexual intimacy with him. Trenor seizes the opportunity to create an obligation on Lily's part, and Lily knows that some expectation for repayment exists. Rosedale also appreciates Lily's beauty, but values her as an avenue of entrée into the social elite. He hopes to marry Lily and through their union achieve the social status to match his financial success. In his approach, Rosedale tends to be more forthright, openly admitting that he offers Lily the financial resources that would underwrite her social power.

In her encounters with her aunt Mrs. Peniston, Lily faces the judgment of Old New York, one that asserts the primacy of decorum and propriety, but thrives on gossip that makes and breaks reputations. Mrs. Peniston prefers "the brilliant and unreliable Lily" to the "neutral-tinted dulness" of cousin Grace Stepney (106). Anxious that her own future not be characterized by that same dullness, Lily assumes that she will be the beneficiary of her aunt's estate. When Grace Stepney's "dull resentment" of Lily's preferred status turns to "active animosity" (129) over a dinner party slight, she uses rumor and innuendo to alter Mrs. Peniston's view. She tells Mrs. Peniston tales of Lily's relationship with Gus Trenor and of Lily's gambling debts. Although Mrs. Peniston initially disregards these remarks, Grace has planted the seeds of suspicion.

In Chapter 12, Wharton presents what appears to be Lily's moment of triumph at the Wellington Brys' party. Lily performs in the *tableau vivant* as Mrs. Lloyd from a painting by Sir Joshua Reynolds. The narrative explains Lily's strategy in choosing this part, for "she had shown her artistic intelligence in selecting a type so like her own that she could embody the person represented without ceasing to be herself" (141–42). Her diaphanous draperies reveal much, but Lily knows that her primary source of power over men in her culture is her ability to generate desire (Joslin, *Edith Wharton* 59). Her beauty causes Selden to believe that he now sees the true Lily, a woman for whom he feels a profound attraction. In the brief encounter they share following

Lily's performance, Selden confesses his feelings, they kiss, and Lily disappears, evoking the fairy-tale quality of the moment. Like Cinderella, however, Lily must leave the party. What she faces in the days that follow again undermines everything that she has worked so hard to achieve.

Lily's downfall follows on the heels of her success. The narrative foreshadows this turn of events, noting that Lily "had a fatalistic sense of being drawn from one wrong turning to another, without ever perceiving the right road till it was too late to take it" (135). Believing that she can keep Gus Trenor at bay with a few kind words and half-hearted attention, Lily agrees to visit the Trenor house on the evening following the Brys' party. Trenor invites Lily while his wife is away, planning to coerce Lily into sexual relations if he cannot seduce her with gifts. When Lily discovers that the money she has received comes from Trenor's own funds rather than from investments he has made for her, she recoils in shock and shame. She verbalizes the code of their social world to protect herself from Trenor's advances, but leaves his house knowing that she must clear her debt with him to redeem her sense of self. Unfortunately, as she flees Trenor's house, Lily is observed by Selden, who assumes the worst.

In need of comfort from someone who will expect nothing in exchange, Lily goes to Gerty Farish. Gerty provides safe space for Lily, whose vulnerability leaves her feeling emotionally homeless. Upon her return to Mrs. Peniston's, Lily sets in motion a chain of events that will leave her literally homeless. She admits to Mrs. Peniston that she has accrued gambling debts, watching as her aunt's "face seemed to be petrifying as she listened" (181). Mrs. Peniston, made ill by thoughts of what has transpired, dismisses Lily, foreshadowing her disinheritance in Book II. Lily retreats to her room, hoping that Selden will arrive to save her.

Instead, Lily discovers that Rosedale has come to call. He again puts forth his proposal in distinctly monetary terms. This grates upon Lily, but she knows that she cannot afford to alienate him. After her vision of a chivalrous rescue vanishes with the discovery that Selden has departed for Havana, Lily feels the web that surrounds her pulling tighter, limiting her options. Escape appears from an unexpected source when Lily receives an invitation to travel from Bertha Dorset. Having in her possession the love letters that she has purchased from Mrs. Haffen, Lily thinks she has the power "to overthrow with a touch the whole structure of [Bertha's] existence" (109), an assumption that allows her to accept the invitation with a false sense of security.

The tone of Book II becomes more deterministic as Lily's downward spiral accelerates and proves inescapable. Lily moves from place to place, staying in each a briefer time, searching for somewhere to call home. The space where she resides continues to shrink with each move until she reaches the small room in the boarding house. As the forces of her social world and her economic realities bear down upon her, Lily attempts to resist their crushing weight, but finds that she lacks the strength and support to bear them.

At the opening of Book II, Lily believes that she has evaded the personal and financial woes that beset her in New York. Cruising the Mediterranean with the Dorsets, she again enjoys a place in the leisure sphere. Bertha takes advantage of Lily's dependent state, expecting her to keep George occupied, while Bertha pursues her recreational dalliance with Ned Silverton. Lily discovers that the rules of the New York social game continue in force, and that she remains vulnerable. When Bertha publicly expels Lily from the yacht to deflect attention from herself, she effectively strands Lily, who realizes that she has nowhere to turn.

Upon her return to New York, Lily learns that further disaster awaits her, financial as well as social. Mrs. Peniston has died, leaving her estate to Grace Stepney and a small cash legacy to Lily. In the aftermath of the funeral, Wharton employs symbolic gestures to convey Lily's expulsion from the social elite, particularly as the women close ranks around Grace Stepney. Realizing that she no longer has a place in Mrs. Peniston's house, Lily again turns to Gerty Farish for shelter. Throughout the ordeal that follows, Gerty provides emotional support that Lily finds nowhere else, but Gerty cannot alleviate Lily's desperation.

Lily must find some way to support herself. When Judy Trenor brushes her off, Lily perceives that her situation is dire, for where "Judy Trenor led, all the world would follow" (239). When Grace Stepney also refuses assistance, Lily turns to Carry Fisher, a woman whose advice she had spurned earlier. Carry arranges for Lily to accompany the Gormers, a newly wealthy couple who are attempting to enter the elite, on their journey to Alaska. Her association with them marks a shift in Lily's social position, for the "Gormer *milieu* represented a social out-skirt which Lily had always fastidiously avoided" (244).

Her contact with the Gormers initially proves satisfactory, and Lily finds her taste for luxury reawakened. As she reestablishes her position, Lily discovers that she cannot free herself from association with the Dorsets' marital problems. Carry Fisher urges Lily to provide

George Dorset with the proof he needs to end his marriage, thus making him available as a marriage partner. Lily rebuffs this suggestion, all the more so when George pleads his own case with her. Meanwhile, Bertha Dorset makes a social call upon Mrs. Gormer, repeating gossip about Lily and dangling before Mrs. Gormer the opportunity of joining Bertha's social circle. Frustrated by Bertha's maneuver, Lily realizes that "the whole weary work of rehabilitation must begin again" (265).

To accomplish this rehabilitation, Carry Fisher recommends that Lily marry Rosedale, a prospect that Lily finds less objectionable than she once did. To Carry, marriage offers protection from Bertha Dorset's schemes, especially marriage to a man with Rosedale's money. When Lily meets with Rosedale, however, she discovers that her value to him has diminished. In her current situation, she cannot offer him the social connection he desires. Rosedale remains attracted to Lily, so he puts forth a business proposition to help her. He urges Lily, with his financial backing, to use the letters she has to disarm Bertha. Lily rejects his plan for what she sees as the "essential baseness of the act" (272). Rosedale assumes that she wants to protect Selden.

Finding herself in desperate financial straits, Lily accepts a job as a secretary-companion to Mrs. Norma Hatch, a divorcee from the West. Mrs. Hatch lives at the Emporium, a fashionable New York hotel, while hoping to form her own liaison with the New York elite. To the elite, Mrs. Hatch's multiple divorces make her an unsavory individual, and Lily's association with her only worsens Lily's plight, a view shared by Selden. He encourages Lily to leave the Emporium and follow a more prudent course by moving in with Gerty. Lily resists this path, seeing in it the sacrifice of the little independence she has left. Eventually she leaves Mrs. Hatch's employ, but not soon enough for "public vindication" (298) or Selden's satisfaction.

Through Gerty's and Carry's efforts, Lily secures a place at "Mme. Regina's renowned millinery establishment" (299). Here Lily discovers that, unlike trimming her own hats, making them for others requires a level of skill that she lacks. Her anxieties and the effects of her insomnia leave her emotionally raw and unable to cope with the criticism of her supervisor. At the end of her workday, Lily avoids mingling with her coworkers, even though she feels desperately lonely. She knows that her days in the milliner's workroom are numbered.

On the way to her shabby room in the boarding house, Lily stops at the druggist to obtain a sleep aid and literally bumps into Rosedale.

Shocked by her condition, he takes her for a cup of tea, and Lily honestly describes her financial situation. Returning to her room, Lily faces another dark night, wrestling with thoughts from her conversation with Rosedale. Again, money lies at the root of her distress as she struggles against the temptation to ignore the debt to Trenor and use her legacy to buy her own shop. She also contemplates accepting the loan from Rosedale in part as compensation for using the letters in her possession to vanquish Bertha Dorset. These inner debates leave Lily sleepless and further weakened.

The last days of Lily's life are marked by gestures of closure, from her encounter with Selden to her writing of checks when her legacy is finally paid. Lily, carrying the incriminating letters, initially plans a confrontation with Bertha. When she nears Selden's apartment, thoughts of him make her plan to use the letters repugnant. Instead she goes to Selden's, remembering the comfort she once found there. Lily tries to explain what he has meant to her, how his words and ideas have changed her. Knowing that she no longer inspires in him feelings that could warm her emotionally, Lily asks Selden to make up the fire to chase away her chill. After he does so, she surreptitiously tosses the packet of letters into the fire. While they burn, she kisses Selden on the forehead, a gesture of benediction and farewell.

On her way to the boarding house, Lily encounters Nettie Struther, a young woman who once benefited from Lily's charity. Nettie invites Lily to sit in the warm kitchen of her home while Nettie prepares her baby's supper. Amid this scene of simple domestic satisfaction, Lily hears Nettie's story of how marriage to a man who believed in her saved her life. Lily holds Nettie's child, feeling the comfort of human touch, but knows that she has no hope of a similar rescue.

Strengthened by this brief encounter with kindness, Lily returns to her room and puts her possessions in order. While doing so, she receives the check bearing payment of her legacy. Again Lily struggles with her impulses, but her ethical sense prevails. She addresses an envelope to her bank in which she encloses her legacy for deposit and writes a check to Trenor, clearing her debt. Finished organizing her paperwork, Lily takes the chloral that lets her rest. As sleep overtakes her, she has visions of the day's encounters and thinks of a word that she must say to Selden "that should make life clear between them" (341).

The next morning Selden sets out for Lily's, also having "found the word he meant to say to her" (342). When he arrives, he finds Gerty

Farish there ahead of him. She guides him to Lily's room where Lily lies dead from an overdose of chloral. Gerty assures him that the overdose was accidental, that the doctor will treat it so, avoiding the scandal of suicide. Through this gesture, Gerty frees Selden from the burden of responsibility for what has happened. During his brief time alone in Lily's room, Selden discovers that she has discharged the debts she carried. As he kneels beside Lily's bed, he believes the word that makes all clear passes between them in silence. Many readers believe the word is *love,* but Wharton intentionally leaves it unstated, underscoring how the inability to communicate openly has thwarted the relationship between Lily and Selden from the start. Feminist critics suggest that in giving Selden these final moments with Lily, Wharton represents the ways in which men hold the power to define women and their lives, that Selden will have the final word about who and what Lily was.

CHARACTERS

In this novel, Wharton presents three main characters: Lily Bart, Lawrence Selden, and Bertha Dorset. Each reflects traits associated with characters in sentimental romances and melodramas, but they are not stock figures. Wharton presents them as complex characters whose strengths and weakness are revealed through their actions and motives. Wharton's ability to create unique beings about whom the reader cares contributes to the emotional power of the novel's ending.

As the protagonist of the novel, Lily Bart reflects certain attributes of the sentimental heroine. Like many of these heroines, Lily is an orphan who must fend for herself in the social realm. Not an innocent by conventional standards, Lily nevertheless has a trusting nature and a degree of naiveté about the world around her. These traits, along with her tendency to ignore the warning signs of danger, make her vulnerable to the scheming of others; however, Lily has aspirations that distinguish her from the typical sentimental heroine. She craves luxury and social power. She often perceives herself as a "victim of the civilization which produced her" (7), but needs the creature comforts and affirmation that civilization bestows. She does not want to be on the margins of the social world like Selden who attends parties; she wants to be at its center like Judy Trenor, giving parties and exercising power through invitations.

Shaped by her parents' marriage and their financial collapse, Lily perceives that her need for beautiful surroundings reflects her mother's influence. Lily's mother believed that their financial collapse was a social disgrace. Treating beauty as a tradable commodity, Mrs. Bart instilled in Lily a belief that Lily could recover their other assets, that she would "get it all back, with [her] face" (30). Such coaching by Mrs. Bart creates in Lily a need to please her audience (Wolff, *Feast* 112), and Lily frequently performs expected roles to garner affirmation.

Through her interactions with Selden, Lily recognizes another self—one that values principles and craves freedom of expression. Under Selden's influence, Lily feels ambivalent about her materialistic desires. When she thinks at times about the social elite, she feels "a stealing allegiance to their standards, an acceptance of their limitations" (52). Applying Selden's standards, she knows that the elite are "brutal and self-engrossed" (51), causing her distress when she thinks of being the same. This other self beckons Lily to live by a code that values the individual over money or possessions, that values doing right over scoring the best deal. Much of Lily's internal conflict, especially throughout Book II, derives from the tension between her two sensibilities. She wrestles with the obligation of her debt and the temptation to use Bertha's letters to annihilate her arch-rival. This inner turmoil makes her vulnerable, but ultimately earns Lily the reader's sympathy as she heeds the prompting of her better self.

Similar to Lily Bart, Lawrence Selden has conflicting impulses toward the social elite. Because he stands at its outskirts, Selden believes that he can judge this circle impartially. Seeing their faults and failures, he believes himself above its members, taking satisfaction in personal superiority because he cannot compete financially. Influenced by his reading of Emerson, Selden critiques the unbridled consumption of the world around him. He believes that he can create a world for himself free from the corruption that he condemns, and he encourages Lily to aspire to that same world (Joslin, *Edith Wharton* 52).

Through Selden's character, Wharton also develops the implications of the double standard that governs the lives and reputations of men and women. Drawn to attractive women such as Lily Bart rather than to so-called good women like Gerty Farish, Selden has had an adulterous affair with Bertha Dorset. Even though various characters suspect this relationship, it has no effect on Selden's social standing or reputation. When he sees Lily leaving the Trenor house, he assumes that she is having an affair with Gus. Selden, judging Lily according to the standards of his social world as well as through his own feelings of betrayal, rejects her. Although he has felt heroic impulses toward Lily (see the "Allusions" section later in this chapter), his own instinct for self-protection, emotional and social, causes him to fail Lily at times of her greatest need for understanding or compassion. He cannot overcome the prejudices with which he was raised and believes that Lily is no longer deserving of his help.

As Lily's antagonist, Bertha Dorset provides both a profound contrast in character and an important study in female power. Her ability to manipulate situations reveals that Bertha knows the world in which she lives, and knows how to read the signs and gestures that indicate people's weaknesses. Bertha assumes that those who are her opponents will take advantage of situations if she does not. Trapped in a marriage to a man who bores her, Bertha takes satisfaction in creating turmoil in the lives around her. She seduces young Ned Silverton and then drops him when his presence becomes a nuisance. Still attracted to Selden, she resents Lily's apparent claim on his attention.

Bertha is an excellent strategist and knows her opponent well, while Lily underestimates Bertha and pays the price. From her first appearance in the novel, Bertha undermines the efforts Lily makes to secure her position in the social elite. Each time Bertha reappears, she has devised some new means to embarrass Lily, from engineering the engagement of Percy Gryce to expelling Lily from the yacht in Monte Carlo. She works behind the scenes, visiting Mrs. Sam Gormer to cultivate her allegiance when it appears that Lily may be making her way back into society. Bertha's appearances in the novel are limited, but her presence is felt throughout the narrative. Her efforts to vanquish her rival contribute to Lily's downfall.

ROLE OF MINOR CHARACTERS

The minor characters who appear in the novel can be divided into two groups: the secondary figures who play substantial roles, and the truly minor figures who enact limited parts. All of these characters allow Wharton to convey the texture of the social world in which Lily exists. The secondary characters affect Lily's life, some through the value systems they uphold, others through the power that they hold over Lily.

Mrs. Peniston, Lily's aunt, retains the traditional values of her youth with a "high sense of family obligation" (129) and a frugality that ensures her own comfort, but leaves Lily perpetually short of cash. When describing the ritual opening of the house in October, Wharton underscores Mrs. Peniston's love of tradition and routine. Her household inventory resembles an examination of conscience, suggesting that as long as Mrs. Peniston's house is in order, so too is her emotional and spiritual state. This love of order, as well as her frugality, foreshadows Mrs. Peniston's lack of sympathy for Lily's financial plight. She blames Lily for allowing the element of chance (gambling) to influence her life.

While Mrs. Peniston represents the security and status of Old New York, Gerty Farish and Grace Stepney reflect Lily's options should she not find a suitable marriage partner. Their lives present aspects of the dependence and submissiveness that Lily hopes to avoid. Gerty Farish, a woman of good family but with little money and few marriage prospects, has dedicated her life to social work. As a figure who exists on the margins of the social elite, Gerty depends upon kind gestures from her friends, whether these gestures are for her charities or herself. Gerty knows that Lily views her humble surroundings and restricted life with distaste, yet she remains generous toward Lily even when angry with her. Grace Stepney, on the other hand, feels no such charitable impulses toward Lily. The recipient of hand-me-down dresses and secondhand gossip, Grace watches the social world from the sidelines. She knows that she must curry favor to preserve the little security that she has, and she works diligently to play the devoted relative before Mrs. Peniston. She, too, believes that Lily looks down on her, but bides her time until she can take revenge. After she inherits Mrs. Peniston's estate, Grace holds a social and financial position from which she takes retribution.

For single women in the novel, marriage represents an avenue toward financial security. For the outsider Sim Rosedale, marriage provides an avenue toward social acceptance. Rosedale's business acumen puts him on firm footing with men of wealth, but his lack of family connections and his Jewish background limit his social standing. His presence in the novel is significant, however, for as an outsider he "can speak about subjects that are taboo to the others" and exists as more than a "flat stereotype" (Goldman 26). He talks openly to Lily about her financial situation, initially through his proposal of marriage and then later through his offer of financial backing. In each case, he believes he offers mutually profitable arrangements. Not a sentimental man, Rosedale shows more compassion for Lily than most of the other characters in the novel.

Also straddling the line between insider and outcast, Carry Fisher knows that the women in the elite view her with condescension. A divorcee, Carry guides those attempting to break into the elite, trading her knowledge for the hospitality that spares her own small financial resources. Her willingness to accept gifts of money from married men such as Trenor in exchange for the attention she bestows upon them irritates their wives, but they perceive in Carry little threat to their marriages. Often bemused by Lily's idealism, Carry has a realistic picture of the social world she inhabits and what she needs to do to survive in it. Similar to Rosedale, she evaluates situations in monetary terms, and encourages Lily to do the same.

The Trenors serve as a representative couple of the new social order. They are not from established families, but have secured their position as insiders. Gus Trenor has succeeded financially, and his wealth enables Judy to exercise social power. Initially sympathetic to Lily, Judy attempts to support her efforts to make an appropriate match. When she sees Lily repeatedly discard her chances, hears rumors about Lily and Gus, and learns of the Monte Carlo fiasco, Judy severs her ties. She will not expend her influence where it will not pay. Gus, who feels neglected by his wife, believes his gifts of money have purchased his right to Lily. His less refined nature remains close to the surface, as noticed by Selden who sees that "the beast was predominating" (163) after the Brys' party. An avid consumer like most in his social circle, Trenor resents being denied that for which he has paid.

In addition to the secondary characters who have more lasting effects on Lily, Wharton makes use of numerous minor figures. Some of these characters, such as Mrs. Bart, the Wellington Brys, the Sam Gormers, and the lesser aristocrats who appear in Monte Carlo, allow Wharton to convey the shallowness of the social elite and those who aspire to join them. Others, such as Mrs. Haffen and Nettie Struthers, advance the plot or highlight aspects of Lily's character.

THEMES

A complex novel, *The House of Mirth* presents many issues that Wharton finds provocative. An avid reader of social and scientific thought, Wharton considers the implications of social Darwinism, the relationship between economy and culture, and the power of social conventions. Within these contexts, Wharton also explores the position of women in early twentieth-century elite culture.

Competition lies at the heart of the narrative and underscores the struggle for resources and power that occurs at all levels of society. Wharton considers this issue through the lens of social Darwinism and its concept of survival of the fittest. In the world that Wharton depicts, only those who are able to adapt to their environment, to play by the social and economic rules, survive and prosper. Lily wants to compete in her social world, but too often she listens to her heart or conscience, making her vulnerable to the actions of others. At the beginning of the novel, Lily is described as "highly specialized," as though she has evolved further than most on the evolutionary scale (5). In Book II, however, Wharton suggests that part of Lily's problem stems from her over-refinement, that she lacks the stamina to function in the teeming world of the urban working class.

The competition in which characters engage is fostered by the American economic system anchored in industrial capitalism and consumerism. Throughout the novel, characters appraise the value of people and things, turning everything into commodities that can be exchanged in the marketplace. Wharton reveals how this thinking affects those in all social classes, for even someone like Mrs. Haffen puts a price upon the letters she has to offer. Throughout the narrative, Wharton makes use of the language of finance and investment, employing words and phrases such as *speculation, go into partnership,* and *ventures* to intensify the reader's awareness of this marketplace mindset. Wharton demonstrates how monetary power translates into purchasing power, especially for the men in the novel who see women as decorative or sexual objects available for ownership. In a world where appearances mean everything, gossip (or knowledge) also becomes a source of power that carries financial value. Grace Stepney uses gossip to secure her financial future through what she says about Lily to Mrs. Peniston. The letters Lily holds can be a source of power and financial security, but only if she will use them.

Wharton is also keenly conscious of the power of social conventions and the danger of defying those conventions when one does not have economic security. Lily often feels conflicted about whether to live to please others or to please herself, but she knows that her well-being, financial and otherwise, depends upon others' approval. She often thinks about the costs of her actions when she tests the boundaries of convention, such as in her first visit to Selden's apartment. When she goes to his apartment again late in the novel, she does so freely because she feels she has nothing left to lose.

In the social and economic culture that Wharton depicts, women are denied open, public power and authority. A woman's realm is the social world, but her place in it depends as much upon her husband's financial success as upon her own skills as a hostess. Wharton indicates that women do not have sufficient outlets for their talents and abilities; instead, they serve as embodiments of cultural values and expectations. Wharton demonstrates how such objectification damages a woman's sense of self. Women often act covertly to exercise whatever power they have, especially in personal relations. Bertha Dorset best exemplifies this, but other characters engage in lesser forms of the same actions. Lily Bart perceives these limitations as shaped by class and gender expectations. Although she attempts to resist them, she finds it nearly impossible to do.

SYMBOLS

Wharton makes use of symbols to expand the levels of meaning in her novel. In keeping with the novel of manners tradition, Wharton often describes the accessories that decorate settings and the gestures that accompany behavior. She invests these details with symbolic implications that relate to the values and mores of the world she depicts or that convey additional insights into characters and their motives. For example, Lily's letter seal, a ship accompanied by the word *Beyond!,* reflects both Lily's desire for escape and her romantic sensibility (Joslin 50).

The gesture of smoking a cigarette carries numerous symbolic implications. When Bertha Dorset requests a cigarette from Lily during the train ride to Bellomont, her act symbolizes the degree of freedom she enjoys as a wealthy, so-called modern woman uninhibited in the public sphere. To protect her reputation, Lily denies that she smokes, knowing that to Gryce it symbolizes improper behavior for a woman. Lily enjoys smoking in the company of Selden, finding that it symbolizes her freedom to be herself with him. Sharing cigarettes with Selden also carries a sexual charge because the shared cigarettes substitute for the kiss not exchanged between Lily and Selden until later in the novel.

The letters that Lily buys from Mrs. Haffen also serve as a multifaceted symbol. They represent Bertha's transgression of her marriage vows, as well as her claim on Lawrence Selden. When Lily possesses the letters, they symbolize to her a source of power that makes her

Bertha's equal. Lily's decision to burn the letters in Selden's fireplace symbolizes her sacrifice of power and security out of love for Selden.

ALLUSIONS

Wharton makes many allusions to fairy tales and to classical literature that allow her to suggest the timelessness of Lily's story. The allusions to fairy tales such as "Cinderella" add to the romantic aspect of Lily's story, raising the expectation that her rescue will come at the hands of a handsome prince. Some of the allusions to classical mythology reinforce this expectation.

When he believes he is in love with Lily, Selden thinks of himself as Perseus to Lily's Andromeda. A brave hero in Greek mythology, Perseus, with the aid of the deities Athena and Hermes, killed the Gorgon Medusa. On his return from this victory, he rescued the princess Andromeda, the daughter of a vain woman. When Perseus freed her, Andromeda was about to be sacrificed to a sea monster as punishment for her mother's offenses. Selden thinks about the fact that Andromeda had to depend upon Perseus's strength after her ordeal, much as he hopes Lily will depend on him for her rescue.

Other references to classical literature suggest the darker side of Lily's experience. The references to the work of Aeschylus, often considered the first tragedian of Greek drama and a favorite of Nietzsche, evoke human suffering and calamity experienced through the agency of unseen powers. This suffering, however, serves a purpose as a vehicle for knowledge, as Wharton demonstrates through Lily's increased level of perception in the last chapters of the novel.

The many references to the Fates and the Furies also link Lily's story to classical tragedy and suggest that her future is controlled by a power outside herself. The Fates were three female figures who spun the thread of life, assigned a destiny, and cut the thread at death. Terrifying in appearance, the Furies, also three figures of mythology, pursued sinners and inflicted punishment. The references to the Fates and Furies suggest that Lily, like some figures in classical tragedy, suffers from hubris, or ambition and over-confidence, which contributes to her fall.

ALTERNATIVE READING: NEW HISTORICISM

A critic who takes a new historicist approach examines the relationship between a work of literature and the historical contexts in which it was produced and originally read. A new historicist argues that such contexts are not simply background information, but are vital to a full understanding of the work. Contrary to the argument advanced by practitioners of New Criticism who assert that any work of art stands by itself as a unified and coherent whole, new historicists believe that a work of literature cannot be interpreted without reference to the era in which it was written. They do not see history as a progressive, evolutionary process, but they do believe that the changes taking place in any given era affect its literature. Critics who take this approach are interested in more than just the facts of a particular time period. They examine values and attitudes, especially as they are conveyed through language and symbols.

New historicists believe that an author engages in interpretation of his or her culture and then reflects that interpretation in the written text. To gain a wider view of a particular era, new historicists often look to nonliterary sources for insights into cultural concerns. They may examine political tracts, newspapers, advice manuals, advertisements, and illustrations as a means of identifying how people responded to issues and conflicts, how people conceived of their daily life. These nonliterary sources often reflect the trends and values of popular culture rather than high art, but reveal the wider contexts within which a work of literature expresses meaning. New historicists also draw upon the work of theorists who have explored aspects of culture. Some, such as Michel Foucault, emphasize the importance of identifying bases of power within a culture and examining how those who hold power determine what is considered true and acceptable, normal and sane. Others, such as Mikhail Bakhtin, suggest that any text or discourse is dialogic, that it contains many independent voices that may be in conflict with each other. Some of these voices may be subversive, contesting the dominant ideology of the culture, while others defuse challenges to the culture or appear to support its codes and conventions.

The class hierarchy at the turn of the twentieth century dominates the social world of *The House of Mirth*. The novel openly presents the pressure exerted by the newly wealthy to break into the elite circle, but Wharton also reveals how the world of the elite relies upon the often unacknowledged presence of the lower classes. Many of these lower-class characters remain unnamed and unnoticed throughout the text. Most are voiceless, although a few emerge as speakers who openly criticize the assumptions and values of Lily Bart's world.

Even the silent characters find means of expressing their presence through gestures that can be read as acts of resistance to the elite's expectations. These acts of resistance reveal how a change occurring within American culture intensifies the disruption faced by the elite not only from those near the top of the economic ladder, but also from those near the bottom.

The existence of what was termed the servant problem initiated commentary in American magazines as early as the 1840s. In the decades following the Civil War, the problem intensified, becoming the subject of newspaper articles, letters to the editor, and advice columns in women's magazines. While these sources of information and commentary were directed at the middle class, the servant problem also affected the elite. As the turn of the twentieth century approached, many social reformers addressed this issue. Noting that the conditions of service were "tinged with feudalism" especially in the form of a master-servant relationship, Jane Addams, known for her settlement work at Hull House, sought to restructure the nature of domestic service (Sutherland 242). She and others who advocated change believed domestic service should be governed by a specific contract and established hours, more in keeping with modern industry.

The presence of modern industry had a direct effect on domestic service. By the turn of the twentieth century, according to historian Susan Strasser, the number of women seeking employment through factory work created a shortage of servants, especially for those mistresses who did not accept new technologies as a sufficient replacement for full-time workers (163). As more opportunities arose for paid work with fixed hours and a set hourly wage, women hesitated to enter domestic service with its twenty-four hour work schedule and payment in kind (room and board along with cast-off clothing). The status of domestic service, in general, declined steadily during the last decades of the nineteenth century (Strasser 167).

Servants, both male and female, appear throughout *The House of Mirth,* their presence taken for granted. While Gerty Farish can afford only one woman who does the washing and the cooking, the wealthy employ numerous individuals, their duties differentiated by gender and by specific assignment within the household. Little is said in the novel about their lives, but in practice live-in female servants were almost always single and entirely dependent upon maintaining the goodwill of their employers. Their conduct also served as a means of measuring their employer's status. Lily's mother had complained about the "slatternly parlour maids" (32) employed in various relatives' homes, seeing them as a sign of falling standards.

This question of standards and the need for household staff to maintain them is evident in the home of Mrs. Peniston. Mrs. Peniston, who maintains rigorous domestic order, depends upon her house staff to accomplish all of the rituals of that order to her satisfaction. A frugal woman, she has few modern conveniences, in part because "servants were simply cheaper than machines" (Sutherland 246). She checks on their work through her inventory of linens and by "passing her lace handkerchief" across the surface of a statue, after which she remarks, "'I knew it—the parlour maid never dusts there!'" (113). Mrs. Peniston also expresses her irritation at the inability of the maid to draw the blinds down evenly on the front windows. It never dawns on her on these occasions that such omissions might be silent acts of resistance on the part of individuals who have no voice in her world.

Married women who performed domestic service were hired as day-laborers, as were many immigrant women. These day-laborers frequently performed heavy and/or dirty work viewed as demeaning by those women who held full-time posts; however, this form of domestic employment gave workers a greater degree of independence, as demonstrated by Mrs. Haffen, the char-woman. When she first appears, Mrs. Haffen scrubs the stairs in Selden's apartment building, her position forcing Lily to press against the wall to pass her. Mrs. Haffen stares at Lily, unsettling her with a critical appraisal. Mrs. Haffen then appears at Mrs. Peniston's, again scrubbing stairs on her hands and knees. She fixes a stare on Lily with "unflinching curiosity" (104) and later in the day asks to see her. When she offers to sell Lily the letters Bertha had written to Selden, Mrs. Haffen bargains over the price, telling Lily "the poor has got to live as well as the rich" (111). Mrs. Haffen pays no deference to Lily's social station; her willingness to look Lily in the eye, to bargain with her, and to express her opinions directly all reflect overt acts of resistance to the ideas of hierarchy and superiority assumed by the elite.

The conditions for domestic employees at all levels help to explain Lily's choices when she seeks employment. She remarks upon her own experiences of servitude when called upon to perform various tasks to pay back friends such as Judy Trenor for their hospitality and "the dresses and trinkets which occasionally replenished her insufficient wardrobe" (28). Lily sympathizes with her own maid who was on call at all hours, and even admits to herself that she envies her maid's more regular wages. When her own fortunes precipitously decline, Lily seeks a position that will be viewed as acceptable for a woman of genteel breeding. She works as a secretary-companion to Mrs. Hatch, but this places her in a situation similar to that of a domestic who is paid in kind, not with a salary.

Even though housework was relatively well paid, and room and board supplemented wages (Strasser 169), the issue of becoming a servant marks a class shift unacceptable to Lily, no matter how desperate her circumstances. She also prefers to live in a shabby room in a boarding house rather than accept the restrictions inherent in a servant's job. To maintain her independence, Lily needs a cash income, something she can earn through set wages. She chooses a form of manufacturing over domestic service, genteel though her choice of millinery may appear. Her co-workers are "fairly well-clothed and well paid," although they bear the pallor caused by the "unwholesomeness of hot air and sedentary toil" (297). They view Lily with a degree of amusement, for her lack of skill with a needle makes her unsuitable for the workroom. She realizes that she is not even their equal, let alone their superior, when it comes to productive work. She is also surprised by the "insatiable curiosity and contemptuous freedom" (301) with which they discuss the patrons of the shop, revealing a more extensive knowledge of the elite world than Lily has of theirs. Knowing that she does not have the ability or the stamina to survive in this world of work, Lily embarks upon the acts of closure that bring her life and the novel to its end.

6

Ethan Frome (1911)

When she built her home The Mount in the Berkshires in 1901–02, Edith Wharton believed that she had found a healthful environment where she could escape the pressures of city life and the social demands of resorts such as Newport, Rhode Island and Bar Harbor, Maine. As she began to explore the region more extensively, however, Wharton discovered that behind the bucolic façade existed a world as problematic and individuals as troubled as those in the city. Wharton perceived in this region "villages still bedrowsed in a decaying rural existence, and sad, slow-speaking people living in conditions hardly changed since their forbears held those villages against the Indians" (*A Backward Glance* 898). In *Ethan Frome,* Wharton explores the lives of individuals who have been stunted by circumstances, whose daily routines reinforce the sense of inescapable frustration.

This short novel remains Wharton's best-known work, praised by contemporary reviewers for its convincing realism. Some critics cautioned, however, that it was too tragic and depressing. Wharton claimed that the first pages of the novel were written in French, an exercise she undertook to improve her vocabulary, but as she worked on the English manuscript, the volume became more important to her. She explained, "It was not until I wrote 'Ethan Frome' that I suddenly felt the artisan's full control of his implements" (*A Backward Glance* 941). In *Ethan Frome,* the harsh winter climate of Starkfield,

Massachusetts, mirrors the emotional coldness within the Frome farmhouse. The three central characters, Ethan, his wife Zeena, and her cousin Mattie Silver, have become living emblems of lives crippled by frustrated hopes and thwarted dreams. In the chilling conclusion, Wharton anticipates the bleakness of Jean Paul Sartre's *No Exit* (1944) and other existentialist works of the twentieth century. This tightly constructed narrative still surprises readers. Its power and mystery have appealed to filmmakers as well, as seen in the 1960 version by Alex Segal and John Madden's interpretation in 1993.

POINT OF VIEW

In *Ethan Frome*, Wharton consciously experimented with point of view and created a frame story to establish the narrator's sensibility. Wharton saw the narrator as an intermediary between the individuals he has observed and the audience to which he relates the tale.

The narrator, an unnamed persona, begins by explaining his presence in the region. Working temporarily in the Starkfield area, he is employed at the electric generating plant at Corbury Junction. As an outsider and someone connected to the forces of modernization, the narrator sees Starkfield and its inhabitants as part of a disappearing past. He draws a contrast between what he sees as the "vitality of the climate" and the "deadness of the community" (65), especially during the winter. He wonders how people are affected by what he perceives as the negation of life and sees in Ethan Frome's story an opportunity for discovery. He admits that the tale he has heard from townsfolk is limited by "perceptible gaps" between facts and that "the deeper meaning of the story was in the gaps" (65). This admission reveals that the narrator is not simply an objective recorder of what he hears from others, but has engaged in an imaginative reconstruction of Ethan's story, filling in those gaps as he sees fit. The narrator also creates an air of suspense surrounding the question of Ethan Frome at the outset to justify his interest in the past and to engage the reader in pursuit of the answer.

During his stay in Starkfield, the narrator lodges with Mrs. Ned Hale, who tells him more about the community and its residents, though she hesitates to speak of the Fromes. Readers have noted the similarities between this situation and that of the narrator Lockwood and Nelly Dean in *Wuthering Heights*. When Wharton's narrator returns from his night at the Frome farmhouse, he hopes to trade his observations for the details Mrs. Hale can supply about the past. He probes with careful questions, encouraging her to reveal what cannot be known by an outsider, much as a Jamesian narrator might do. Wharton's narrator expresses his sympathetic response to Ethan and his plight, and sees something noble in his character. His mention of Mrs. Hale's comment at the end of the novella invites the reader to choose how to respond to Frome, with pity for a beleaguered man as does Mrs. Hale, or with understanding and admiration as does the narrator.

SETTING

The town of Starkfield and its surroundings, drawn from the hill country of western Massachusetts, provide the setting for the novel. In the frame story, the narrator describes the region. He comments on the length of the winter, on its severe beauty but draining cold. He compares the efforts of residents to endure the season to a garrison withstanding a long siege, suggesting a battle waged between man and nature. This description of Starkfield as a battleground is important to the tale that follows, for Ethan's story can be read as a contest of wills, an emotional battle that produces no winner. The narrator mentions the isolation that had characterized the region in earlier times and suggests that the long, snowy winter still threatens to cut people off from their neighbors. This physical isolation, coupled with the natural reserve of the inhabitants, makes for a lonely existence, especially in a region where privacy is not lightly violated.

Nowhere is this reserve and isolation more evident than within the Frome household. The house serves as the center of conflict, though the climax of the central narrative occurs outdoors. The farmhouse shows signs of neglect that reflect the financial struggles of the Fromes: It has "shutterless windows" (88), "thin clapboards" (92) and "loose-hung windows" (92). Until the arrival of Mattie Silver, the Frome household is characterized by "long intervals of secretive silence" interrupted by one of Zeena's "abrupt explosions of speech" (80). This silence reveals the emotional repression that makes possible the co-existence of Ethan and Zeena, though the tensions between them smolder beneath the surface. The kitchen of the farmhouse serves as a barometer of the emotional tenor of the household. On winter nights the kitchen has "the deadly chill of a vault" (90), except on the evening of Zeena's absence, but even then "its ancient implications of conformity and order" (109) exert a restraining influence over Ethan and

Mattie. Upon Zeena's return, the kitchen again looks "cold and squalid" (116) despite the fact that the stove is lit and Mattie is present. When the narrator finally enters the farmhouse kitchen, he finds all the signs of a failed domesticity, including broken china on a greasy table and the fire almost out. This scene reveals the complete breakdown of the characters' inner lives, the chaos and turmoil that Ethan still tries to hold at bay with his moments of routine in the outside world.

While the house serves as a prison, Ethan often finds comfort in the outdoors. From his youth, Ethan has been sensitive to nature's beauty and "even in his unhappiest moments field and sky spoke to him with a deep and powerful persuasion" (79). Ethan also finds that he does his clearest thinking outdoors as though nature's austere clarity pares away the distractions that tend to interfere. Nature is powerful, however, and presents danger to those who are careless, as Ethan reveals when he speaks of the great elm at the turn of the Corbury Road. When other avenues of escape are closed to Ethan and Mattie, the natural world still beckons, as they go sledding before Mattie's departure. The natural world seems to offer permanent escape when Mattie urges Ethan to take them "Right into the big elm . . . So 't we'd never have to leave each other anymore" (148). But nature is indifferent to the desires of human beings, an aspect of the literary naturalism that influences this short novel.

PLOT AND STRUCTURE

In devising the frame story for *Ethan Frome,* Wharton draws upon a narrative convention that was popular at the turn of the twentieth century. The frame story's origins date back to earlier works of literature, such as *The Arabian Nights* and *The Canterbury Tales,* but many nineteenth-century novelists incorporated this device, including Mary Shelley in *Frankenstein* and Emily Brontë in *Wuthering Heights.* The frame story allows a writer to create an impression of veracity for the story within the story. It may also allow the author to create the illusion of objectivity on the part of the narrator, who is identified as an observer rather than a participant in the central action.

The opening segment of the frame story serves a number of purposes: It introduces the narrator and gives some insight into his sensibility. It provides background information on the region and its winter climate as well as presents snippets of Ethan's story as the narrator hears it from local residents. It also creates an aura of suspense that impels the reader into the narrative that the frame story introduces.

The narrator provides glimpses and then a sustained picture of Ethan Frome as he appears during the narrator's stay in Starkfield. Curious as to the cause of Frome's limp and the red gash on his forehead, the narrator sees Frome as a "ruin of a man" (63). He first observes him from a distance, noting the regularity of his behavior, the predictability of his routine. When the narrator hires Frome to transport him to the train station, he hopes to converse, but discovers Frome to be a laconic companion. This silence encourages the narrator's speculation about Frome's history; similar to the gaps in others' stories, it adds to the mystery about Frome.

During a snowstorm that makes further travel impossible, the narrator accompanies Frome to his house. Upon entering its precincts, the narrator states that he "found the clue to Ethan Frome" (74) and breaks off the frame story. The narrative that ensues recounts events that occurred twenty-four years earlier as the narrator relates his version of Ethan's life and the accident that has left Frome maimed physically and psychologically. The central events occur over a three and a half day period, but Wharton provides information about the characters' pasts through Ethan's reflections and the narrator's descriptions. While the narrator's chief interest lies in what has shaped Ethan Frome, Frome's wife, Zeena, controls much of the action in the narrative.

The narrative of Ethan's past opens with young Ethan waiting for Mattie as a town dance comes to a close. There to walk her home, Ethan watches Mattie as she enjoys a last dance and parts from her friends. Although a married man, Ethan feels possessive toward Mattie and jealous of her dance partner, Dennis Eady, whose youth, freedom, and financial security heighten Ethan's sense of inadequacy. While he waits for her outside the dance, Ethan reflects upon what Mattie's arrival at the Frome household has meant to him. Her presence has given him an opportunity to share his appreciation of nature and "there were other sensations, less definable but more exquisite" (79) that drew him to her. He believes that her youthful gaiety and attractiveness can free him from the stifling condition of his life. While these thoughts bring Ethan a sense of comfort, he also harbors feelings of anxiety over his wife's growing displeasure with Mattie and whether she has detected Ethan's interest in the young woman.

Ethan's optimism seems capable of overcoming his fears until Zeena confronts him and Mattie upon their return to the Frome farmhouse. The house has a funereal atmosphere, standing in darkness with a dried cucumber vine appearing like "the crape streamer tied to a door for a death" (88). The contrast between Mattie's lively beauty and Zeena's haggard looks stand out immediately. When Zeena opens the door, she appears corpse-like, as the lamplight "drew out of the darkness her puckered throat and the projecting wristbone of the hand that clutched the quilt, and deepened fantastically the hollows and prominences of her high-boned face" (89). Zeena overshadows both Ethan and Mattie, her dour mood quickly dispelling their happiness. She resents their youthful energy and suspects that their relationship threatens her own security. They submit to her authority as she stands between them on the stairway, a symbolic position that suggests Zeena's ability to separate Ethan and Mattie more permanently. Ethan perceives this power as a threat to his happiness and believes he can thwart it.

Ethan's attraction to Mattie and his fear of Zeena's retribution generate the tension of the first three chapters. Toward the close of Chapter 3, Zeena announces her intention of going to Bettsbridge to consult a doctor, leaving Ethan and Mattie alone in the house overnight. Ethan and Mattie see this as a reprieve from Zeena's oppressive presence. It serves as a test, however, through which Zeena will gain proof of what she has suspected, that her husband's loyalties have shifted to another woman. The presence of Zeena's cat throughout this episode reinforces the impression of a trap that has been laid for unsuspecting prey. In some ways, Zeena plays a cat-and-mouse game with Mattie, for Zeena knows that she holds power in this conflict, her rights supported by family opinion and by law. She waits for the right moment to pounce.

After Zeena leaves, Mattie makes the most of her opportunity to be the ideal woman Ethan imagines, whose potential for domestic accomplishments would awaken if she were to marry a man she loved. When she greets Ethan at the door, Mattie stands in the same pose that Zeena held the night before, but the effect of the light is to throw into relief Mattie's youthful charm. Ethan sees how the ribbon she has run through her hair "transformed and glorified her" (103), especially in contrast to the image of his wife. Mattie appears a welcoming domestic angel who has created an atmosphere of harmony and comfort. In her efforts to do so, Mattie raids Zeena's treasures, both literally and figuratively. She brings out the red pickle dish, a wedding gift that Zeena has deemed inappropriate for everyday use. The supper begins with a feeling of contentment, but the presence of Zeena's cat and the repeated mention of Zeena's name creates discomfort for Ethan and Mattie. When the two simultaneously clasp the milk jug, the only physical contact they have during this night alone, the cat backs away and knocks the pickle dish from the table. The breaking of the dish shatters the mood of the evening, and Ethan finds that his efforts at romantic banter after dinner fall flat, leaving Mattie embarrassed. Though Ethan thinks he can conceal the broken dish from Zeena, this symbolic evidence of betrayal sets in motion the final power struggle of the Fromes' marriage.

The conflict simmering between Ethan and Zeena erupts into the open upon Zeena's return from Bettsbridge. For Zeena, the security of being a married woman is worth preserving, and to protect her marriage, Zeena has engineered plans to force Mattie's departure. She has already hired a girl from Bettsbridge to come as a replacement, using doctor's orders as her justification. When she discovers the broken pickle dish, her suspicions of illicit behavior are confirmed, and she becomes impervious to Ethan's attempts to persuade her to reconsider.

Determined to resist Zeena's will for as long as he can, Ethan realizes that he has no real possibility of circumventing her plans. He spends a sleepless night trying to imagine alternatives for himself and Mattie, but acknowledges that he hasn't the means to pursue those alternatives. Instead, he insists upon taking Mattie to the train depot himself, stopping along the way for the promised coasting ride. They opt for a final sled run, Mattie urging Ethan to crash into the great elm to achieve together a romantic escape in death. Charged with an undercurrent of sexual tension, this episode ends in failure. As Ethan attempts to drive them headlong into the elm, Zeena's face appears before him, throwing him momentarily off course. When they do strike the tree, both are injured, but not killed; as Ethan comes to he hears Mattie make "a small frightened *cheep* like a field mouse" (150) and recognizes that she must be in pain. As in his other attempts to escape, Ethan's gesture proves futile. His last thought in the narrative of the past reflects the powerful hold that routine has over him, for he thinks about feeding his horse.

At the culmination of this tale of frustrated escape, the narrator returns to the frame story, entering the Frome house in Ethan's company. He again creates an aura of mystery through the use of unidentified voices to bring the full shock of recognition home to the reader. Paralyzed before the kitchen stove sits the once vital Mattie Silver, now a living symbol of the destruction wreaked on three lives. Mattie resembles Zeena with "hair as grey as her companion's, her face as bloodless and shrivelled" (173–74). Another burden for Ethan, Mattie's crippled body and soured spirit serve as constant reminders of his failure and their entrapment. The novella ends with a final conversation between the narrator and Mrs. Ned Hale, who has always been sympathetic to Ethan. She sees little difference between the living Fromes and the dead, except that among the dead "the women have got to hold their tongues" (181). This remark reinforces the perception of Ethan as a beleaguered man, unable to escape his nagging wife or his dismal fate. Wharton suggests, however, that none of the main characters can break free of the limits that poverty and social roles have placed upon them. In the face of the bleak determinism that controls the lives of the characters, the only heroic action is endurance.

CHARACTERS

The three main characters are seen through the sensibilities of the narrator. His sympathy toward Ethan allows him to present both the positive and negative aspects of Ethan's character. In his treatment of the two women, however, the narrator tends to emphasize Mattie's attractive qualities and Zeena's negative traits. He presents Zeena as though she has always appeared as she does when he sees her, whereas the profound change in Mattie contributes to the power and surprise of the ending.

Ethan Frome has qualities that make him stand out from those around him, despite what has happened to him. He has a "careless powerful look" (63) that intrigues the narrator who wonders what the source of that power might be. On their rides together Ethan appears "like the bronze image of a hero" (68), suggesting a figure who has risen above the ordinary, who has met his trials triumphantly. Yet this impression stands in ironic contrast to the evidence of Ethan's life. The narrator probes the details of Ethan's story to discover what generates that heroic aura. One might argue that it is Ethan's endurance in the face of numerous hardships that gives him stature, but cannot bring him happiness.

As a young man Ethan believes that his chance to rise is linked to his ability to escape Starkfield. For years the gravestones in the family burial ground have "mocked his restlessness, his desire for freedom and change" (88), but in his youth and again in Mattie's youthful presence, he briefly thinks escape is possible. His first attempt occurs when he attends engineering school in Worcester, Massachusetts. There he enjoys the subject that he studies and camaraderie with his classmates, but his freedom is short-lived. His parents' declining health calls him back to their farm. As an only child, Frome cannot shirk his filial duty to care for his aging parents. When Ethan's mother sickens, depressed by her isolation, cousin Zenobia Pierce comes to care for her. Zeena's presence initially frees Ethan to resume the activities in which he feels comfortable, to "go about his business and talk with other men" (70). After his mother's death, Ethan proposes marriage to Zeena, more out of fear of loneliness than out of feeling for her, ironically turning her into an element of his entrapment.

Alienated from his wife, whose invalidism drains off his resources, Ethan is receptive to Mattie's friendly overtures. Her presence seems to rejuvenate him and restores his hope that something positive still awaits him in life. Mattie clearly awakens Ethan's sexual desire, and much of the natural imagery that Ethan associates with Mattie has sexual connotations (Ammons, *Argument* 65). Ethan sees their relationship in idealized romantic terms, however, and tries to maintain his chivalric role as her protector and defender. Some of his gestures, such as kissing the fabric that she sews rather than Mattie herself, suggest that Ethan sees Mattie as unattainable, a figure he has placed on a pedestal in his imagination. It also underscores Ethan's hesitancy to act, a failure for which he repeatedly rebukes himself.

When Zeena demands that Mattie leave, Ethan suffers a night of turmoil in which he evaluates his life and his prospects. He believes that he is "too young, too strong, too full of the sap of living, to submit so easily to the destruction of all his hopes" (129). He assumes that the one pleasure left to Zeena is to torture him and that his life with her will be a waste. Unfortunately, he cannot find a way out of his predicament: He does not have the means, personal or financial, to escape. He identifies life with Zeena as imprisonment and life with Mattie as freedom, but he struggles with the fact that he cannot obtain his freedom by cheating others. He becomes increasingly aware of the ironies of his situation, but realizes that his knowledge cannot change things. In another of the ironies that define Ethan's life, his failed sled run with Mattie turns her into part of his entrapment, leaving him to provide for her care and support as well as Zeena's.

While Ethan receives sympathetic treatment from the narrator, Zenobia (or Zeena) Frome receives his antipathy. In the narrator's version of Ethan's story, Zeena appears decrepit. She removes her false teeth at night and spends her days detecting new symptoms of her numerous ailments. As the narrator remarks, she is only seven years older than Ethan but at thirty-five is "already an old woman" (95). Like Ethan's farm, she drains his energies and offers him little sustenance. She has put her "self" into storage, much as she has her wedding gifts. This self-protective act may be a response to her own feelings of entrapment and her realization that Ethan has no desire for her. It seems that Zeena has resigned herself to a life of invalidism and isolation, but when her security is threatened by Mattie's presence, Zeena acts decisively.

When she arrived at the Frome farmstead to nurse Ethan's mother, Zeena knew the nature of her situation. She was hoping to escape the life of drudgery and exhaustion that characterized the experience of women in rural New England. As a single woman in a small village, she had few prospects for initiating her escape. Only through marriage could she achieve a secure place and an identity in the community. As a married woman, Zeena has a house to call her own, although she hopes it will be sold to enable her to move on to better things. When Ethan's farm attracts no buyers, Zeena realizes that she too is trapped in Starkfield. She resents what has happened to her and uses invalidism as a means of exerting control over her husband and punishing him for what she perceives as his failure to get ahead.

To intensify her villainous role and to convey the impression that Zeena commands a superhuman power over Ethan and Mattie, the narrator likens her to a witch. His descriptions of her appearance emphasize her crone-like features, her "bloodless" complexion, marked by "creases" and "querulous lines" (95). Zeena's interest in doctoring and remedies both as a patient and as a home-practitioner links her to the tradition of herbalism that was also associated with witchcraft and magic. In colonial New England, it was believed that witches were motivated to cause harm to others out of "pride, discontent, greed or envy" (Karlsen 6). Ethan frequently attributes these feelings to Zeena and sees them as factors that shape her behavior. Ethan needs to see Zeena as a witch, as an enemy who is larger than life, to justify psychologically and ethically his desire to leave her. To admit that she is only a disappointed and sickly woman makes his own motives and desires seem selfish and cruel. When the sickly Zeena again finds herself needed by Ethan and Mattie, she is "raised right up when the call came to her" according to Mrs. Hale (155) and has cared for both of them for twenty-four years. This sudden change suggests that much of Zeena's dour manner has been the result of her lack of purpose in life.

In contrast to Zeena, Mattie Silver appears as an image of youth and beauty to Ethan and to the narrator. Ethan sees her as a redeeming angel and as a fragile being who needs his protection. Ethan imagines that she will evolve into the so-called angel of the house, a popular female image from the nineteenth century. He believes she will keep a kitchen tidy as his mother once did and make him feel at home in the farmhouse. Mattie also serves as a mirror for Ethan, her reflective quality suggested by the name *Silver.* When Ethan is with her, he sees the self that he hopes to be, a man who still has the potential to make something of his life. More sensitive to the nuances of Zeena's words and gestures, Mattie at times signals to Ethan to be careful in what he says or does.

To Ethan and the narrator, Mattie is a wholly different creature from Zeena, but her circumstances reveal that her situation is not unlike the one her older cousin faced. Left in desperate circumstances through her father's death and business failures, Mattie has attempted to make her way in the world. With no training or skills, she could only find work that physically exhausted her. Having depleted her resources, Mattie is forced to accept the role of a domestic in the Frome household. That room and board is all she receives for her work makes her dependent upon Zeena's goodwill, for Mattie has no finan-cial resources that will allow her freedom. Her only hope of escape is tied to her ability to attract a suitor whose offer of marriage would remove her from the household. Her attraction to Ethan contributes to her entrapment because he can do nothing to free them from "his barren farm and failing saw-mill" (93). When Mattie faces the reality of her departure from the farm and her need to attempt once again to survive in a world that offers no place for her, she urges Ethan to take the last sled ride. She imagines that they will escape together in death, never imagining that she will be imprisoned by her own body as well as by her circumstances.

ROLE OF MINOR CHARACTERS

The minor characters serve as a source of information for the narrator both about Ethan's story and about the general conditions in Starkfield at the time of his accident. Harmon Gow and Mrs. Ned Hale are contemporaries of Frome's and know about the events that have shaped his life. They also provide insight into the values and expectations that shape the culture of the region and provide the yardstick by which Frome measures himself and his success or failure. The minor characters also serve as a measure of the way change has affected the region. The prosperity of Dennis Eady, the declining fortunes of Mrs. Ned Hale, and the retirement of Harmon Gow when the trolley replaced the stage, all signal the way market forces and aspects of progress affect people positively and negatively.

THEMES

Ethan Frome presents one of Wharton's most open explorations of the role of determinism in human experience. Determinism holds that individuals do not act freely to shape their own fate and future; instead, their lives are controlled by the forces of heredity, nature, and the social environment. Writers who explore the presence of determinism see human beings as more limited figures than did their romantic and realist counterparts. In this short novel, Wharton explores how all three factors have had an influence, especially on Ethan's life.

His family background affects Ethan, both in terms of his obligation to his parents and through the presence of the family burial ground that reminds him of his history. Wharton reveals that the isolation and demands of rural life have taken their toll on this family, from Ethan's father's death to his mother's mental breakdown. Wharton implies that there may be a hereditary weakness in the family line, something that accounts for the continuing decline. Ethan fears that this weakness may be mental or psychological, and that Zeena has been affected as well because she has started to withdraw as his mother did when she became ill.

The natural world also presents a hostile environment in the novel, one that, as the naturalists suggest, has no regard for human beings or their suffering. Ethan's farm barely provides a subsistence living, the thin soil and short season making the region unsuitable for large-scale farming. Likewise, his sawmill and lumber business do little to supplement his meager income. The most obvious struggle imposed by nature comes during the winter months in which the novel is set, for the bitter cold and deep snows make travel difficult, if not impossible, intensifying the sense of isolation and disconnection from the larger world.

The social environment also has an impact on Ethan and on Zeena and Mattie. The gender roles and expectations of late nineteenth- and early twentieth-century New England limit the possibilities for self-realization for all three characters. When Ethan's mother falls ill, Ethan must assume the domestic duties of the household, something for which he is unprepared and puts him into what is seen as a woman's sphere of activity. Zeena's arrival initially frees Ethan, as she assumes the running of the household and caring for his mother. Zeena brings a level of order back into the household that makes it possible for Ethan to return to the work of the farm and sawmill, activities deemed appropriate for men of his time. After Ethan marries Zeena, their relationship changes, for she becomes a dependent he must support and he feels trapped once again. Both Zeena and Mattie are also limited by the gender roles of their time; neither can go out into the world to support herself in other than menial, unskilled jobs. Both are in effect dependent upon marriage for their support and for their social definition. The conditions of dependency generate the bitterness that affects all three characters.

As in her other writings, Wharton also explores the tension between duty and self-fulfillment. This theme runs throughout *Ethan Frome,* but is pronounced during Ethan's night of questioning. He thinks about the possibilities of simply leaving Zeena and the farm, but he knows he cannot do so. He feels the power of his obligations, his need to do the right thing by Zeena, even though he has come to detest her. He also knows that he cannot obtain money from his neighbors under false pretenses; he cannot take advantage of others to steal some happiness for himself. He has also worried about Mattie and struggles not to take advantage of her. He does not want to ruin her reputation by engaging in a sordid affair. When he thinks of their being together, he thinks in terms of marriage, believing it is his duty to preserve her honor.

Although *Ethan Frome* is one of Wharton's bleaker works, not all of her themes are negative. Through the narrator and the frame story, she also explores the power of imagination to construct narrative from the bits and pieces of life. She, like Henry James, is interested in how the impressions of life, the details, manners, and gestures that characterize experience can be transformed into a unified whole. She also considers the role of the storyteller in framing a coherent tale, bringing order and meaning out of the raw material of life. Through such creative acts, individuals can, at least temporarily, rise above the deterministic aspects of life.

SYMBOLS

Wharton uses a number of symbols to enlarge the scope of meaning in this tightly woven narrative. None is more striking than the red pickle dish. This dish becomes a symbol with multiple meanings, often reflecting the critical perspective of the reader as well as the point of view of the characters. Initially to Zeena, the dish represents something that is too valuable for daily use, something that needs to be protected and hidden, possibly her own heart. Its color also suggests the sexual passion that she may have hoped for in marriage, but has now relinquished. To Mattie, the dish represents a pretty object (like Mattie herself) that will enhance a table setting and make it more colorful. For her, too, its color evokes the passionate attraction she feels for Ethan. The broken dish represents the broken relationships within the narrative. Ethan's inability to repair the dish suggests his inability to conceal the truth from Zeena or to remedy the problems in his life. For Zeena, the broken dish ultimately becomes the sign of her broken marriage. She laments that if she had listened to the village gossip sooner and sent Mattie away, she could have prevented the damage to her marriage as well as to her prized possession.

THE SUPERNATURAL

As in some of her short stories, Wharton uses elements of the supernatural, especially as a means of addressing the psychological tensions between the characters. The motif of ghosts and haunting runs throughout the narrative, most often associated with Zeena. Although Ethan wants to see Zeena as an insubstantial shade, a powerless ghost who cannot control him, Zeena haunts him in his dreams and during his waking hours.

When Ethan and Mattie are alone in the house, they sense Zeena's presence as though she sees all they do, adding to the tension that leads to the breaking of the pickle dish. Zeena's most powerful haunting of Ethan occurs during the sled ride with Mattie. Just as he heads toward the great elm, Zeena's face looms before him, causing him momentarily to swerve, losing a fraction of the momentum that impels him toward his fate. This vision makes her seem inescapable and all powerful, a figure of judgment who oversees all that Ethan does.

Enhancing the characterization of Zeena as a witch, Wharton suggests that her pet cat is her one ally in the household. The cat, traditionally assumed to be a witch's familiar or animal accomplice, seems to act in Zeena's stead, promoting her efforts to keep Ethan and Mattie apart. It sits rocking in Zeena's chair as though Zeena herself were present, and stays in the kitchen with Ethan and Mattie as though keeping an eye on them. The cat's attempt to get to the milk jug precipitates the breaking of the pickle dish, ensuring that Zeena has evidence to discover upon her return.

ALTERNATIVE READING: MARXIST CRITICISM

Marxist literary criticism examines the ways in which economics, class structure, and ideologies (a set of beliefs and the images that reflect them) shape a culture and are revealed in its literature. Karl Marx (1818–1883), author of the *Communist Manifesto* (1848), argued that economic activity established the base of a culture and provided the foundation for its intellectual, political, and legal systems (superstructure). He asserted that the culture's ideology shapes the consciousness of human beings so that an individual's sense of self and expectations in life are conditioned by his or her acceptance of the dominant ideology.

Marxist criticism explores historical and sociological contexts as well as economic structures to analyze the complex nature of social relations in a given era. Marx believed that such relations were dynamic, that history reflected a process called dialectical materialism. In this process, change occurs through the continuing struggle of opposites, including the struggle between the ruling class and the oppressed classes. For Marx, the main conflict of the industrial age was waged between the capitalists (ruling class) and the proletariat (working and oppressed class) over who would own and control the means of production, who would own and control the products of labor. Later Marxist theory also critiqued the role of the middle class or bourgeoisie, seeing it as aligned with the interests of capital and focused on preserving the status quo to maintain its own security. Marxist criticism has evolved during the twentieth century into a broad range of approaches. When examining a literary text, a Marxist critic asks questions such as: How is the economic system or power of the marketplace evident within the narrative? Who controls the means of production and/or the access to power within the culture? How is the dominant ideology present and privileged in the text?

In *Ethan Frome,* the economic structure of the time and the values associated with it govern the characters' understanding of themselves and their relationships. They view their lives in terms of debt and compensation, and believe that power or authority is determined by one's ability to control resources, one's ability to pay or collect payment from others. This sensibility derives in part from the Calvinist heritage of New England that held that prosperity was a sign of God's favor and poverty a sign of punishment. Under the influence of industrial capitalism, this concept evolved into a Protestant work ethic that asserted that hard work brings rewards and laziness results in poverty. Such thinking puts the burden of responsibility for economic success and social status upon the individual rather than questioning the distribution of resources in the economic system. For Ethan, Zeena, and Mattie, frustration emerges in part from their inability to secure the economic resources that would grant them a degree of autonomy in their lives.

As a farmer and sawmill operator, Ethan is tied to old, land-based activity. His location in Starkfield and his lack of education make it impossible for him to rise in the system of industrial manufacturing and capitalism that defines the emerging twentieth century. Ethan stands in sharp contrast to the narrator whose employment in the electric industry provides his connection to the future and to a source of power, both literally and figuratively. In the Industrial Age, both masculinity and class status are determined by a man's ability to participate in the marketplace, to control the use of resources. Ethan's inability to make his farm productive or to collect payment from those who owe him for lumber undermines his sense of manhood. His lack of capital also impedes his attempts to exercise authority, whether in his marriage or in conversations with his hired man.

During Ethan's dark night when he attempts to find a way out of the trap he finds himself in, all his thoughts revolve around the link between money and freedom. He recalls the story of a man in a nearby town who had run off with the woman he loved, divorcing his wife and leaving her the farm. His ex-wife sold the farm and used the proceeds to open a lunchroom, going into business for herself. When the man returned with his new wife and child, he too had prospered in the West. Ethan considers doing the same. He then recalls that his property is "mortgaged to the limit" (131) and feels the weight of his economic dependency crush his hopes for a new life. Ethan defines his marriage in economic terms, believing that Zeena's ability to ease his burden during his mother's illness "magnified the sense of what he owed her" (97). He resigns himself to the reality that he is a "prisoner for life" (131), but blames himself rather than the economic system that governs his life.

Like Ethan, Zeena measures everything in terms of cost and payment. Because a woman had fewer options for participation in industrial capitalism, Zeena depends on her relationships with others to define her place in the social and economic system. She believes that Ethan owed her marriage as compensation for having tended his mother during her last illness. Zeena sees Ethan's farm as the source of capital that will permit their move into a city and into a middle-class life. When the farm attracts no buyers, Zeena realizes that her situation is little better than when she had been single; she is trapped in a rural life that thwarts her hopes to rise in status.

Having bartered herself in exchange for the economic opportunity she thought marriage would bring her, Zeena feels she must find a new avenue of compensation. She makes Ethan pay for her frustrated dreams through her invalidism. Not only does it consume his meager financial resources, it also deprives him of the domestic services a farmer's wife was expected to provide. Through her invalidism, Zeena achieves some degree of leisure associated with a middle-class life. While Zeena may not be happy in her marriage, she defends the status quo. When her marriage is threatened by Mattie's presence, Zeena acts to preserve the one source she has for her own financial security and identity.

Mattie, like Zeena, depends on her relationships to others to define her place in the economic and social world. Because she has no other resources, Mattie must market herself and treat herself as a commodity to participate in the marketplace. Her attempts at being a wage-earner before her arrival at the Fromes', including bookkeeping and clerking in a department store, have resulted in failure and the breakdown of her health. One option for her survival is to make a good match, to marry a man with financial resources. Early in the novel, she appears in the company of Dennis Eady, a young man who will inherit his father's business and who enjoys the benefits of his family's prosperity.

When Eady invites her to ride in his sleigh, Mattie must decide whether she can barter her physical charms for the security of a marriage proposal. Her reluctance to objectify herself may account for her decision to walk home with Ethan instead.

To remain in the Frome household requires that Mattie accept a degree of dependency that limits her freedom, both personal and financial. The other option available to her, should she move to the city, is prostitution. To a Marxist critic, prostitution defines the nature of a woman's relationship to the capitalist economic system, whether she commodifies herself for monetary gain or marriage. Neither of these situations provides a woman with autonomy, however, and Mattie's final decision to seek escape through death suggests the depths of her entrapment. Ironically, even this attempt to determine her own fate fails her, and she is reduced to a state of utter dependence. The loss of her vitality and personality turn her into an object, a symbol of the powerlessness that subsumes Ethan and Zeena as well.

Summer (1917)

Edith Wharton was keenly aware of how ties to places as well as people shape identity. A witness to the chaos generated by World War I, she perceived how the loss of security, the loss of a home, affected an individual's sense of self and expectations for the future. Published while Edith Wharton was actively engaged in relief work during World War I, *Summer* (1917) presents a multifaceted search for identity and purpose, in some ways a search for self and home. Wharton claimed that she wrote the novel "in fits and starts" because of her war work (*Letters* 397), yet she presents a carefully constructed narrative that reveals her continuing attention to detail.

In the novel, Wharton returns to the "decaying rural existence" she had first explored in *Ethan Frome,* a world defined by limited options and frustrated hopes (*A Backward Glance* 898). Within this environment, Wharton traces the experiences of Charity Royall, who evolves from a rebellious adolescent to a woman faced with the difficult choices that impending motherhood thrusts upon her. Similar to other Wharton protagonists, Charity must wrestle with the codes and values of her community, including those that define woman's place and those that define Charity as an outsider. In her youthful exuberance, Charity believes that she can defy the codes of her world and be the independent agent of her own destiny. Wharton, however, uses Charity's experiences to reveal the constraints that affect women regardless of class or background.

Writing to her friend Gaillard Lapsley, Wharton referred to *Summer* as "the Hot Ethan" because of its treatment of intense emotions, including passion and anger (Lewis 396). While similar in some ways to *Ethan Frome, Summer* treats different questions and issues. Continuing to explore how social expectations curtail a woman's freedom, Wharton draws upon elements of the seduction novel and the sentimental romance, but modifies them to suit her own purposes. Some early reviewers noted this similarity, observing that her plot is "as old as civilization itself, one of those constantly recurring tragedies" (*New York Times Book Review* 253). Others were critical of Wharton's tone and treatment of characters, accusing her of being "too callous in the uses to which she has put this seduction" (*New Republic* 311). This novel continues to provoke debate among present-day readers who disagree over its meaning and the implications of the ending.

SETTING

Given her appreciation for the ways that place shapes an individual, Wharton devotes much attention in this novel to the setting, using it to enhance the development of themes and to provide further insights into characters. Unlike the frozen landscape of *Ethan Frome, Summer* is governed by the season for which it is named. Its warmth and fair weather provide a degree of freedom and mobility that encourage Charity Royall's journey toward self-discovery. From late spring through autumn, Charity moves from adolescence into womanhood as Wharton alludes to the traditional association of human growth with the cycle of the seasons. Wharton connects Charity's sexuality to the fruitfulness of summer, drawing upon a metaphor that foreshadows Charity's pregnancy. Charity's relationship with Lucius Harney follows the course of a summer romance as well, intense but temporary. The closing chapters of the novel occur in autumn. During this time of harvest and preparation for the long New England winter, Charity makes decisions that determine her future. She accepts a marriage that will provide respectability and security for her and her child, but Wharton suggests that this marriage entails the dormancy of Charity's passion and zest for life.

In addition to the seasonal aspects of setting, various locales play a significant part. Through contrasts between locations, Wharton conveys many of the underlying themes and tensions of the narrative. The regional setting for the action lies in western Massachusetts among the scattered hill towns whose sterility and rigidity Wharton had probed in *Ethan Frome.* In *Summer,* Wharton develops three important locations as parameters for the action: the village of North Dormer, the town of Nettleton, and the Mountain. Each influences Charity's attempts to define and understand herself, and each offers a different set of values or codes by which its inhabitants respond to life.

North Dormer, as its name implies, is a sleepy New England farming village, marked by a slow pace and emptiness even on a mild June afternoon. The town has stagnated because it has no rail connection or telegraph office, underscoring its isolation and lack of progress. The absence of shops and entertainment venues deprives North Dormer's inhabitants of contact with contemporary culture. The town's one cultural resource, the Hatchard Memorial Library where Charity works, more closely resembles a mausoleum than an active lending library, adding to the stultifying atmosphere of the town. Charity thinks of the library as "her prison-house" (162), an emblem of her confinement.

North Dormer's lack of connection to the outside world has fostered a rigid social structure and a conservative sensibility. Respectability is highly valued. For the community, the concept of respectability serves as a means of distancing itself from the lawlessness of the Mountain. Townsfolk frequently remind Charity that she is privileged to live in North Dormer, which offers her the "blessings of the most refined civilization" (161), rather than amid the squalor and presumed licentiousness of her birthplace. This fear of sexual promiscuity and the chaos associated with it particularly affects the attitudes toward women's behavior in the village. For women, respectability can be maintained only through marriage or unimpeachable virginity. A woman's reputation rests on the assumptions townspeople make about her, and Wharton notes, especially through Charity's experiences, how gossip functions as a tool for controlling women's premarital sexual activity. Those women who violate the norms suffer ostracism, as in the case of Julia Hawes, or the continuing taunts of resentful in-laws, as does Rose Coles, who was "married to make things right" (280). Men also face the test of respectability, but Wharton shows how the double standard provides greater leeway for their personal indiscretions as the community places greater emphasis on men's roles in the public sphere.

The neighboring town of Nettleton presents aspects of urban life that initially stimulate Charity's desire to discover what lies beyond North Dormer. Nettleton has a railway station, shops, restaurants, and a theatre, affording its inhabitants the variety of the marketplace. The tiny French café with its "queerly flavoured things" and a waitress who speaks "in unintelligible words" (227–28) adds a cosmopolitan air to Charity's visit. In this setting, Charity contemplates the possibilities of travel and new experiences. She believes that urban life offers variety and access to culture that can reduce her feelings of boredom and of inferiority. She envies and admires individuals such as Annabel Balch who enjoy the pleasures of cities like Springfield, and believes that Harney has "the air of power that the experience of cities probably gave" (182). Charity further assumes that the city or large town offers privacy and anonymity, unlike North Dormer where everyone knows everyone else's business.

To Charity, Nettleton has many attractive qualities, but the town reveals grim aspects of adult experience. Charity has heard of the house on Lake Avenue and Wing Street, the address of the woman doctor and abortionist Dr. Merkle. When Charity sees the house while riding through town a "shiver of cold ran over her" (229). She knows that Julia Hawes has remained in Nettleton after seeking the services of Dr. Merkle, finding herself no longer welcome in North Dormer. Julia's ostracism reflects the limited options available to women who have violated North Dormer's code of respectability. Charity also discovers that Nettleton may be a smaller town than she has assumed. When she encounters Royall in the company of Julia Hawes at the end of the fireworks display, Charity realizes that Nettleton offers no real escape from the world she has known.

Throughout much of the novel, the Mountain exists as a mysterious place, a dark figure on the landscape. A place of wildness, the Mountain is home to untamed nature and lawless people. The residents of North Dormer believe the Mountain to be a place of danger and disgrace, symbolizing the primitive state to which people devolve when they abandon the institutions of social order. To come from the Mountain carries a stigma of shame, and Charity does not like to be reminded that it is her birthplace. She believes, however, that the Mountain too may afford her an escape from the constricted life in North Dormer.

The reality that Charity discovers on the Mountain undercuts the romantic image that she has formed under Harney's influence. When she goes to the Mountain in search of her mother and a place among her people, she discovers a small band eking out a hardscrabble existence on the unforgiving terrain of New England's granite hills. Through this direct encounter, the Mountain loses its power as a symbol of escape for Charity. It no longer appeals to her as a place where she can make a home among her own people, for she realizes that she has even less connection to the Mountain's inhabitants than she does to those of North Dormer.

To intensify the connection between people and place, Wharton develops significant contrasts among the many houses that serve as stages for action. She calls attention to houses in part through Lucius Harney's efforts to sketch those that reflect the region's earlier history (and more prosperous times) for an architectural volume. The house that predominates is that of Lawyer Royall. Although it is not a building Harney plans to sketch, Royall's house defines the town, standing at one end of the main street while the church stands at the other. This arrangement suggests that law and religion serve as the anchors of the community's values and traditions.

Other houses or shelters invite comparison to Royall's. The Hyatts', with its remnants of architectural detail suggesting its prosperous beginnings, has given way to general neglect and poverty apparent in paintless clapboards and broken windows. The cabins on the Mountain, little more than one-room shacks, are even further removed from the stable home Charity has known. The most significant contrast to Royall's house appears in the abandoned house that Charity and Harney reclaim for their romantic trysts. The little house sits in a neglected garden that evokes images of fallen Eden, complete with an old apple tree in the dooryard. When Charity and Harney first arrive, the house is a "long-empty shell" (243), but as the space becomes reanimated by the passionate energy they share, signs of domestic comfort appear. When Royall confronts them there, he calls attention to the temporary and artificial nature of this domestic scene. He asks Harney, "Is this the home you propose to bring [Charity] to when you get married?" (265), knowing that they are merely squatters with no rightful claim to the place. Their lack of legal right to the property calls attention to the illegitimacy of their relationship in the eyes of the community.

PLOT AND STRUCTURE

Summer unfolds in a fairly simple plot that follows the experiences of Charity Royall as she interacts with other characters and the world around her. While Charity believes the changes occurring in and around her are momentous, Wharton emphasizes the daily activities of Charity's life, the ordinariness of much of what occurs. The narrative can be read as an example of a female *bildungsroman,* a novel that follows the course of a young person's development and eventual integration into the adult society of his or her time. In the eyes of North Dormer, Charity's integration into the adult community will come through marriage and domestic responsibilities. Charity, however, hopes to achieve self-definition by resisting the customary behaviors and expectations for young women in North Dormer. Throughout the novel, Charity feels torn between desire for marriage and rejection of it. She feels that avoiding marriage is the only way of avoiding surrender to the patriarchal code that defines the mediocrity of North Dormer. To express this tension within the novel, Wharton alternates Charity's moods between feelings of elation associated with freedom and of despair associated with frustration. She also alternates Charity's primary interactions through much of the novel between scenes of connection with Harney and scenes of confrontation with Royall.

At the opening of the novel, Wharton positions Charity on the threshold of the Royall house, looking out to the world, suggesting her potential for growth and transformation (Wolff 273). Wharton uses the word *initiation* at two key points in the novel to identify changes that are taking place for Charity. Wharton labels Charity's first trip outside North Dormer an initiation because it brings her a new perspective on the wider possibilities of the world beyond her village. She also labels Charity's journey to the Mountain a "tragic initiation" because the knowledge gained there forces her to admit her lack of autonomy. Between these two "initiations," Wharton establishes various stages through which Charity must pass on her quest for self-knowledge and freedom.

Just as the physical starting point of Charity's journey is the threshold of the Royall house, so her mental and emotional state has been shaped by her life with Royall. Theirs is a complex relationship, made so in part by the fact that Royall never adopted Charity. Although he has served in a parental role through much of her life and she feels an attachment to him, both are conflicted over the nature of their relationship as Charity approaches womanhood. Charity, reflecting her adolescent sensibility, defines their coexistence as a power struggle, one that has been dramatized in Royall's inappropriate sexual advance. In evaluating her feelings toward him, Charity frequently recalls the night Royall came to her room seeking sexual favors and how she fended off his approach. His actions have damaged her trust in him and she sees him as "a hideous parody of the fatherly old man she had always known" (173).

In Charity's view, Royall's shame over his inappropriate behavior parallels the shame she feels over her Mountain origins, making them in a sense equals. Confident that Royall's shame has weakened his ability to control her, Charity believes that she has gained the upper hand in the struggle between them. She refuses Royall's offer of marriage, negating any legitimacy in his feelings for her. However, she fears his reprisals, believing that he, like the town of North Dormer, will exact some form of retribution from one who defies expectations. Charity feels alienated from Royall and sees in him the same hypocrisy that she believes characterizes all of North Dormer.

While Charity nurses her "fierce revulsion" toward Royall (177), she encounters Lucius Harney. Charity's first encounter with Harney reawakens her desire to know more about the world because he represents something foreign to and, in Charity's eyes, better than North Dormer. Although her initial response upon seeing him is to retreat into Royall's house, to the world she has known, Charity watches Harney, attentive to his movements and gestures. Their relationship gets off to a rocky start, however, when Charity accuses him of betraying her lack of diligence to Miss Hatchard. Harney charms her into believing that he had no such intention, but Wharton's early mention of betrayal foreshadows the relationship's problematic end. Charity freely accepts Harney's assurances that she can trust him because she seeks compensation for her lost trust in Royall. She also feels reassured when Harney speaks of the Mountain in romantic terms. He sees it as a "curious place," an "independent little kingdom" inhabited by "rough customers" who "have a good deal of character" (190). Charity begins to see her birthplace in a different light. Her curiosity about her family connections on the Mountain is reawakened and she wonders whether her Mountain origins may explain some of her own "revolts and defiances" (190).

After the connection between Charity and Harney is established, the narrative traces its progress from friendship to romance. For Harney, the romance is a part of his summer excursion, but his architectural studies and his life beyond North Dormer are always available to him. For Charity, the relationship becomes the focal point of her existence, affecting how she interprets everything that occurs around her and how she sees herself. Charity also reads Harney's behavior and emotions as similar to her own, evident when she watches him from outside Miss Hatchard's house. Wharton suggests that Charity may see what she hopes is true rather than what is.

To mark succeeding stages in the relationship between Charity and Harney, Wharton uses three events that stand out from the daily routine: the Fourth of July trip to Nettleton, the Old Home Week celebration, and the confrontation at the abandoned house. These events place Harney and Royall in opposition to each other and reveal Royall's continuing influence on Charity, even when she tries to ignore him. Wharton also enlarges the context for Charity and Harney's relationship through the presence of Julia Hawes in Nettleton and Annabel Balch at Old Home Week. These two women establish the ends of the spectrum between scandal and respectability against which Charity measures herself.

Wharton underscores the significance of the Fourth of July excursion to Nettleton by placing it at the center of the novel. She also connects the holiday's commemoration of Independence Day with Charity's decision to assert her own freedom of choice. This episode is the first that takes place outside the precincts of North Dormer and marks the start of Charity's movement away from the inexperience that has governed her life. The day proves to be one of wonder and excitement as Harney shows Charity much of what Nettleton can offer. Harney buys her a pin and Charity wears it like a badge of membership that entitles her to attend the day's festivities in his company. Their celebration is capped off by the fireworks display at the lake, during which Charity realizes that her emotional and sexual exuberance is reflected in the bright colors that burst over their heads. At the end of the display, Harney kisses her and "with a sudden vehemence . . . wound his arms about her" (234), further inspiring her passionate desires.

Unfortunately, the day does not end on this high note. While leaving the lake, Charity encounters Royall in the company of Julia Hawes. Royall berates Charity for her disheveled appearance while he stands before her in a drunken state. Worse, he calls her a whore while he has spent his day in the company of prostitutes. Humiliated by this public scolding, Charity wants to escape the moment to avoid further scandal and to preserve the purity of her feeling for Harney. She also believes she must escape from Royall's house and his abusive authority. Harney convinces her to stay in North Dormer, however, to preserve her reputation and live down Royall's accusations.

The second celebration for which Charity prepares is North Dormer's Old Home Week, an event that occurs toward the end of August. For many rural communities, Old Home Week marks the close of the summer season and reasserts the community's claim upon its members, even those who have moved away. Charity has selected a white silk dress to wear for the occasion, "to let North Dormer see that she was worthy of Harney's admiration" (254). When she sees the dress and its accompanying veil laid out like a bridal outfit, Charity tells herself that she no longer depends on her earlier dreams of marriage because "warmer splendours had displaced them" (255). In gazing at her ensemble, Charity discovers that she will wear a pair of Annabel Balch's cast off shoes and wonders if she has been a stand-in for Annabel all along.

At the ceremony itself, Charity has a series of epiphanies. One is her recognition of Royall's abilities as a public speaker and of his honesty in acknowledging the personal failure that brought him back to North Dormer. She begins to grasp the standard against which he measures himself and why others in the community respect him. Her next realization is more personally troubling. As Royall resumes his seat, one of the decorations falls to reveal Harney in the company of Annabel Balch. Charity has fretted over Harney's mention of other young women and now "the vision of their two faces had blotted out everything. In a flash they had shown her the bare reality of her situation" (259). As Charity struggles to comprehend what she sees, she sickens and faints at Royall's feet. Charity tries to pass this off as the effects of the heat of the day and the length of the speeches, but she fears that she is pregnant.

During the interval between the Fourth of July and Old Home Week, Charity and Harney have engaged in a sexual relationship. As their relationship becomes intimate, Charity feels emotionally attached to Harney and believes she can trust him, telling him of Royall's sexual advances. She also believes that she has freed herself from the constraints of North Dormer's morality, that she has control over her life and its direction, symbolized by the mobility provided by her rented bicycle. For Harney, their liaison is part of his summer vacation, the "two golden rainless August weeks" (251) during which he enjoyed the Edenic setting of the abandoned house and Charity's company. Just as Adam and Eve had to face the consequences of their actions after tasting of the tree of knowledge, so Charity and Harney are surprised after Old Home Week by Royall's visit to the abandoned house and his pointed questions. Royall challenges Harney regarding his long-term intentions toward Charity and castigates Charity for violating the norms of sexual propriety. Charity denies that marriage matters to her and professes to Harney that she doesn't regret her actions. Charity realizes that their romance is waning, however, for "she waited to be caught in his arms, but he turned away from her irresolutely" (266).

In addition to her concerns over her relationship to Harney, Charity suspects that her bouts of faintness and illness signify a pregnancy. Charity verifies her condition, but she does not want to trap Harney into marriage. Having sought freedom for herself, she does not want to restrict his freedom. She also does not want to redefine their relationship as one in which she has been the victim of his seduction. When she receives the letter that she perceives is his "avowal of Annabel Balch's prior claim" (278), Charity realizes that Harney is not strong enough to break from the social conventions of his class. She believes she must now face her future alone, but she holds out hope for acceptance and connection on the Mountain, her last avenue of escape.

Wharton has already taken Charity through a series of tests and challenges that measure the strengths and limits of her character. Her journey to the Mountain serves as the final trial before the novel moves toward resolution. This is in keeping with the structure of the *bildungsroman,* for it often includes a spiritual or psychological crisis through which the central character must pass to reach maturity and an understanding of the larger world. For Charity, the journey to the Mountain proves to be her "dark night," when she engages in her most sustained introspection and contemplation of her place in the world. Wharton conveys the paradox of Charity's situation: Her night on the Mountain marks the physical high and emotional low points of her journey. She has finally reached the place of her origins, but must acknowledge the lack of sustenance on the Mountain for her and her child. She believes that she now bears responsibility for her child's future and that she must act to provide for its well-being, despite her own needs.

Charity's realizations on the Mountain govern the resolution of the novel. On her descent, Charity encounters Royall, who has come to find her. For his efforts, "she felt a softness at her heart which no act of his had ever produced since he had brought her the Crimson Rambler" (298). He persuades her to enter his carriage and again proposes marriage, but he does not mention her pregnancy. Charity, benumbed by the rush of experiences she has had, accepts his offer and goes with him to Nettleton to be married. She knows a life with Royall offers stability and social respectability for her and her child, even if she must sacrifice her own freedom and happiness to attain it. While in Nettleton she reclaims the pin she has left with Dr. Merkle, seeing it as a remembrance of her summer of freedom, something she wishes eventually to give to her child. At the end, Charity approaches the threshold about to re-enter Royall's house. Wharton has brought her back to her starting point, underscoring the limitations that her circumstances have placed upon her.

This ending has provoked controversy among critics and readers. Some see Charity's marriage as permitting her integration into the adult community and preventing her from reliving her mother's experience (Wolff 291; Waid *Underworld* 114-15). Others perceive the underlying question of incest as a key to Wharton's critique of marriage and patriarchy (Ammons 137) or see Charity's reclaiming of the brooch as a subversion of patriarchy (Skillern "Good Girl" 134). Still others find the use of humiliation and coercion on the part of Royall as undermining any positive aspects of this union (Raphel 298-99). Although Charity returns to the house from which her journey began, Wharton does not imply that she has found the home she has been seeking. The ambiguities of the ending leave that issue unresolved and suggest that Charity may have to create that space for herself and her child.

CHARACTERS

As in many of her novels, Wharton presents three main characters whose interactions and confrontations impel the plot forward and reveal the underlying tensions within the narrative. These characters have mixed natures, the blend of strengths and failings that make them believable and that influence their motives and actions. Of the three, Charity Royall is the most fully developed and through her eyes the reader often views Lucius Harney and Lawyer Royall.

A headstrong and proud young woman, Charity Royall refuses to allow North Dormer to govern her sense of self. She feels conflicted about her identity, however, for her guardian, Lawyer Royall, never legally adopted her. She believes that Royall christened her Charity to reinforce her feeling of dependence and presumably gratitude as well. As the narrative progresses, Charity becomes more conscious of the sources of her identity. She wonders about her birth mother as a young woman and questions whether she is related to Liff Hyatt, whose mental slowness and awkwardness of movement mark him as an outsider. In addition, Charity reveals typical adolescent insecurities as she compares herself to Annabel Balch, whom she envies for her blue eyes and more privileged social status.

Charity finds her own life routine and stifling. She chafes against the restrictions placed upon young women in North Dormer and harbors a barely contained anger that flares whenever she experiences disappointment. She sees her work at the library as futile, often leaving early to escape the dank interior for the open fields and warm sun outdoors. Being outdoors brings her comfort, especially because the natural world affirms the naturalness of her own feelings and desires. As the novel progresses, Charity becomes more conscious of her desirability but fears that her physical attractiveness is not enough, that her ignorance and inexperience create an insurmountable gulf between herself and Harney. She tries to put this and other troubling issues out of her mind, but they are often hovering at the edge of her consciousness.

Charity prides herself on her ability to exert control in situations. After her sexual relationship with Harney has begun, however, Charity allows him to direct her course of action, "in a fatalistic acceptance of his will" (248). At this point, Charity comes closest to the female characters who appear in seduction novels because she seems willing to surrender her decision-making abilities for romance. Unlike those characters who often suffer ostracism and death when abandoned, Charity refuses to succumb. During her brief sojourn on the Mountain, Charity senses her insignificance but believes she must draw upon her inner reserves of strength for the well-being of her child. She accepts a marriage that is a compromise, a surrender to the social forces that surround her, but she does not surrender her entire sense of self.

While Charity Royall may be the most rounded character in *Summer,* Lucius Harney resembles a stock figure from the seduction novel. He is a young man from a more privileged background who takes his social position and individual freedom for granted. He is charming and, in Charity's eyes, sophisticated and well educated. His mobility and opportunities intensify Charity's feelings of confinement; a relationship with Harney appeals to Charity in part because she believes that she can share the freedom he enjoys. Similar to the male characters in many seduction novels, Harney uses words to gain his own ends. From the time he denies his betrayal at the library to the letter he writes excusing himself from making a commitment to Charity, Harney's phrases place himself and his actions in the best light. He also condemns Royall's carnal impulses toward Charity, but moments later embraces her, asking her to surrender to his own sexual desire. Harney serves as a vehicle for Charity's initiation into sexual knowledge, but Wharton does not treat him as a villain. In naming him Lucius, she associates him with light and with something luscious that appeals to the senses. She does, however, reveal selfish aspects of his character that govern his responses when making a significant decision. Like his counterparts in other seduction novels, Harney leaves town when a crisis occurs, taking advantage of his freedom.

Lawyer Royall is the most complex figure in the novel. In a letter to Bernard Berenson, Wharton expressed her satisfaction that Berenson liked this character, claiming, "Of course, *he's* the book!" (*Letters* 398). Royall, a man in midlife, has been in a slow process of decline, brought about by temper, alcohol, and loneliness. At one time he had potential to make a name for himself in the law, but some unnamed personal failure brought an end to these hopes. He retreated to North Dormer at his late wife's insistence and has spent his life working for insurance companies and handling the minor cases of a rural practice. North Dormer sees him as the leading light intellectually, but the respect his neighbors have for him does not provide him with companionship or a sense of purpose. His midlife crisis prompts his carousing with prostitutes and drunken young lodge men who mock him while they accept his money. Even he does not believe his claim that "it's not too late for me" to find a prosperous line of work (217).

Royall's many failings are made plain, especially during his angry outbursts, but Wharton suggests greater depth to his character. The anger that he expresses toward Charity often reflects his own feelings of frustration and isolation. He seeks an emotional response from her, even if all he gets in return is her anger. At times he attempts to use his patriarchal authority to coerce Charity into compliance with his wishes, but he discovers that she is as headstrong as he, which he begrudgingly admires. For all his faults, Royall struggles on, persevering in life despite his disappointments and frustrations. He provides Charity with a stable home even after the death of his wife and he attempts to make Charity happy, seen in his gift of the Crimson Rambler and his offer to secure Harney's marriage proposal for her. Charity has been the one responsibility that has given meaning to his life, and the threat of losing her frightens him more than he can admit. His actions after Charity's journey to the Mountain reveal a man who believes that her desperate situation has renewed his opportunity to act out of noble purpose, to live up to his name and the standards by which he judges the life around him.

ROLE OF MINOR CHARACTERS

Wharton includes a number of minor characters who convey the attitudes and expectations that shape the world in which Charity functions. The male characters such as Liff Hyatt and the Reverend Miles have a limited impact on Charity, but the female characters provide further definition of women's roles and options. Annabel Balch, Ally Hawes, and Julia Hawes serve as foils to Charity. Miss Hatchard and Dr. Merkle delineate the differences in attitude between the village and the town.

Annabel Balch embodies the ideal of the fair heroine of romance fiction, with her blond hair and blue eyes in contrast to Charity's darker coloring. In the romance tradition, the fair heroine is associated with purity and sexual naïveté; lackluster and reserved, the fair heroine ultimately wins the hero of the romance. Annabel represents an unattainable ideal to Charity, especially because she also enjoys the social and class advantages that Charity lacks. At the Old Home Days ceremonies and dance, Annabel functions as a silent standard against which Charity measures herself. While Charity is involved with Harney, she believes that she has triumphed over Annabel; but like other fair heroines of romance, Annabel holds Harney's commitment to marriage in the end.

While Annabel stands at one end of the spectrum of young womanhood, Julia Hawes occupies at the other. Julia, exiled from North Dormer for violating the codes that govern women's sexual conduct, has become a prostitute. Hardened by her experience in the city, Julia views others with cynicism and laughs at Charity's naïve ideas. Julia's younger sister Ally represents the typical young woman of North Dormer. From a family of limited means, Ally earns money to support herself and her mother by working as a respectable seamstress. She maintains secretive contact with her older sister, but fears the repercussions of open visits to her. She depends on the benevolence of women like Annabel Balch for her meager pay. Her "pale face . . . like the ghost of wasted opportunities" (221) reflects the exhausting nature of her work. Ally has no desire to leave whatever security North Dormer offers her.

In the town of North Dormer, Miss Hatchard claims the role of leading citizen whose place is ensured as the descendent of one of the founding families of the town. Prim and proper, she embraces all the pomp and ritual of Old Home Week and any other event that venerates the memory of the town's founders. She uses her propriety as a shield to avoid confronting anything she deems unpleasant or sordid, such as the truth of Royall's behavior toward Charity. She represents North Dormer's vision of maiden spinsterhood: an innocuous presence within the community who does nothing that will unsettle the status quo.

In contrast to Miss Hatchard, whose wealth and status exempt her from paid labor, Dr. Merkle works as a physician in Nettleton. While Miss Hatchard avoids any direct mention of the human body or sexuality, Dr. Merkle's livelihood depends on her frankness in doing so. She is solicitous when Charity first consults her, but proves to be a hard-edged businesswoman when it comes to payment for her services. Like Julia Hawes, Dr. Merkle is hardened by what life in the city demands of her, and she is willing to use Charity's lack of sophistication and experience against her.

THEMES

In keeping with the nature of a *bildungsroman,* Wharton explores the relationship between an individual and the community. She focuses particularly on the individual's desire for autonomy and the community's pressure to conform to its code. She also explores how the institutions of a society contribute to its stability and reflect its values, including the institution of marriage. Wharton considers how these institutions and values perpetuate the imbalance of power between men and women and how this affects the relationships between them. She inquires into the relationship between innocence and experience and what knowledge costs. Further, Wharton addresses issues of specific interest in the era in which she is writing, including the influence of heredity and aspects of determinism in human experience.

The conflict between the individual's desire for autonomy and the community's claims on an individual serves as the thematic focus of much American literature. It also appears as a continuing theme in much of Wharton's work, including *The House of Mirth* and *The Age of Innocence.* In *Summer,* the code of North Dormer is often articulated by Lawyer Royall, from his censure of Charity's promiscuous behavior to his condemnation of the moral laxity on the Mountain. He and others in the village uphold the rule of law and the institutions it supports, especially when they think of the chaos and degradation on the Mountain. The village believes that its institutions, including the church and the home, provide stability in the social order and security for individuals. In exchange for these benefits, the individual has a duty to uphold and improve the life of the community, to sacrifice individual satisfactions for the good of the whole. Wharton sees the danger in this thinking, however, because it serves to reinforce the status quo and to excuse individuals and the community from questioning the validity of long-held beliefs and practices.

In a novel in which marriage serves as a sign of integration into adult life, Wharton also examines how marriage as an institution reflects the values of a culture. She perceives that in a world that clings to tradition and the subordinate status of women, marriage cannot be a partnership of equals. Despite the many times Charity thinks of herself as Royall's equal, their marriage entails a continuation of her dependency, what Elizabeth Ammons calls "perpetual daughterhood," in which a woman continues to obey the dictates of a patriarchal order (*Argument* 141). Throughout much of the novel, Charity has resisted the idea of marriage, much as she has resisted the values of North Dormer, in an attempt to achieve a degree of self-realization and independence. Wharton suggests that abandoning this independence is the cost of the security Charity seeks at the end.

Wharton is also interested in the cost of knowledge, the sacrifices that an individual makes in the course of moving from innocence to experience. In her treatment of Charity and Harney's sexual relationship, Wharton makes numerous allusions to the story of Adam and Eve in the Garden of Eden. Adam and Eve gain sexual knowledge as well as the knowledge of good and evil through their actions. The cost of this knowledge is high, however, for they are driven from Eden and discover that they must toil for their bread and eventually suffer death.

The admonition to Eve during the expulsion from Eden is particularly relevant for Charity. Eve is told, "in pain you shall bring forth children" (Genesis 3:16), pain that for Charity is psychological and emotional as well as physical. Wharton also raises the possibility of a "fortunate fall" for Charity in that her knowledge gradually results in greater depth of character. She has come to value something about her inner self, as represented by the pin she reclaims that compensates for her loss.

Also reflected through Charity's questions and experiences, the role of heredity and familial legacies contributes to the tension of the novel. Charity often wonders whether she is like her birth mother and what she has inherited from her origins on the Mountain. She wonders about Liff Hyatt's mental slowness, whether it signifies a family legacy resulting from inbreeding among the Mountain's inhabitants. She also thinks about her similarities to Royall, comparing "their terrible equality of courage that sometimes made her feel as if she had his blood in her veins" (218), even though they have no biological tie. Dale Bauer suggests that Wharton raises these issues in light of her own critical response to the eugenics movement, popular during the early twentieth century. Eugenicists argued that a society can produce better offspring through genetic control, but Wharton questioned their arguments for evolutionary progress (Bauer, *Brave* 29–32).

SYMBOLS AND ALLUSIONS

In *Summer,* clothing and jewelry function as symbols that give voice to things that Charity cannot articulate. Her choice of clothing is especially significant at the Fourth of July celebration and the Old Home Week ceremony. For the Fourth of July festivities, Charity chooses to wear a new white muslin dress, signifying her innocence and girlhood. The bonnet she wears, however, reveals another facet of her; its cherry-colored lining and red roses represent her sexuality and the passionate core of her being (Skillern 122). This pairing of the two colors connotes Charity's blend of innocence and sexuality. Again at the Old Home Week ceremony, Charity wears a white dress, as do the other young women who form the chorus. Because Charity is no longer a virgin, the white dress no longer symbolizes her purity but represents the public mask she must present to North Dormer. In contrast to these two special outfits, the clothing Charity wears for her wedding is her everyday attire, nothing that makes her stand out in a crowd. Wharton uses this clothing to suggest that Charity has resigned herself to the ordinary circumstances of her outward life.

The pin that Harney buys for Charity also assumes a symbolic role at the time of its purchase and again when Charity redeems it from Dr. Merkle. When she and Harney enter the jewelry store in Nettleton, Charity admires a "gold lily-of-the-valley" (226), a flower associated with innocence and purity. Harney indicates that the blue pin, its stone "blue as a mountain lake," is preferable (226). Charity believes her choice reflects a want of "discrimination," but Harney is also guiding her away from a symbol of innocence toward something more complex in its meaning. As the narrative progresses, the blue stone comes to represent for Charity her inner life and the depth of her being that cannot be changed or taken from her by social expectations (Skillern 134). She uses the pin as collateral for payment to Dr. Merkle, but knows she must get it back as she enters into her married life. The pin represents for her that part of herself that is not ordinary, that she will not surrender to her marriage vows and hopes to pass on as a legacy to her child.

ALTERNATIVE READING: FEMINIST CRITICISM

Feminist scholars analyze the condition of women in society and explore how gender expectations affect the experiences of women and men. They question how gender influences an individual's ability to exercise power, participate in the public sphere, and engage in self-definition or self-realization. Feminist scholars may critique a male-centered or male-dominated culture (patriarchy) that imposes limitations on women through definitions of appropriate behavior. They may look for signs of a latent matriarchy, a covert source of female power that is perpetuated through the mother-daughter relation. Feminist critics raise these issues when they read literary texts, seeing them as representations of a particular culture's values. Because *Summer* includes many elements of a female *bildungsroman*, aspects of the novel lend themselves to feminist analysis. One issue that has provoked interest on the part of readers and critics is Charity's search for a mother figure, and the role the mother and motherhood plays in Charity's understanding of herself.

In the nineteenth century, the mother-daughter relationship created what Carroll Smith-Rosenberg has called an "apprenticeship system" through which daughters learned to navigate the social codes and expectations that defined their world (16). While this "apprenticeship system" diminished in significance by the end of the century as more opportunities for women's education became available, the mother-daughter relation still provided an important avenue for socialization and served as a source of support. In *Summer,* Wharton makes the absence of a mother-daughter relationship a central aspect of the novel. The narrative begins and ends at Royall's house, but the house is defined by his patriarchal rule rather than as the center of female power depicted by many of Wharton's regionalist predecessors. Without a mother figure to guide her, Charity must find her own way through the maze of possible roles and behaviors, trying on different attitudes, moods, and even identities in her attempts to understand herself and her potential. Her quest for knowledge of herself and her origins can be read as a search for the mother and for the knowledge of what motherhood means, personally and socially.

In the late nineteenth-century culture that continued to shape the world of North Dormer, the mother's role was still a significant one, defined by her activity within the domestic sphere. A woman was expected to make her home a sanctuary for her family and to support the social order by creating order within her home. Royall's house presents an image of stability, but lacks the fully realized domesticity that a woman of that era would have been expected to provide. The death of Royall's wife when Charity was about eight years old left Charity without a maternal influence and the household without a guiding force. Charity has never learned to do those things that make a household run smoothly, nor has she developed a sense of the house or garden as an outlet for her creativity. The house shows signs of neglect in its untended yard and faded appearance. The lack of domestic care affects the inhabitants of the house as well, for Royall often appears disheveled and Charity unruly.

During much of the novel, Charity does not know whether her birth mother is living or dead, even though she often thinks about her. Because establishing a relationship with her seems an impossibility, Charity looks to other women in the novel to function as mother substitutes. Unfortunately, none of the women with whom Charity has contact can provide her with the guidance or care that she needs. Both Miss Hatchard and Dr. Merkle fail Charity in various ways, and neither sees herself as being obligated to provide Charity support, emotional or otherwise.

Although Miss Hatchard has hired Charity to work at the library, she has little sympathy for her, always associating Charity with the taint of her Mountain origins. When Charity seeks her out after Royall's inappropriate sexual behavior, she realizes that "Miss Hatchard had no help to give her and that she would have to fight her way out of her difficulty alone. A deeper sense of isolation overcame her" (171). Miss Hatchard's own "long immaturity" (171) has left her ill-equipped to respond to Charity's need. She often speaks of standards, but they have become a shield to hide behind whenever Miss Hatchard wishes to avoid something "unpleasant."

Charity experiences a similar feeling of isolation at her appointment with Dr. Merkle. During their first conversation, Dr. Merkle's "smile grew more motherly" (276) and at their second meeting she claimed she "just put it to [her] as [her] own mother might" (309) in demanding payment, but Dr. Merkle is only concerned with her own financial benefit and the opportunity to take advantage of Charity's inexperience. Because her medical practice includes providing abortions, Dr. Merkle comes across as a figure antagonistic to motherhood, irritated that Charity refuses the kind of help she can offer.

While Charity's foster mother died during Charity's childhood, her birth mother still lives on the Mountain. When measured by the standards of motherhood as defined in North Dormer, Charity's mother fails miserably. A mother was expected to be the first teacher of her children, their first and most profound moral and spiritual guide. A woman labeled an unfit mother was thus a failure in the eyes of the community. When Charity hears Lawyer Royall describe her mother as just such an individual, she is horrified and feels her own self-confidence plummet. She believes that her mother was a terrible woman for giving her away, a woman who felt nothing for her own child.

During the course of the novel, however, Charity often wonders whether any aspects of her mother have been transmitted to her. When she discovers that she is pregnant, Charity begins to think more about connections to her mother, especially those defined by the female body and biological destiny. When everyone else in her life has failed her, Charity resolves to find her birth mother, to find answers to the many questions about herself. While Charity journeys up the Mountain, she learns from the minister that her mother is dying. Feeling even greater urgency to make some connection with her mother while she can, Charity arrives at the Mountain only to find her mother dead.

Charity's first sight of her mother is of a repellent corpse in ragged clothes, sprawled on a dirty mattress. Any romantic notions that Charity has held about her mother are dashed by this image, but only at her mother's deathbed does she comprehend the hardships of her mother's life. After the burial, Charity stays on the Mountain and briefly experiences its harsh conditions during her sleepless night in the cold of an unheated cabin. This causes Charity to acknowledge her mother's lack of resources and to reevaluate her mother's decision to give her to someone who could provide a better life for her. She comes to see her mother's decision as a sacrifice to spare her child, the same impulse Charity feels when she thinks she must save her child from a life on the Mountain. Charity begins to consider this implication of motherhood, the need to relinquish her own desires for the sake of someone dependent upon her.

Charity has discovered that the women that she knows cannot provide her with resources to make it on her own. They do not form a latent matriarchy to counterbalance the patriarchal expectations of their world and cannot offer her any alternatives that she finds palatable. When she encounters Royall on her journey down the Mountain, she accepts his proposal because she sees no other viable option. Wharton suggests, however, that Charity draws strength from a better understanding of her mother's choice. It has given her a new sense of worth that enables her to accept responsibility for the well-being of her own child.

8

The Age of Innocence (1920)

In the aftermath of World War I, Edith Wharton assessed the transformation of America. She saw Americans confront the greater instability and unpredictability of life in the wake of a worldwide conflict. Conscious of the nostalgia people felt for the decades between the Civil War and World War I, Wharton sensed that the idealized images of this period created an artificial picture of a less troubled time. Wharton saw how concepts such as duty and responsibility bolstered social stability during this era, but she also recognized how they limited self-realization. In *The Age of Innocence,* she explored the values, mores, and conduct of Old New York in the 1870s when life seemed orderly and safe. In her novel, she probed beneath the period's so-called innocence to reveal a world on the threshold of significant change.

In 1921, Wharton received the Pulitzer Prize for *The Age of Innocence.* The award brought her less satisfaction, however, when she learned that it had been given to her rather than to Sinclair Lewis for *Main Street,* the prize committee's first choice. The trustees of Columbia University, who granted the award, based their decision in part on a desire to avoid further offending the Midwestern readers already troubled by Lewis's novel. Their actions reflected the same attempts to avoid unpleasantness that Wharton critiqued in her novel. Wharton wrote to Lewis acknowledging his achievement, initiating a valued friendship with him. He, in turn, dedicated his novel *Babbitt* to her in 1922.

Praised by reviewers for its "mastery of plot, character and style" when it appeared (Phelps 1), *The Age of Innocence* remains one of Wharton's greatest achievements. The compelling story of love and temptation between Newland Archer and Ellen Olenska has attracted filmmakers as well as readers. As early as 1923, Wesley Ruggles interpreted the novel in a silent film. A more recent version, directed by Martin Scorcese in 1990, captures the richly detailed setting and costume of the era. Within this beautiful environment, characters struggle to accept the demands of duty and self-sacrifice that restrict their personal freedom but preserve their social world.

SETTING

In *The Age of Innocence,* Wharton presents the world of Old New York at a time when Society was a small, well-defined circle. Although America had endured the turmoil of the Civil War in the decade prior to the novel's opening, the upheaval caused by that conflict has had little impact on the world of the social elite. The characters in the novel express no awareness of the world outside their own small sphere, protected by the various efforts made to ensure their privacy. Although the world around them has already witnessed evidence of increasing class competition and the impact of industrialization, their concept of social hierarchy pertains to a ranking of families in Society based upon purity of lineage and ties to the colonial founders of New York.

As in *The House of Mirth,* New York City serves as the center of the action in *The Age of Innocence,* but the era in which the novel is set is less familiar to Wharton's readers. To evoke the atmosphere and quality of life in the 1870s, Wharton makes frequent reference to daily activities far removed from those of her audience in 1920, such as the lighting of oil lamps and tending of fireplaces. She captures for readers the ambiance of a particular historical era, carefully describing clothing styles, furniture, decoration, even the foods served at dinner parties. To remind her readers that the setting precedes the age of the automobile and the freedom it embodies, Wharton presents in detail the carriages in which characters ride as well as the quality of teams of horses. All of these details contribute to the realism of the novel, but they also give readers the impression that they are stepping back with the narrator into a world that no longer exists.

In the 1870s, the effects of the Gilded Age are just beginning to redefine the city and the degrees of wealth that distinguish its elite. Most social activity occurs at dinner parties in people's homes, or at select public locales such as the opera. Although a figure such as Mrs. Struthers at the margins of this social circle gives parties with music on Sunday evenings, the more conservative members of the elite frown upon such activity. Established families see themselves as responsible for maintaining standards and for fending off any attempts to deviate from the accepted order of life. When they travel to resorts such as St. Augustine or Newport, these families take along much of their household staff to ensure as little disruption of the routines of life as possible. During their travels they maintain an exclusive distance from others, preferring the security of the known to encounters with anything or anyone new. Even when Newland takes May to Europe after their wedding, her need for predictability and custom outweighs his longing for adventure.

In sharp contrast to the uniformity of the upper-class households with which Archer and his circle are familiar, Wharton describes the strikingly different interiors in which Ellen Olenska feels at home. Unlike the staid and predictable decoration of Old New York homes, Ellen's surroundings are individual and exotic. She uses decorative elements, especially color and the texture of fabric, because they appeal to her, not because they are what everyone expects to see. When Archer goes to Ellen's apartment for the first time, he admits that her drawing room is "unlike any room he had ever known" (1071). Wharton suggests that Ellen's surroundings mirror her difference in sensibility from that of the New York world she has hoped to re-enter, and that they, like her behaviors, distinguish her as an outsider.

PLOT AND STRUCTURE

The Age of Innocence focuses on the awakening of Newland Archer and his ultimate resignation, his acceptance of being a "good citizen" that requires his sacrifice of "the flower of life" (1291). Although Archer feels that he is trapped by his social world and circumstances, determinism plays a more subtle role in his fate than it did for Lily Bart in *The House of Mirth*. Similar to Lily Bart, Archer desires the freedom to achieve self-realization, but feels the powerful hold that his social world and its expectations place upon him. Various characters give voice to these expectations, but throughout the novel, Archer sees his entire social world rather than a single individual as his antagonist.

Divided into two books, the narrative traces the public relationship between Newland Archer and May Welland as they perform the social rituals associated with betrothal and marriage. Their public relationship creates a front behind which develops the relationship between Archer and Ellen Olenska, a relationship that forces Archer to question many of the truths he has accepted about his own life and the world in which he lives. In juxtaposing these two relationships, Wharton uses the contrasting elements of realism and sentimental romance to reinforce the tensions between Archer's outward and inner lives. The details of Archer's relationship with May and the social contexts that surround them establish the verisimilitude of the realist novel. Beneath this surface, however, Archer's relationship with Ellen Olenska incorporates the emotion and suffering of sentimental fiction. This suits Wharton's purposes, for as Hildegard Hoeller explains, the emotional distress that sentimental characters experience underscores the conflict between individual choices and social conventions (*Dialogue* 26). Book I of *The Age of Innocence* explores the growing tensions generated by these competing relationships, mirroring the tensions between satisfying individual desires and conforming to convention. Book II presents the triumph of convention that governs the remainder of Archer's life.

The opening chapter of the novel presents in microcosm Archer's world and its values. The formality of the evening, underscored by the characters' attire, reveals the social regimen followed by those in Archer's circle. When he stands in the club box at the opera, his position suggests that Archer shares the point of view of his peers, that he accepts a way of life predicated on tradition and standards. The first chapter also places before him and the reader the two women who symbolize the opposing directions Archer's life might take, who embody the inner struggle he will endure through much of the novel. Initially, Archer gazes at the performance on stage, then at his soon-to-be fiancée, May Welland. May's innocence is underscored by her response to the aria from *Faust,* as she finds in it reassurance of Archer's devotion to her. As Archer watches May, he prides himself on his greater worldly experience, that he understands love and sexuality in a way that May does not. He considers himself more knowledgeable and progressive than most in his social circle, but he too feels surprise at seeing Countess Olenska in May's company. By appearance alone, Ellen Olenska stands out from those around her, attracting the attention and comment of the men who stand with Archer. The hint of scandal associated with her makes her presence more remarkable and piques the curiosity of Archer's companions.

In the chapters that follow, Wharton expands the picture of Archer's social world, particularly through the families that populate it. He soon learns the obligations of family ties, when family solidarity with Ellen moves up the announcement of his and May's engagement. Until this announcement takes place, Archer is nominally free, but after his intentions toward May are made public, he is drawn into a pattern of rituals and traditions that make him feel that he is losing control of his life. He must make family visits to May's relatives, including Mrs. Manson Mingott, the matriarch of the Mingott-Welland line, and support the family position regarding Ellen's return to New York society following her separation from her European husband. While he chafes at these expectations, Archer finds reassurance in his knowledge that May embodies all the conventions of his social world and that their union will affirm rather than challenge his place in it.

When members of the social elite snub the Mingotts, refusing their invitation to a party for Ellen, Mrs. Archer feels called upon to support her son in his new familial relation. She makes her own claims on family solidarity, seeking advice and action from the van der Luydens, who occupy the uppermost echelon of the social elite. When the van der Luydens intervene to preserve society, they assert their supremacy to teach a lesson to the impudent Lawrence Lefferts and his ilk. Their actions reinforce the importance of mutual support among elite families to ensure against the fragmenting of their world. The dinner hosted by the van der Luydens for their cousin, the visiting Duke of St. Austrey, follows all the rules of Old New York etiquette, proving to be a predictable and rather dull event. During the evening, Ellen's failure to follow these rules to the letter attracts notice, but because of her foreign title, she, like the Duke, is excused from overt criticism of unconventional ways.

Ellen's foreignness makes her an attractive but problematic individual in Archer's world. Her upbringing by an eccentric aunt and her years of living abroad have given her a different view of life. She welcomes friendships with artists and writers, as well as others deemed questionable by Old New York, such as Mrs. Struthers. Ellen tells Archer that she wishes to become "a complete American again" (1067), and believes he will be an ally in this process. Initially Archer thinks that he supports Ellen and sympathizes with her plan because May wishes it, but he deceives himself. He is drawn to what Ellen offers him, including a richer emotional and intellectual life. Archer begins to have proprietary feelings about Ellen, resenting any intrusions during their time together, especially from Beaufort, whom he views as a rival for Ellen's affections.

As the rituals of his engagement to May continue, Archer finds himself wavering between the two women and what they represent. He feels a "joy of possessorship" with May, seeing her as someone he can shape into the woman he wants her to be, but he finds frustration in the predictability and sameness of their life (1081–82). In Ellen he identifies something that appeals to the less conventional side of himself, something that inspires rebellion against the world that he knows. Upon leaving Ellen's after his first visit, he stops at a florist's to order May's lilies-of-the-valley, a flower associated with innocence and purity. While there, he sees a bouquet of sun-gold roses, dramatic and sensual; he sends these to Ellen, a choice that indicates how he perceives her. His decision to send each woman a bouquet indicates Archer's conflicting desires; he remains unable to choose between the safety represented by May and the daring of Ellen.

In an attempt to reinforce his feelings of loyalty to May, Archer accepts the family charge to convince Ellen that she should not pursue divorce to regain her freedom. While the family claims that their efforts are to protect Ellen from scandal, they also have a financial interest in preventing the loss of her dowry and any monetary settlement that her husband might make. Before he meets with Ellen, Archer reads documents that have been sent to his law firm by Count Olenski. Although Archer prides himself on his worldly experience, his own naïveté affects how he responds to what he learns about Ellen's return to America. In her marriage to Count Olenski, Ellen has implied that unspeakable things have occurred. Wharton never provides the details of what initiated Ellen's departure, only that what occurred made her marriage intolerable. When Archer reads Count Olenski's countercharge, he wonders whether Ellen has compromised herself. As he begins to construct their relationship along the lines of romance, Archer needs to preserve his view of Ellen as an innocent victim and the count as a villain. What he reads in the count's letter threatens to undermine this vision.

What he has read affects Archer's discussions with Ellen regarding her divorce and makes it easier for him to uphold the family's position toward her plans. He grounds his arguments in terms of the sanctity of marriage and the need to avoid inflicting pain or embarrassment on those for whom one cares. While making these statements, Archer is moved by Ellen's expressions of idealism about America and its valuing of individual freedom above custom and tradition. His conversations with her cause Archer to think more about the nature of freedom and whether he wishes to reclaim his own. As his engagement to May proceeds along at a slow and steady pace, Archer invests more of his emotional energy in his growing attraction to Ellen.

When May goes to St. Augustine with her parents, Archer pursues the opportunity to meet with Ellen, who has retreated to the Skuytercliffe mansion of the van der Luydens. Walking the grounds of Skuytercliffe, Archer and Ellen seek shelter in the Patroon House, which Archer sees as the setting of Dutch still life, "magically created to receive them" (1121). For Archer, the structure resonates with the romance of the past and the possibilities of romance in the present. He attempts to elicit from Ellen some sign of her feelings for him, some expression of her need for him. During their conversation, Archer has a romantic vision of Ellen, "stealing up behind him to throw her light arms about his neck. While he waited, soul and body throbbing with the miracle to come" (1122), Archer acknowledges his desire for Ellen. He begins to fashion her into an ideal figure, one that forces the reader to wonder whether Archer is falling in love with the woman or the image he creates of her. Archer's romantic vision is undercut just as he imagines Ellen embracing him; he looks out the window to see Beaufort approaching. This undermining of Archer's romantic dream recurs in the novel each time Archer envisions Ellen as the object of his desire: He enters into romantic fantasy, only to have it disrupted by the intrusion of reality.

In an effort to repress his own doubts about himself and his betrothal, Archer goes to St. Augustine and urges May to shorten the period of their engagement. Not confident in his ability to do the right thing, Archer looks to forces outside himself to eliminate temptation and resolve his indecision. May confronts him about the possibility that his affections lie elsewhere, that he is uncertain of his feelings for her. Striking closer to the mark than is comfortable for Archer, May retreats behind references to an old affair. Not recognizing her remark as a warning sign, Archer believes that May remains unaware of his feelings for Ellen.

In a scene that develops the power of emotion associated with sentimental romance, Archer returns to New York and meets with Ellen once again. He attempts to embrace her, but she steps away, informing him that his own arguments against divorce have made their relationship impossible. Archer confesses that what he read in the count's letter influenced his actions, and he finds himself discomfited when Ellen claims that she had nothing to fear from that letter. An emotional exchange ensues during which each character confesses deep feelings for the other, ending with the outpouring of Ellen's tears. When Archer embraces her, she states, "I can't love you unless I give you up" (1153), articulating the theme of renunciation that underlies much sentimental fiction and foreshadows the outcome of the crisis in Book II. Knowing that Ellen does care for him, Archer returns home to discover a telegram from May indicating that his wish has been granted, that their wedding date has been moved up to the Tuesday after Easter, a month away.

Book II opens with Archer's wedding, replete with all the tradition and ritual that Old New York can muster. The familiarity of the ritual allows Archer to proceed mechanically through the day, but as he and May, as husband and wife, enter their carriage, "suddenly the same black abyss yawned before him and he felt himself sinking into it, deeper and deeper, while his voice rambled on smoothly and cheerfully" (1163). In a painful irony, Archer discovers that his wedding night is to be spent in the Patroon House, reminding him that May is a substitute for the woman he wishes were his.

In his attempts to live up to the expectations of his world, Archer reverts to his "old habits of mind" (1170). He finds May's conventionality frustrating, however, and feels that there is a "slight hardness" in her, that her happiness shines "like a light under ice" (1168). He believes May's chilly demeanor stifles his own self-expression and makes him long for the emotional closeness he felt with Ellen. When Archer mentions visiting Italy on their honeymoon, a land associated with warmth and passion, May dismisses it as an impossibility given their winter obligations, echoing the coldness Archer perceives in her. May's discomfort at meeting Mrs. Carfry and her inability to converse with new acquaintances highlights May's shortcomings for Archer. When in Newport, May feels at home and can demonstrate those qualities, including her athletic ability, that make her an attractive individual. Archer feels pride in his wife and a certain satisfaction in the way other people admire her, but he feels that something is missing for him in their relationship.

When opportunities to see Ellen arise, Archer pursues them. He attempts to find her in Newport, deceived by his own romantic vision in which he mistakes one of the Blenkers' daughters for Ellen. He then invents an excuse to go to Boston in search of Ellen. There he spends the day with her, attempting to realize his romantic dream on a boating excursion. Their distance from land at first seems to free Archer and Ellen from the rules and expectations of their world, but Ellen mentions the fine and good things that characterize New York life. She admits feelings for Archer, but tells him that he must accept their situation as it stands. She unsettles him further by mentioning her husband's new offer and the possibility of her accepting it.

Archer feels that his personal world is in turmoil, that he must enact the charade of a happy young husband while his real love retreats from him. When Archer returns to New York, he hears rumors about Beaufort's impending financial collapse, a situation that places a number of elite families into turmoil. The distress caused by Beaufort's crisis heightens the Mingott-Welland family's need for stability and continuity. They redouble their efforts to have Ellen's situation settled to their satisfaction, if not her own. During this crisis Archer discovers that the family no longer trusts him to represent their point of view. His defense of Ellen and his conduct have raised suspicions, as Archer realizes when questioned by Sillerton Jackson. Other family members, including Mrs. Mingott, probe his feelings to test his loyalty to the family and to May.

Moreover, May suspects Archer's obsession with Ellen. She listens to Archer's pretexts for going to Washington with a knowing silence and then encourages him to see Ellen while he is there. The narrative explains that she has given him a hint about her suspicions "in the only form in which well-bred people of [their] kind can communicate unpleasant things to each other" (1228). This hint serves as a warning that May will not be a passive spectator in what occurs, that she will do whatever she can to preserve her marriage. Her ability to control situations surfaces during the emergency of old Catherine Mingott's stroke; she sends Archer off with a telegram that summons Ellen to New York. As Archer departs, May remarks that he and Ellen will miss each other in transit. The tension between May and Archer increases during Archer's prevarication over his change in travel plans. May dispels the tension through her careful responses, while Archer accepts them at face value, assuming she is still the naïve young woman that he watched at the opera. Blind to May's piloting of their relationship, Archer believes he can deceive her as long as he remains careful. When the tension between them escalates again, Archer even contemplates the freedom he might enjoy should May die, sentiments that reflect his frustration and feelings of entrapment.

In a series of scenes that recalls the emotional power of their last meeting before Archer's wedding, Ellen's return from Washington precipitates the climax of the novel. During their shared carriage ride to Mrs. Mingott's, Ellen expresses her feelings for Archer but explains why they must remain apart. She uses the term "mistress" to describe what she would be to him, introducing morality to bolster her argument. Archer's marriage has redefined his relationship to Ellen, and he realizes that he could become like Beaufort and Lefferts, men he has despised for deceiving their wives. When Ellen and Archer meet again at the Museum of Art, Ellen knows that Archer still holds false hopes of escape and attempts to jar him into facing reality. Testing Archer's feelings for her and his integrity, she offers to meet him once for a sexual encounter and then return to her husband. Ellen tries to determine whether Archer truly cares about her as a person, morally and emotionally, or whether she has become only an object of desire for him. Frustrated by their situation, Archer angrily accepts her offer but senses it will not come to pass.

While his emotions swirl beneath the surface, Archer continues to engage in the social events that define his world. He and May attend dinner at the van der Luydens' and then go to the opera. When they return home, Archer plans to tell May his true feelings. Instead, she informs him that Ellen will return to Europe, but does not provide a reason. Upon leaving the room, May remarks on her torn and muddied wedding dress, another sign that she is no longer the innocent that Archer married.

To affirm their familial and social ties, May plans to host the farewell dinner for Ellen. Archer sees the event as a ritual of solidarity prior to sending off an offending member of the tribe, and his dreams of escape vanish as Ellen says farewell. When May and Archer are alone, she informs him that she is pregnant, using accepted forms of indirection to communicate this news. She does, however, admit that she had told Ellen of her condition two weeks earlier, when she thought it a possibility but not a fact. Archer sees that May's "blue eyes are wet with victory" (1288). She has succeeded in using the claims of family solidarity and counted on Ellen's integrity to preserve her marriage and secure her own future.

The last chapter of the novel takes place twenty-six years later. Archer reviews his life and sees himself as the "good citizen" (1291).

He admits that Ellen "had become the complete vision of all he had missed" (1291), preserved in his romantic dream, one that he believes he has kept secret. When he speaks with his son Dallas and discovers that May has known his "secret" all along, he is pleased, but does not consider the implications. He sees the deceased May as she looked the first time he saw her. For him, she too has never been a fully realized individual, but a representation of the values and expectations that have shaped his world through the duties of marriage. Through his son, who is engaged to Fanny Beaufort, he realizes that times have changed, that the so-called tribe's control over the social world has diminished considerably. Not only does Dallas have greater freedom in choosing his spouse, but he can be more direct in conversation as well. Archer agrees to travel with Dallas to Paris, knowing that Ellen resides there. When Dallas goes to Ellen's apartment to visit, however, Archer remains on the street below. He does not want to confront the changes time has wrought, but to preserve the image, to find consolation in his fantasy. In this bittersweet closure, Wharton suggests that Archer chooses his romantic and sentimental vision over the woman he professed to love.

CHARACTERS

In *The Age of Innocence,* Wharton again focuses on three central characters who form a triangle of conflicting duties and passions. As Archer, May, and Ellen attempt to determine their identities and their futures, they negotiate the codes and expectations that govern the world of Old New York.

Newland Archer, the central character, stands at a turning point in his life when the novel opens. He is about to marry May Welland and enter into the adult roles and responsibilities defined by his social network. He considers himself mature and confident, yet the narrative frequently mentions his insecurities about his identity and place in the world. Smug and self-satisfied, Archer believes himself both more worldly than and morally superior to many in his circle. He fails to realize that he has never been tested, that he has been paying lip service to values and beliefs that are not necessarily his own. He also thinks of himself as a risk-taker, yet throughout the novel he remains indecisive, looking to others to make choices or take actions that will absolve him of the need to do so.

The limited third-person narrative conveys information primarily from Archer's point of view so that the perception of events and other characters is shaped by his sensibility. Wharton uses this technique to her advantage to reveal Archer's blind spots, particularly his tendency to see only the surfaces of individuals and not their depths. He quickly categorizes people and makes assumptions about them, seldom revising his initial impressions. When he looks at May, Archer believes he sees the embodiment of everything his culture expects from women; that she will be a mirror who will reflect his own ideals, not an individual who has her own needs and desires. Archer believes that his relationship with Ellen has initiated his true awakening to life and its possibilities, but even in this situation, Archer often responds with preconceived notions. He has constructed an image of Ellen with which he has fallen in love, but he often fails to see the complex woman who exists behind the image.

Archer has many blind spots about himself, and these are often accentuated through Wharton's use of both verbal and situational irony. His biggest blind spot hides the fact that he does little to shape the direction of his own life. Ultimately, Archer lives as a "dilettante," a term used to describe him at the outset, and one that identifies an individual who has only superficial interest in the arts or an area of knowledge. He cannot commit himself to anyone or anything with a true passion—not May, Ellen, a career, or politics. The only satisfaction he expresses at the end of the novel comes from his relationship with his children, but even there he is receding into the background as his children begin their own marriages and families.

When she first appears in the novel, May Welland projects the aura of innocent maidenhood, seated between her mother and her aunt, clutching her bouquet of lily-of-the-valley. As she watches the performance of *Faust,* her attention focuses on the love aria, not the bargain that Faust makes with Mephistopheles. As the narrative develops, more of May's nature emerges. She is optimistic, athletic, and at times perceptive, more so than Archer gives her credit for being. Her athletic prowess marks her as a more modern figure than her mother, but May is still constrained by the codes that define her world. She embraces her place in that world and the privilege it affords her. A dutiful daughter, May accepts that marriage and motherhood will define her roles in life.

Initially May takes Archer's love and loyalty as a given, encouraging him to do what he can to help Ellen. When May senses that Archer wavers in his loyalty to her, she acts to secure it. May can use the image of innocence to her advantage. When she asks Archer questions, he takes them at face value, never realizing how May is surveying her situation through them. Perceiving that her future is in jeopardy, she takes decisive action, but does so covertly. She will not violate the rules of decorum that have governed her existence, nor will she sacrifice her identity or future to what she perceives as Archer's whim. The allusions to the goddess Diana in reference to May underscore her determination to protect hearth and home (see the "Allusions" section later in this chapter). May has inherited the strong will of her Granny Mingott, and uses the women's network within her family to assist her in removing Ellen as a threat.

In contrast to May Welland, Ellen Olenska first appears as the so-phisticate, a woman who has lived amid the aristocracy of Europe and has seen the world. Her style of dress is exotic to New York eyes and her manner, especially in her interactions with men, foreign. She is regarded with a certain degree of pity for the "incoherent education" (1063) she received under the guidance of her aunt, Medora Manson, although it has provided her first-hand encounters with art, music, and literature. As a woman who has left her husband and seeks a divorce, Ellen places herself in a threatening position in New York. As an unattached woman who possesses worldly and sexual knowledge, she embodies what Old New York sees as the potential for social chaos. These factors pique the interest of many of the men in Archer's circle and raise concerns among the women, motivating the family's desire to keep Ellen under someone's control.

Ellen, however, reveals her own naïveté and idealism in her statements about what it means to be an American, to enjoy freedom and self-definition. Her ideas about America are those formed in her child-hood, not an idyllic time, but one less troubled than her adulthood in Europe. At one of their early encounters, she tells Archer, "I don't always remember that everything here is good that was—that was bad where I've come from" (1067), explaining how her disillusionment in Europe has affected her perspective. She associates Archer with her childhood and assumes that he too believes in independence and self-determination. While Ellen learns through her experiences that New York does not endorse independence for women, she has a strong degree of integrity. She is not willing to inflict on May the pain infidelity causes, despite her own feelings for Archer. Further, she is not willing to sacrifice her own newly gained freedom for a life lived in secrecy, similar to that of Lydia Tillotson in "Souls Belated."

Through her treatment of the two female characters, Wharton interrogates the tradition of American romance, inverting some of its patterns to suggest a greater complexity of life than romance accommodates. In traditional American romances, the fair heroine is associated with purity, naïveté, and virtue. She lacks cunning or the ability to manipulate others. The dark heroine, associated with passion and sexuality, also tends to be more experienced in reading her social world and in being able to manipulate aspects of that world for her own ends. Wharton uses the surface differences between May and Ellen to allude to these traditional roles and then blurs the distinctions by giving each some attributes associated with her opposite; therefore, May engages in covert strategies to preserve her engagement and marriage to Newland while Ellen naïvely looks upon the society to which she has returned and preserves her integrity. By inverting the expected pattern, Wharton calls attention to Archer's superficial understanding of the two women who affect his life, hinting that in responding to each he relies upon stereotype rather than actuality.

ROLE OF MINOR CHARACTERS

Many of the minor characters who populate the novel form the extended family network for Newland, May, and Ellen. Some of these characters are well developed and can be seen as secondary rather than minor; others appear briefly to serve a specific purpose. This network of characters conveys the values, beliefs, and behaviors of Archer's world, some by rigidly adhering to them, others by flouting them. They also reveal the gender expectations and limits imposed by the social code, further defining the conflicts faced by the central characters. Few outsiders appear, reinforcing the closed nature of this New York society.

Two secondary male characters, Lawrence Lefferts and Julius Beaufort, serve as foils to Archer, who consciously compares himself to each of them. Lefferts and Beaufort have similar natures, although they hold different status in the social world. Lefferts enjoys his social station through his lineage and family name, although it does not carry the level of prestige he would like to believe. Regarded as an authority on the rules of decorum and form, he exercises power through the manipulation of opinion. While he passes condescending judgment upon others for their failure to follow good form, he uses his own public performances of decorous behavior to shield his extramarital affairs, signifying the discrepancy between appearances and reality. Beaufort, on the other hand, exercises power because of his knowledge of the marketplace and his ability to manipulate finances. Unlike Lefferts, Beaufort has an obscure past, his social position secured through his marriage to Regina Dallas. Both men see marriage as a matter of convenience and the women in their social sphere as naïve creatures easily deceived. Archer initially measures his difference from these two men, seeing himself as more genuine and morally superior. As his interest in pursuing a relationship with Ellen intensifies, Archer recognizes his similarities to them, a fact that disturbs him.

Other male characters reveal the life of a man of leisure, the potential future for Newland Archer. Sillerton Jackson's major interests are the quality of meals and the quantity of the gossip he digests. An aging bachelor, Jackson has no children but has become a specialist in the genealogies of all the ruling families. His knowledge gives him a degree of authority in his world that he might not otherwise enjoy. Mr. Welland, May's father, has become a hypochondriac who thinks of nothing but his own symptoms. Humored by his wife, he is averse to any risk, preferring to shelter himself in the safety of his own home or in warmer climes. He represents the potential ineffectuality of men of his class who will be left behind as the social and financial world changes.

The extremes for female characters are represented through the solidity of Catherine Mingott and the flightiness of Medora Manson. As the matriarch of the Mingott-Welland clan, Catherine exerts a degree of authority enjoyed by few in her world. The status and power that have accrued to her are manifest in her size; people must go to her rather than she to them. Old Catherine has achieved this level of regard through her ability to combine an adventurous spirit with a spotless reputation. She is perceptive and strong willed, often having the final word on any situation that involves her family. Her stroke occurs just as two major crises confront her, Beaufort's financial collapse and the threat to May's marriage. The instability of both the market and the marriage, the two institutions that have been the underpinnings of her world, strike at Catherine's own well-being.

In contrast to Catherine, Medora Manson, who reared Ellen, wanders through the novel as she does through life, her eccentricities placing her outside the circle of influence within the family. The family sees her as misdirected but harmless; Ellen perceives Medora's vulnerability to the influence of figures such as Agathon Carver, a fortune hunter who drops Medora when he discovers she has no funds to bankroll his schemes. Her rootlessness and limited resources make her dependent upon the indulgence of others, including Catherine, who subsidizes Medora to create a degree of stability for her.

Occupying the middle ground between these two women, most of the other female figures who appear in the novel form the bedrock of their social world, but exercise their authority less openly than Catherine. Archer's mother and his sister Jenny are products of the seemingly sheltered life they lead, but they, like Sillerton Jackson, thrive on gossip and enjoy the way it affirms their insider status. Mrs. Welland, May's mother, has been the more forceful figure in her marriage, but she controls by appearing to accommodate, much as May begins to do with Archer.

THEMES

As do many of Wharton's novels and stories, *The Age of Innocence* explores the tension between self-realization and self-sacrifice. Wharton probes the resistance to change embedded in the social world of the elite and how it affects the possibilities that characters envision for themselves. As in *The House of Mirth,* economic forces affect characters' lives in *The Age of Innocence,* but in subtler ways. Wharton questions the nature of the leisure enjoyed by the elite and the various means by which individuals seek to alleviate the boredom they feel. In the novel, Wharton also examines the problem of communication and the manipulation of language, how the inability to speak directly affects relationships and expectations.

Early in the novel, Newland celebrates the signs of continuity in his world, seeing some predictable routines as amusing, others as necessary. As his own awakening to new possibilities for his life occurs through his relationship with Ellen, these routines and customs become increasingly restrictive to him. Archer struggles with impulses to satisfy his desires while simultaneously feeling constrained by a lifetime of training to do his duty. His awakening forces him to admit the degree of boredom that defines the world of his peers, unabated by the material resources at hand. He also begins to see how the routines and customs of his social world operate as a means of resisting change, of slowing the inevitable shift in power and influence that is already underway in New York.

The costs of perpetuating the illusion of stability and its accompanying innocence exist in the tension between appearances and realities, a focus of the novel of manners. Wharton depicts the ways in which so-called good form is used by various characters to hide unpleasant truths. Strict adherence to the rules of outward form inhibits the development of individual talents, something that Wharton chafed against in her own upbringing. These costs are particularly high for women who are treated as decorative ornaments in public, even if they keep their families functioning in private.

Wharton sees the manipulation of language as one of the means by which Old New York perpetuates its false innocence. She notes the frequent use of the *double entendre* (literally a statement with two meanings, the second either risqué or suggestive of impropriety) among Archer's circle. Archer prides himself on recognizing the implications of such remarks, but such remarks also indicate that things exist within the culture that are not openly acknowledged. The prevalence of gossip reinforces this impression as characters privately exchange knowing remarks about the conduct of others, knowledge they disavow in public. As in *The House of Mirth,* the problem of communication affects the interaction between men and women. The inability to speak openly, to use language precisely and accurately, preserves a superficial politeness during encounters but allows for misreading of motives and actions.

ALLUSIONS

Aware of the value of literary allusions as a form of shorthand, Wharton makes effective use of them in *The Age of Innocence.* While there are numerous minor references within the novel, three significant ones appear: the performance of *Faust* in the opening chapter, the mention of the play *The Shaughran* in Chapter 13, and the frequent mention of the goddess Diana and imagery related to her in the descriptions of May Welland.

The allusions to *Faust,* both to Part I of Goethe's drama and to the opera by Gounod, serve several purposes within the novel. In Part I of Goethe's work, Faust, who has become bored with his life, makes a bargain with the devil, Mephistopheles. He promises that Mephistopheles can claim his soul if Faust ever admits that he experiences total contentment, that he has exhausted the limits of knowledge. Until this occurs, Mephistopheles will be Faust's servant, providing him with new experiences and stimulants. After making this bargain, Faust falls in love with Margaret (Marguerite), who embodies innocence. He impregnates but then abandons her; Margaret kills her child and goes to prison, redeemed at her death when she rejects Faust and what he has become. The allusion to Goethe's *Faust* thus underscores the theme of the quest for knowledge, especially as a means of alleviating boredom. Newland Archer believes he seeks a deeper knowledge of life through the books he reads and then through his relationship with Ellen. Initially he has fallen in love with the innocent May, but he contemplates abandoning her when he believes his love for Ellen will bring him greater contentment.

The play *The Shaughran,* written and produced by Dion Boucicault, was popular in the mid-1870s. The play contains multiple complications, including the separation of lovers, unjust imprisonment, and other elements of melodrama. In the end, Conn, the wanderer, saves his friends, the lovers are reunited, and the villain arrested. The scene described in Wharton's novel is one acted without words, something Archer feels intensifies the dramatic moment. He attempts to correlate this scene with his own encounters with Ellen, applying the melodramatic sentimentalism to his own experience.

In many of her works, Wharton makes use of allusions to classical literature and mythology. In *The Age of Innocence,* Newland Archer frequently compares his virginal bride to the goddess Diana, seeing May as cool and aloof, as severe as Diana was thought to be. Diana, the Roman name for Artemis, was worshipped as the goddess of nature; she was often depicted as a huntress, carrying a bow and quiver of arrows. May's love for the outdoors and her athletic ability, especially her prowess in archery, elicit such comparisons. In classical times, Diana/Artemis was also worshipped as a protector of women and children, a role that May assumes when she acts to save her marriage and secure the future for her children.

ALTERNATIVE READING: CULTURAL STUDIES

According to critic Terry Eagleton, culture "can be loosely summarized as the complex of values, customs, beliefs, and practices which constitute a way of life for a specific group" (34). Critics engaged in cultural studies, as do those who work with new historicism (see Chapter 5), follow an interdisciplinary path to analyze a work of literature. They see a literary text as one form of discourse (the language used to express a particular area of knowledge or to transact social relations) that interacts with other discourses present within a culture. They not only discern the material forms and underlying assumptions of a culture as present within a literary text, but also find within the narrative indications of an author's engagement with and questioning of those assumptions.

Cultural studies traces its roots back to ideas articulated by Matthew Arnold in the nineteenth century. He believed that culture provided a means by which an individual saw beyond his or her individual needs and drives to recognize ties and responsibilities to a collective whole; therefore, culture served as a means of preventing anarchy or social chaos, in part by encouraging individuals to serve the greater or communal good. Arnold saw literature as an expression of culture and felt that works often labeled canonical or identified as "high" art were those that expressed values and beliefs worth preserving and disseminating.

During the twentieth century, cultural criticism evolved, influenced by developments in sociology, anthropology, and linguistics, as well as Marxist theory. The Marxist theorist Louis Althusser explored how ideology informed culture and shaped the institutions that serve as means of social control (Brantlinger 88–92). Ideology refers to the body of ideas that express the social needs of a particular class, legitimating that class's interests and exercise of power. Images and expectations based on these ideas are disseminated throughout the culture and affect how people in a given time and place perceive reality and truth. Antonio Gramsci, another theorist, explored how hegemony, the predominance of one set of ideas over others, allowed for building social consensus and unity through negotiation (Brantlinger 95–100). These negotiations acknowledge agency for sub-groups within a society whose discourses affect the dominant discourse or expressions of the dominant ideology.

In light of these arguments, practitioners of cultural studies reject the notion that only canonical or high art expresses culture. They explore the ways that multiple cultures co-exist and interact with each other in a given time and place, that various sub-cultures employ images and expectations that challenge or contradict those representing the dominant ideology. These images and expectations appear in popular music and sports as well as minor literatures, film, advertising, and folk traditions, all of which are of interest to cultural critics. When cultural critics approach a work of literature, they analyze how the text represents the dominant ideology, but they also look for disruptions of that ideology's discourse through the presence of characters, events, and images that present cultural alternatives. They consider how these disruptions and alternatives represent the ongoing negotiation over beliefs, values, and meaning that result in the continuing production of culture.

As her travel writings and works such as *French Ways and Their Meaning* (1919) indicate, Edith Wharton found the question of culture a fascinating topic. In *The Age of Innocence,* Wharton uses the customs and practices of the New York elite of the 1870s to create the verisimilitude of a realist novel. She also engages in multiple levels of cultural critique. In keeping with the novel of manners tradition, she exposes the contradictions between expressed beliefs and the actions of individuals, revealing characters' deceptions and self-deceptions through satire and irony. Wharton's treatment of self-sacrifice to serve a greater good and her depictions of Archer reading canonical literary texts and eventually seeing himself as a good citizen, reflect the influence of Matthew Arnold's ideas about culture. Wharton's deeper interests, however, lie in exploring the power that culture exerts over individuals. Fascinated by the ways in which a culture perpetuates itself, Wharton attempts to convey how culture exists as, in Eagleton's words, something "bred in the bone rather than conceived in the brain" (28).

Throughout the novel, characters make assumptions about their lives and the lives of others based on two central precepts of their culture, family and form. When characters say the word *family,* they evoke a multifaceted array of concepts and beliefs. Family encompasses history, lineage, status, defining aspects of identity. Family ties and lineage are sources of power and security; they can protect one from outsiders as well as ensure one's place within the elite. Sillerton Jackson's preoccupation with genealogy, his study of every detail of pertinent family trees, reflects the desire of the elite to regulate its membership and maintain its status.

In the narrative, Wharton uses the word *tribe* as a synonym for *family,* suggesting that the group holds powerful sway over individuals, that survival is its primal instinct. This connection to the primitive also creates the impression that family as a source of identity and status transcends time and place. The elite believe in continuity, the uninterrupted reign of select families who, like the aristocracy of Europe with whom they prize their connections, accept the right to rule as naturally ordained. Their views also imply that social stratification and a ruling elite are a natural outgrowth of the process of civilization.

In the world that Wharton describes, one's identity and membership are reinforced through the practice of *ritual,* another term that appears frequently within the narrative. Through repetition, rituals reinforce within the individual consciousness the values and beliefs of a community, determining the ways in which individuals perceive reality and their place in the world. Many of the rituals mentioned in the novel relate to the customs of courtship and marriage, which the elite sees as the foundation of social order and the means of perpetuating itself. Proper observation of the rituals surrounding courtship and marriage reaffirm both the legacy of the past and the need to maintain exclusivity in the present.

In addition to ritual, *form* manifests the values and beliefs of the social world of *The Age of Innocence*. Form encompasses the rules of etiquette, guides to behavior and conduct that distinguish the elite from the masses. To internalize these rules and act on them effortlessly are the hallmarks of good breeding. To recognize so-called good form means that one perceives the unspoken rules of society, for every gesture and nuance conveys meaning and serves as a sign of membership recognized by others. Wharton reveals the polished surface of this social world, but shows how this surface can be manipulated to conceal common and sometimes sordid behavior.

By foregrounding these concepts in her narrative, Wharton asks whether culture is an omnipotent force regulating the lives of characters. Some readers see Newland Archer as a man entrapped by the culture that has shaped him, unable to break away from the world he has known. Wharton's narrative, however, also reveals the ways in which culture changes or evolves, for she does not see culture as a static entity. In her novel, the elite of Old New York embrace the illusion of permanence, but Wharton demonstrates that they are already engaged in cultural negotiations that will alter the ideas and values they hold. These negotiations occur through interactions with representative individuals who are not from the elite.

One representative individual, Julius Beaufort, gains admission to the elite through his marriage to Regina Dallas. As a man whose position has been secured by wealth rather than his own lineage, Beaufort makes visible the presence of the capitalist economy that perpetuates the existence of the elite. His conduct in both financial and social spheres challenges the expectations of the social circle to which he has aspired. In his financial dealings, he treats other people's money as another commodity in the marketplace, showing little concern for the probity expected by those who have invested with him. In his social relations, he also defies the status quo. He treats his marriage as little more than a means of access to investment capital. His long-term affair with Fanny Ring, which he does little to conceal, stands as an open challenge to the power of the elite to regulate his conduct. The changes that result from Beaufort's presence ease the rigidity of the social hierarchy but do not affect the economic base that stands behind it. His daughter by Fanny Ring may be engaged to Newland Archer's son Dallas at the end of the novel, but wealth derived from the capitalist economy sustains the greater freedom they both enjoy.

Another representative figure encountered by Newland Archer, Ned Winsett works as a journalist but had once aspired to a career in belles-lettres. Archer encounters Winsett as both men leave the theater following the performance of Boucicault's *The Shaughran.* Here Wharton presents, in the form of popular theater, one arena in which negotiations over ideas can occur. The play attracts members of the elite to its performances, even though it is authored by an Irish im-migrant and written to appeal to a wide audience. Winsett provides a perspective on class relations that differs from Archer's own. When he invites Archer to join him for a beer at a German restaurant near the theater, Winsett presents an opportunity for Archer to encounter a different sub-culture, but Archer declines. By no means a radical, Winsett looks critically upon the behavior and superficiality of the elite. His comments provoke Archer's own thoughts on the issue of the "unbridgeable difference between men like Winsett and . . . Archer's kind" (1114). When Archer thinks about Winsett, he focuses on his failures as a way of diminishing the importance of his voice and critique, engaging in a form of misrepresentation. Although Winsett has little effect on Archer in the long run, his presence in the novel and his voice disrupt the narrative's discourse on class.

Set a quarter century later than the rest of the narrative, the last chapter of the novel takes place at the turn of the twentieth century. Through this device, Wharton draws attention to the changes that have occurred, both in daily activities and in underlying values. The greater mobility of characters, the ease of travel, and the freedom to choose one's marriage partner from outside a limited circle reflect the enlarging of what had been Newland Archer's small world. To New-land Archer these changes seem monumental, and Wharton sees in them the seeds of greater changes that appear after World War I. A cultural critic viewing these changes from today's perspective might see them as incremental, as not having altered the underlying ideology that informs Dallas Archer's world.

Bibliography

All pages referenced in the text are to the four volumes of the Library of America edition of Wharton's works, except for *The Writing of Fiction* (New York: Octagon, 1966).

WORKS BY EDITH WHARTON

Verses, 1878 [privately printed]
The Decoration of Houses, 1897
The Greater Inclination, 1899
The Touchstone, 1900
Crucial Instances, 1901
The Valley of Decision, 1902
Sanctuary, 1903
The Descent of Man and Other Stories, 1904
Italian Villas and Their Gardens, 1904
Italian Backgrounds, 1905
The House of Mirth, 1905
Madame de Treymes, 1907
The Fruit of the Tree, 1907
The Hermit and the Wild Woman and Other Stories, 1908
A Motor-Flight Through France, 1908
Artemis to Actaeon and Other Verses, 1909
Tales of Men and Ghosts, 1910

Ethan Frome, 1911
The Reef, 1912
The Custom of the Country, 1913
Fighting France, from Dunkerque to Belfort, 1915
The Book of the Homeless (ed.), 1915
Bunner Sisters, 1916
Xingu and Other Stories, 1916
Summer, 1917
The Marne, 1918
French Ways and Their Meaning, 1919
In Morocco, 1920
The Age of Innocence, 1920
The Glimpses of the Moon, 1922
A Son at The Front, 1923
Old New York: False Dawn, The Old Maid, The Spark, New Year's Day, 1924
The Mother's Recompense, 1925
The Writing of Fiction, 1925
Here and Beyond, 1926
Twelve Poems, 1926
Twilight Sleep, 1927
The Children, 1928
Hudson River Bracketed, 1929
Certain People, 1930
Human Nature, 1933
The Gods Arrive, 1933
A Backward Glance, 1934
The World Over, 1936
Ghosts, 1937

POSTHUMOUS PUBLICATIONS

The Buccaneers [unfinished], 1938.
The Collected Short Stories. Ed. R.W.B. Lewis, 1968.
The Ghost Stories of Edith Wharton, 1973.
Fast and Loose: A Novelette by "David Olivieri." Ed. Viola Hopkins Winner, 1977.
Edith Wharton: Novels [*The House of Mirth, The Reef, The Custom of the Country, The Age of Innocence*]. New York: The Library of America, 1985.
The Letters of Edith Wharton. Ed. R.W.B. Lewis, 1988.
Edith Wharton: Novellas and Other Writings [*Madame de Treymes, Ethan Frome, Summer, Old New York, The Mother's Recompense, A Backward Glance*]. New York: The Library of America, 1990.
The Cruise of the Vanadis. Ed. Claudine Lesage, 1992.
The Buccaneers. Completed by Marion Mainwaring, 1993.
The Uncollected Critical Writings of Edith Wharton. Ed. Frederick Wegener, 1996.

Edith Wharton: Collected Stories, 1891–1910. New York: The Library of America, 2001.

Edith Wharton: Collected Stories, 1911–1937. New York: The Library of America, 2001.

BIOGRAPHIES OF EDITH WHARTON

Auchincloss, Louis. *Edith Wharton: A Woman in Her Time.* New York: Viking, 1971.

Benstock, Shari. *No Gifts from Chance: A Biography of Edith Wharton.* New York: Scribner's, 1994.

Coolidge, Olivia. *Edith Wharton, 1862–1937.* New York: Scribner's, 1965.

Dwight, Eleanor. *Edith Wharton: An Extraordinary Life.* New York: Abrams, 1994.

———. *The Gilded Age: Edith Wharton and Her Contemporaries.* New York: Universe, 1996.

Kellogg, Grace. *The Two Lives of Edith Wharton: The Woman and Her Work.* New York: Appleton-Century, 1965.

Lewis, R. W. B. *Edith Wharton: A Biography.* New York: Harper, 1975.

Lubbock, Percy. *Portrait of Edith Wharton.* New York: Appleton-Century-Crofts, 1947.

Wolff, Cynthia Griffin. *A Feast of Words: The Triumph of Edith Wharton.* New York: Oxford UP, 1977.

CRITICAL STUDIES OF WHARTON'S WORK

Ammons, Elizabeth. *Edith Wharton's Argument with America.* Athens: U of Georgia P, 1980.

Auchincloss, Louis. *Pioneers & Caretakers.* Minneapolis: U of Minnesota P, [1965].

Bauer, Dale M. *Edith Wharton's Brave New Politics.* Madison: U of Wisconsin P, 1994.

Bell, Millicent, ed. *The Cambridge Companion to Edith Wharton.* New York: Cambridge UP, 1995.

———. *Edith Wharton & Henry James: The Story of Their Friendship.* New York: Braziller, 1965.

Bendixen, Alfred and Annette Zilversmit, eds. *Edith Wharton: New Critical Essays.* New York: Garland, 1992.

Bentley, Nancy. *The Ethnography of Manners: Hawthorne, James, Wharton.* New York: Cambridge UP, 1995.

Bloom, Harold, ed. *Edith Wharton.* New York: Chelsea, 1986.

Boydston, Jeanne. "'Grave endearing traditions': Edith Wharton and the Domestic Novel." *Faith of a (Woman) Writer.* Ed. Alice Kessler-Harris and William McBrien. Westport, CT: Greenwood, 1988. 31–40.

Cahir, Linda Costanzo. *Solitude and Society in the Works of Herman Melville and Edith Wharton*. Westport, CT: Greenwood, 1999.

Campbell, Donna M. "Edith Wharton and the 'Authoresses': The Critique of Local Color in Wharton's Early Fiction." *Studies in American Fiction* 22.2 (1994): 169–83.

Coard, Robert L. "Edith Wharton's Influence on Sinclair Lewis." *MFS: Modern Fiction Studies* 31.3 (1985): 511–527.

Colquitt, Clare, Susan Goodman, and Candace Waid, eds. *A Forward Glance: New Essays on Edith Wharton*. Newark, DE: U of Delaware P—Associated UP, 1999.

Craig, Theresa. *Edith Wharton: A House Full of Rooms*. New York: Monacelli Press, 1996.

Cuddy, Lois A. "Triangles of Defeat and Liberation: The Quest for Power in Edith Wharton's Fiction." *Perspectives on Contemporary Literature* 8 (1982): 18–26.

Donovan, Josephine. *After the Fall: The Demeter-Persephone Myth in Wharton, Cather, and Glasgow*. University Park: Pennsylvania State UP, 1989.

Elbert, Monika. "The Transcendental Economy of Wharton's Gothic Mansions." *American Transcendental Quarterly* 9.1 (1995): 51–67.

Erlich, Gloria C. *The Sexual Education of Edith Wharton*. Berkeley: U of California P, 1992.

Fagan, Cathy E. "The Price of Power in Women's Literature: Edith Wharton and Dorothy Parker." *Gender in Popular Culture: Images of Men and Women in Literature, Visual Media, and Material Culture*. Ed. Jane S. Bakerman. Cleveland: Ridgemont, 1995. 227–46.

Fedorko, Kathy A. *Gender and the Gothic in the Fiction of Edith Wharton*. Tuscaloosa: U of Alabama P, 1995.

Fryer, Judith. *Felicitous Space: The Imaginative Structures of Edith Wharton and Willa Cather*. Chapel Hill: U of North Carolina P, 1986.

Garrison, Stephen. *Edith Wharton: A Descriptive Bibliography*. Pittsburgh: U of Pittsburgh P, 1990.

Gimble, Wendy. *Edith Wharton: Orphancy and Survival*. New York: Praeger, 1984.

Goodman, Susan. *Edith Wharton's Inner Circle*. Austin: U of Texas P, 1994.

———. *Edith Wharton's Women: Friends & Rivals*. Hanover, NH: UP of New England, 1990.

Goodwyn, Janet Beer. *Edith Wharton: Traveller in the Land of Letters*. New York: St. Martin's, 1990.

Hadley, Kathy Miller. *In the Interstices of the Tale: Edith Wharton's Narrative Strategies*. New York: Peter Lang, 1993.

Hamblen, Abigail Ann. "Edith Wharton in New England." *The New England Quarterly* 38 (1965): 239–244.

Hays, Peter L. "Edith Wharton and F. Scott Fitzgerald." *Edith Wharton Newsletter* 3.1 (1986): 2–3.

Hepburn, Allan. "A Passion for Things: Cicerones, Collectors, and Taste in Edith Wharton's Fiction." *Arizona Quarterly* 54:4 (1998): 25–52.

Hoeller, Hildegard. *Edith Wharton's Dialogue with Realism and Sentimental Fiction*. Gainesville, FL: UP of Florida, 2000.

———. "Competing Mothers: Edith Wharton's Late Vision of Family Life." *Family Matters in the British and American Novel*. Ed. Andrea O'Reilly Herrera, Elizabeth Mahn Nollen and Sheila Reitzel Foor. Bowling Green, OH: Popular P, 1997. 167–82.

Holbrook, David. *Edith Wharton and the Unsatisfactory Man*. London: Vision; New York: St. Martin's, 1991.

Howe, Irving, ed. *Edith Wharton: A Collection of Critical Essays*. Englewood Cliffs, NJ: Prentice-Hall, [1962].

Hutchinson, Stuart. "Sex, race, and class in Edith Wharton." *Texas Studies in Literature and Language* 42 (2000): 431–45.

Jessup, Josephine Lurie. *The Faith of Our Feminists: A Study in the Novels of Edith Wharton, Ellen Glasgow, Willa Cather*. New York: Biblo and Tannen, 1965.

Jirousek, Lori. "Haunting Hysteria: Wharton, Freeman, and the Ghosts of Masculinity." *American Literary Realism* 32.1 (1999): 51–68.

Johnson, Laura K. "Edith Wharton and the Fiction of Marital Unity." *Modern Fiction Studies* 47 (2001): 947–75.

Joslin, Katherine. *Edith Wharton*. New York: St. Martin's, 1991.

Joslin, Katherine and Alan Price, eds. *Wretched Exotic: Essays on Edith Wharton in Europe*. New York: Peter Lang, 1993.

Kazin, Alfred. "The Lady and the Tiger: Edith Wharton and Theodore Dreiser." *Virginia Quarterly Review* 17.4 (1941): 101–19.

Killoran, Helen. *The Critical Reception of Edith Wharton*. Rochester, NY; Suffolk, Eng.: Camden House, 2001.

———. *Edith Wharton: Art and Allusion*. Tuscaloosa: U of Alabama P, 1996.

———. "Meeting of Minds: Edith Wharton as Mentor and Guide." *American Literary Mentors*. Ed. Irene C. Goldman-Price and Melissa McFarland Pennell. Gainesville: UP of Florida, 1999. 117–130.

Kinman, Alice H. "The Making of a Professional: Edith Wharton's *The Decoration of Houses*." *South Atlantic Review* 65.1 (2000): 98–122.

Koprince, Susan. "Wharton and Longfellow." *American Literary Realism* 31.3 (1999): 21–30.

Laskin, David. *A Common Life: Four Generations of American Literary Friendship and Influence*. New York: Simon & Schuster, 1994.

Lauer, Kristin O. and Margaret P. Murray. *Edith Wharton: An Annotated Secondary Bibliography*. New York: Garland, 1990.

Lawson, Richard H. *Edith Wharton*. New York: Ungar, 1977.

Leavis, Q.D. "Henry James's Heiress: The Importance of Edith Wharton." *Scrutiny* Dec. 1938: 261–76.

Luria, Sarah. "The architecture of manners: Henry James, Edith Wharton, and The Mount." *American Quarterly* 49 (1997): 298–328.

Margolis, Stacey. "The Public Life: The Discourse of Privacy in the Age of Celebrity." *Arizona Quarterly* 51.2 (1995): 81–101.

McDowell, Margaret B. *Edith Wharton.* Rev. ed. Boston: Twayne, 1990.

Merish, Lori. "Engendering Naturalism: Narrative Form and Commodity Spectacle in U.S. Naturalist Fiction." *Novel: A Forum on Fiction* 29.3 (1996): 319–45.

Miller, D. Quentin. "'A Barrier of Words': The Tension between Narrative Voice and Vision in the Writings of Edith Wharton." *American Literary Realism* 27.1 (1994): 11–22.

Montgomery, Maureen E. *Displaying Women: Spectacles of Leisure in Edith Wharton's New York.* New York: Routledge, 1998.

Murray, Margaret P. "The Gothic Arsenal of Edith Wharton." *Journal of Evolutionary Psychology* 10.3–4 (1989): 315–21.

Nettels, Elsa. *Language and Gender in American Fiction: Howells, James, Wharton and Cather.* Charlottesville: UP of Virginia, 1997.

———. "Texts within Texts: The Power of Letters in Edith Wharton's Fiction." *Countercurrents: On the Primacy of Texts in Literary Criticism.* Ed. Raymond Adolph Prier. Albany: State U of New York P, 1992. 191–205.

Nevius, Blake. *Edith Wharton: A Study of Her Fiction.* Berkeley and Los Angeles: U of California P, 1953.

Papke, Mary E. *Verging on the Abyss: The Social Fiction of Kate Chopin and Edith Wharton.* New York: Greenwood, 1990.

Preston, Claire. "Ladies Prefer Bonds: Edith Wharton, Theodore Dreiser, and the Money Novel." *Soft Canons: American Women Writers and Masculine Tradition.* Ed. Karen L. Kilcup. Iowa City: U of Iowa P, 1999. 184–201.

Price, Alan. *The End of the Age of Innocence: Edith Wharton and the First World War.* New York: St. Martin's, 1996.

Price, Kenneth M. and Phyllis McBride. "'The Life Apart': Texts and Contexts of Edith Wharton's Love Diary." *American Literature* 66 (1994): 663–88.

Raphel, Lev. *Edith Wharton's Prisoners of Shame: A New Perspective on Her Neglected Fiction.* New York: St. Martin's, 1991.

Saunders, Catherine E. *Writing the Margins: Edith Wharton, Ellen Glasgow, and the Literary Tradition of the Ruined Woman.* Cambridge: Harvard UP, 1987.

Schriber, Mary Suzanne. *Gender and the Writer's Imagination: From Cooper to Wharton.* Lexington: UP of Kentucky, 1987.

Sensibar, Judith L. "Edith Wharton Reads the Bachelor Type: Her Critique of Modernism's Representative Man." *American Literature* 60 (1988): 575–90.

Singley, Carol J. *Edith Wharton: Matters of Mind and Spirit.* Cambridge, Eng.: Cambridge UP, 1995.

Tintner, Adeline R. *Edith Wharton in Context: Essays on Intertextuality.* Tuscaloosa: U of Alabama P, 1999.

Tuttleton, James W., Kristin O. Lauer, and Margaret P. Murray, eds. *Edith Wharton: The Contemporary Reviews*. Cambridge, Eng.: Cambridge UP, 1992.

Tylee, Claire M. "Imagining women at war: feminist strategies in Edith Wharton's war writing." *Tulsa Studies in Women's Literature* 16 (1997): 327–44.

Updike, John. "Reworking Wharton." *The New Yorker,* 4 Oct. 1993: 198–212.

Vickers, Jackie. "Women and wealth: F. Scott Fitzgerald, Edith Wharton and Paul Bourget." *Journal of American Studies* 26 (1992): 261–64.

Vita-Finzi, Penelope. *Edith Wharton and the Art of Fiction*. London: Pinter, 1990.

Waid, Candace. *Letters from the Underworld: Fictions of Women and Writing*. Chapel Hill: U of North Carolina P, 1991.

Walton, Geoffrey. *Edith Wharton: A Critical Interpretation*. Rutherford, NJ: Fairleigh Dickinson UP, 1970.

Wegener, Frederick. "Charlotte Perkins Gilman, Edith Wharton and the Divided Heritage of American Literary Feminism." *The Mixed Legacy of Charlotte Perkins Gilman*. Ed. Catherine J. Golden and Joanna Schneider Zangrando. Newark, DE: U of Delaware P—Associated UP, 2000. 135–59.

———. "Edith Wharton and the Difficult Writing of *The Writing of Fiction*." *Modern Language Studies* 25.2 (1995): 60–79.

———. "'Rabid Imperialist': Edith Wharton and the Obligations of Empire in Modern American Fiction." *American Literature* 72 (2000): 783–812.

Wershoven, Carol J. *The Female Intruder in the Novels of Edith Wharton*. Rutherford, NJ: Fairleigh Dickinson UP, 1982.

Williams, Deborah Lindsay. *Not in Sisterhood: Edith Wharton, Willa Cather, Zona Gale, and the Politics of Female Authorship*. New York: Palgrave, 2001.

Worth, Richard. *Edith Wharton*. New York: J. Messner, 1994.

Wright, Sarah Bird. *Edith Wharton's Travel Writing: The Making of a Connoisseur*. New York: St. Martin's, 1997.

CRITICISM OF WHARTON'S SHORT FICTION

Bauer, Dale M. "Edith Wharton's 'Roman Fever': a Rune of History." *College English* 50 (1988): 681–94.

Beer, Janet. *Kate Chopin, Edith Wharton, and Charlotte Perkins Gilman: Studies in Short Fiction*. New York: St. Martin's, 1997.

Berkove, Lawrence I. "'Roman Fever': A Mortal Malady." *CEA Critic* 56.2 (1994): 56–60.

Brennan, Joseph Payne. "Can the Supernatural Story Survive?" *American Supernatural Fiction: From Edith Wharton to the Weird Tales Writers*. Ed. Douglas Robillard and Benjamin F. Fisher. New York: Garland, 1996. 253–60.

Dyman, Jenni. *Lurking Feminism: The Ghost Stories of Edith Wharton*. New York: P. Lang, 1996.

Erlich, Gloria. "The Female Conscience in Wharton's Shorter Fiction." *The Cambridge Companion to Edith Wharton*. Ed. Millicent Bell. New York: Cambridge UP, 1995. 98–116.

Fracasso, Evelyn B. *Edith Wharton's Prisoners of Consciousness: A Study of Theme and Technique in the Tales*. Westport: Greenwood, 1994.

Funston, Judith E. "'Xingu': Edith Wharton's Velvet Gauntlet." *Studies in American Fiction* 12 (1984): 227–34.

Inverso, Mary-Beth. "Performing Women: Semiotic Promiscuity in 'The Other Two.'" *Edith Wharton Review* 10.1 (1993): 3–6.

Kaye, Richard A. "'Unearthly Visitants': Wharton's Ghost Tales, Gothic Form and The Literature of Homosexual Panic." *Edith Wharton Review* 11.1 (1994): 10–18.

Killoran, Helen. "'Xingu': Edith Wharton Instructs Literary Critics." *Studies in American Humor* 3.3 (1996): 1–13.

McDowell, Margaret B. "Edith's Wharton's Ghost Tales Reconsidered." *Edith Wharton: New Critical Essays*. Ed. Alfred Bendixen and Annette Zilversmit. New York: Garland, 1992. 291–314.

Mortimer, Armine Kotin. "Romantic Fever: The Second Story as Illegitimate Daughter in Wharton's 'Roman Fever.'" *Narrative* 6.2 (1998): 188–98.

Nettels, Elsa. "Gender and First-Person Narration in Edith Wharton's Short Fiction." *Edith Wharton: New Critical Essays*. Ed. Alfred Bendixen and Annette Zilversmit. New York: Garland, 1992. 245–60.

Olin-Ammentorp, Julie. "Female Models and Male Mentors in Wharton's Early Fiction." *American Literary Mentors*. Ed. Irene C. Goldman-Price and Melissa McFarland Pennell. Gainesville: UP of Florida, 1999. 84–95.

———. "'Not Precisely War Stories': Edith Wharton's Short Fiction from the Great War." *Studies in American Fiction*, 23.2 (1995): 153–72.

Petry, Alice Hall. "A Twist of Crimson Silk: Edith Wharton's 'Roman Fever.'" *Studies in Short Fiction* 24.2 (1987): 163–66.

Plante, Patricia. "Edith Wharton as Short Story Writer." *Midwest Quarterly* 4 (1963): 363–79.

Smith, Allan Gardner. "Edith Wharton and the Ghost Story." *Women and Literature* 1 (1980): 149–59.

Sweeney, Gerard M. "Wharton's 'The Other Two'." *Explicator* 59.2 (2001): 88–91

White, Barbara A. *Edith Wharton: A Study of the Short Fiction*. New York: Twayne, 1991.

TWO NOVELLAS: *MADAME DE TREYMES* (1907) AND *THE OLD MAID* (1924)

CONTEMPORARY REVIEWS OF *MADAME DE TREYMES*

Hawthorne, Hildegarde. "Mrs. Wharton's Heroines." *New York Times Saturday Review*, March 1907, 137.

"Madame de Treymes." *Athenaeum* [England], May 4, 1907, 535.

"*Madame de Treymes.*" *Academy*, May 11, 1907, 465–6.

Moss, Mary. "Mrs Wharton's *Madame de Treymes.*" *Bookman*, May 1907, 303–34.

Smith, Harry James. "Some Recent Novels." *Atlantic Monthly*, July 1907, 131–32.

CONTEMPORARY REVIEWS OF *THE OLD MAID*

Canby, Henry Seidel. "Stories of Our Past." *Saturday Review of Books*, August 16, 1924, 43–44.

Field, Louise Maunsell. "Edith Wharton Shows Us Old New York." *Literary Digest International Book Review*, June 1924, 538–39.

Ford, James L. "Maligning Old New York." *Literature Digest International Book Review*, October 1924, 785–86.

Morris, Lloyd. "Mrs. Wharton Looks at Society." *New York Times Book Review*, May 18, 1924, 1, 24–5.

"Mrs. Wharton." *Times Literary Supplement* [England], September 11, 1924, 553.

CRITICISM OF *MADAME DE TREYMES* AND *THE OLD MAID*

Chambers, Dianne. "Female Roles and National Identity in Kay Boyle's 'Plagued by the Nightingale' and Edith Wharton's 'Madame de Treymes.'" *Critical Essays on Kay Boyle*. Ed. Marilyn Elkins. New York, NY: G. K. Hall, 1997 241–61.

Funston, Judith E. "Clocks and Mirrors, Dreams and Destinies: Edith Wharton's *The Old Maid.*" *Edith Wharton: New Critical Essays*. Ed. Alfred Bendixen and Annette Zilversmit. New York: Garland, 1992 143–57.

Levine, Jessica. "Discretion and Self Censorship in Wharton's Fiction: 'The Old Maid' and the Politics of Publishing." *Edith Wharton Review* 13.1 (1996): 4–13.

McDowell, Margaret B. "Edith Wharton's *The Old Maid:* Novella/Play/Film." *College Literature* 14 (1987): 246–62.

Rae, Catherine M. "Edith Wharton's Avenging Angel in the House." *Denver Quarterly* 18.4 (1984): 119–25.

THE HOUSE OF MIRTH (1905)

CONTEMPORARY REVIEWS

Boutell, Alice May. "A Burst of Enthusiasm." *Critic*, January 1906, 87–8.

Dunbar, Olivia Howard. "A Group of Novels." *Critic*, December 1905, 509–10.

"Fiction: *The House of Mirth.*" *Times Literary Supplement* [England], December 1, 1905, 421.

Hale, E. E., Jr. "Mrs. Wharton's *The House of Mirth*." *Bookman*, December 1905, 364–66.

"*The House of Mirth* and Other Novels." *Nation*, November 30, 1905, 447–48.

"Mrs. Wharton's Latest Novel." *Independent*, July 20, 1905, 150–51.

"A Notable Novel." *Outlook*, October 21, 1905, 404–6.

CRITICISM

Abbott, Reginald. "'A Moment's Ornament': Wharton's Lily Bart and Art Nouveau." *Mosaic: A Journal for the Interdisciplinary Study of Literature* 24.2 (1991): 73–91.

Barnett, Louise K. "Language, Gender, and Society in *The House of Mirth*." *Connecticut Review* 11.2 (1989): 54–63.

Beaty, Robin. "Lilies That Fester: Sentimentality in *The House of Mirth*." *College Literature* 14 (1987): 263–75.

Benert, Annette Larson. "The Geography of Gender in *The House of Mirth*." *Studies in the Novel* 22.1 (1990): 26–42.

Benstock, Shari. "'The Word Which Made All Clear': The Silent Close of *The House of Mirth*" *Famous Last Words: Changes in Gender and Narrative Closure*. Ed. Alison Booth. Charlottesville: UP of Virginia, 1993. 230–58.

Beppu, Keiko. "The Moral Significance of Living Space: The Library and Kitchen in *The House of Mirth*." *Edith Wharton Review* 14.2 (1997): 3–7.

Brazin, Nancy Topping. "The Destruction of Lily Bart: Capitalism, Christianity, and Male Chauvinism." *Denver Quarterly* 17.4 (1983): 97–108.

Brooks, Kristina. "New Woman, Fallen Woman: The Crisis of Reputation in Turn-of-Century Novels by Pauline Hopkins and Edith Wharton." *Legacy: A Journal of American Women Writers* 13.2 (1996): 91–112.

Cain, William E. "Wharton's Art of Presence: The Case of Gerty Farish in *The House of Mirth*." *Edith Wharton Newsletter* 6.2 (1989): 1–2, 7–8.

Clubbe, John. "Interiors and the Interior Life in Edith Wharton's *The House of Mirth*." *Studies in the Novel* 28.4 (1996): 543–64.

Colquitt, Clare. "Succumbing to the 'Literary Style': Arrested Desire in *The House of Mirth*." *Women's Studies* 20.2 (1991): 153–62.

Coulombe, Joseph. "Man or Mannequin? Lawrence Selden in *The House of Mirth*." *Edith Wharton Review* 13.2 (1996): 3–8.

Davidson, Cathy N. "Kept Women in *The House of Mirth*." *Markham Review* 9 (1979): 10–13.

Dawson, Melanie. "Lily Bart's Fractured Alliances and Wharton's Appeal to the Middlebrow Reader." *Reader: Essays in Reader-Oriented Theory, Criticism, and Pedagogy* 41 (1999): 1–30.

Dimock, Wai-chee. "Debasing Exchange: Edith Wharton's *The House of Mirth*." *PMLA* 100 (1985): 783–92.

Dittmar, Linda. "When Privilege Is No Protection: The Woman Artist in *Quicksand* and *The House of Mirth*." *Writing the Woman Artist: Essays on Poetics,*

Politics, and Portraiture. Ed. Suzanne W. Jones. Philadelphia: U of Pennsylvania P, 1991. 133–54.

Dixon, Roslyn. "Reflecting Vision in *The House of Mirth.*" *Twentieth Century Literature* 33 (1987): 211–22.

DuBow, Wendy M. "The Businesswoman in Edith Wharton." *Edith Wharton Review* 8.2 (1991): 11–18.

Esch, Deborah, ed. *New Essays on The House of Mirth.* Cambridge, England: Cambridge UP, 2001.

Fetterley, Judith. "'The Temptation to Be a Beautiful Object': Double Standard and Double Bind in *The House of Mirth.*" *Studies in American Fiction* 5 (1977): 199–211.

Foster, Shirley. "The Open Cage: Freedom, Marriage and the Heroine in Early Twentieth-Century American Women's Novels." *Women's Writing: A Challenge to Theory.* Ed. Moira Monteith. Sussex; New York: Harvester; St. Martin's, 1986. 154–74.

Friman, Anne. "Determinism and Point of View in *The House of Mirth.*" *Papers on Language and Literature* 2 (1966): 175–78.

Gabler-Hover, Janet and Kathleen Plate. "*The House of Mirth* and Edith Wharton's 'Beyond!'" *Philological Quarterly* 72 (1993): 357–78.

Gargano, James W. "*The House of Mirth*: Social Futility and Faith." *American Literature* 44 (1972): 137–43.

Gerard, Bonnie Lynn. "From Tea to Chloral: Raising the Dead Lily Bart." *Twentieth Century Literature* 44 (1998): 409–27.

Goldman, Irene C. "The Perfect Jew and *The House of Mirth*: A Study in Point of View." *Modern Language Studies* 23.3 (1993): 25–36. Rpt. in *Edith Wharton Review* 16.1 (2000 Spring): 1, 2–9.

Goldner, Ellen J. "The Lying Woman and the Cause of Social Anxiety: Interdependence and the Woman's Body in *The House of Mirth.*" *Women's Studies* 21 (1992): 285–305.

Goldsmith, Meredith. "Edith Wharton's Gift to Nella Larsen: *The House of Mirth* and *Quicksand.*" *Edith Wharton Review,* 11.2 (1994): 3–5, 15.

Herman, David. "Economies of Essense in *The House of Mirth.*" *Edith Wharton Review* 16.1 (1999): 6–10.

Hochman, Barbara. "*The Awakening* and *The House of Mirth*: Plotting Experience and Experiencing Plot." *The Cambridge Companion to American Realism and Naturalism: Howells to London.* Ed. Donald Pizer. Cambridge: Cambridge UP, 1995. 211–35.

———. "The Rewards of Representation: Edith Wharton, Lily Bart and the Writer/Reader Interchange." *Novel: A Forum on Fiction* 24.2 (1991): 147–61.

Hoeller, Hildegard. "'The Impossible Rosedale': 'Race' and the Reading of Edith Wharton's *The House of Mirth.*" *Studies in American Jewish Literature* 13 (1994): 14–20.

Horne, Philip. "Beauty's Slow Fade." *Sight and Sound* 10 (Oct. 2000): 14–18.

Hovet, Grace Ann and Theodore R. Hovet. "TABLEAUX VIVANTS: Masculine Vision and Feminine Reflections in Novels by Warner, Alcott, Stowe, and Wharton." *American Transcendental Quarterly* 7 (1993): 335–56.

Howard, Maureen. "On *The House of Mirth*." *Raritan* 15.3 (1996): 1–23.

Hutchinson, Stuart. "From *Daniel Deronda* to *The House of Mirth*." *Essays in Criticism* 47 (1997): 315–31.

Karcher, Carolyn L. "Male Vision and Female Revision in James's *The Wings of the Dove* and Wharton's *The House of Mirth*." *Women's Studies* 10.3 (1984): 227–44.

Kassanoff, Jennie A. "Extinction, Taxidermy, Tableaux Vivants: Staging Race and Class in *The House of Mirth*." *PMLA* 115.1 (2000): 60–74.

Kaye, Richard A. "Literary Naturalism and the Passive Male: Edith Wharton's Revisions of *The House of Mirth*." *Princeton University Library Chronicle*, 56.1 (1994): 46–72.

Koprince, Susan. "Edith Wharton's Hotels." *Massachusetts Studies in English* 10.1 (1985): 12–23.

———. "The Meaning of Bellomount in *The House of Mirth*." *Edith Wharton Newsletter* 2.1 (1986): 1, 5, 8.

Langley, Martha R. "Botanical Language in Edith Wharton's *The House of Mirth*." *NMAL: Notes on Modern American Literature* 5 (1980): Item 3.

Lidoff, Joan. "Another Sleeping Beauty: Narcissism in *The House of Mirth*." *American Quarterly* 32 (1980): 519–39.

Michelson, Bruce. "Edith Wharton's House Divided." *Studies in American Fiction* 12 (1984): 199–215.

Miller, Carol. "'Natural Magic': Irony as Unifying Strategy in *The House of Mirth*." *South Central Review* 4.1 (1987): 82–91.

Moddelmog, William E. "Disowning 'Personality': Privacy and Subjectivity in *The House of Mirth*." *American Literature* 70 (1998): 337–63.

Montgomery, Judith H. "The American Galatea." *College English* 32 (1971): 890–99.

Olin-Ammentorp, Julie. "Wharton's 'Negative Hero' Revisited." *Edith Wharton Newsletter* 6.1 (1989): 6, 8.

———. "Edith Wharton's Challenge to Feminist Criticism." *Studies in American Fiction* 16 (1988): 237–44.

O'Neal, Michael J. "Point of View and Narrative Technique in the Fiction of Edith Wharton." *Style* 17 (1983): 270–89.

Orr, Elaine N. "Contractual Law, Relational Whisper: A Reading of Edith Wharton's *The House of Mirth*." *Modern Language Quarterly* 59 (1991): 53–70.

Pickrel, Paul. "Vanity Fair in America: *The House of Mirth* and *Gone with the Wind*." *American Literature* 59 (1987): 37–57.

Pizer, Donald. "The Naturalism of Edith Wharton's *The House of Mirth*." *Twentieth Century Literature* 41 (1995): 241–48.

Radden, Jennifer. "Defining Self-Deception." *Dialogue* 23.1 (1984): 103–120.

Restuccia, Frances L. "The Name of the Lily: Edith Wharton's Feminism(s)." *Contemporary Literature* 28 (1987): 223–38.

Riegel, Christian. "Rosedale and Anti-Semitism in *The House of Mirth*." *Studies in American Fiction* 20 (1992): 219–24.

Rooke, Constance. "Beauty in Distress: *Daniel Deronda* and *The House of Mirth*." *Women and Literature* 4.2 (1976): 28–39.

Sapora, Carol Baker. "Female Doubling: The Other Lily Bart in Edith Wharton's *The House of Mirth*." *Papers on Language and Literature* 29 (1993): 371–94.

Seltzer, Mark. "Statistical Persons." *Diacritics* 17.3 (1987): 82–98.

Showalter, Elaine. "The Death of the Lady (Novelist): Wharton's *House of Mirth*." *Representations* 9 (1985): 133–49.

Shulman, Robert. "Divided Selves and the Market Society: Politics and Psychology in *The House of Mirth*." *Perspectives on Contemporary Literature* 11 (1985): 10–19.

Singley, Carol J. "Edith Wharton and Partnership: *The House of Mirth, The Decoration of Houses*, and 'Copy.' " *American Literary Mentors*. Ed. Irene Goldman-Price and Melissa McFarland Pennell. Gainesville, FL: UP of Florida, 1999. 96–116.

Tintner, Adeline R. "Two Novels of 'the Relatively Poor': *New Grub Street* and *The House of Mirth*." *NMAL:-Notes on Modern American Literature* 6.2 (1982): Item 12.

Totten, Gary. "The Art and Architecture of the Self: Designing the 'I'-Witness in Edith Wharton's *The House of Mirth*." *College Literature* 27.3 (2000): 71–87.

Town, Caren J. "The House of Mirrors: Carrie, Lily and the Reflected Self." *Modern Language Studies* 24 (1994): 44–54.

Trilling, Diana. "*The House of Mirth* Revisited." *The American Scholar* 32 (1963): 113–28.

Tyson, Lois. "Beyond Morality: Lily Bart, Lawrence Selden and the Aesthetic Commodity in *The House of Mirth*." *Edith Wharton Review* 9.2 (1992): 3–10.

Vella, Michael W. "Technique and Theme in *The House of Mirth*." *Markham Review* 23.3 (1970): [17]–[20].

Von Rosk, Nancy. "Spectacular Homes and Pastoral Theaters: Gender, Urbanity and Domesticity in *The House of Mirth*." *Studies in the Novel* 33 (2001): 322–50.

Waid, Candace. "Building *The House of Mirth*." *Biographies of Books: The Compositional Histories of Notable American Writings*. Ed. James Barbour and Tom Quirk. Columbia: U of Missouri P, 1996. 160–86.

Wershoven, C. J. "*The Awakening* and *The House of Mirth*: Studies of Arrested Development." *American Literary Realism* 19.3 (1987): 27–41.

Westbrook, Wayne W. "*The House of Mirth* and the Insurance Scandal of 1905." *American Notes and Queries* 14 (1976): 134–37.

Wolff, Cynthia G. "Lily Bart and the Beautiful Death." *American Literature* 46 (1974): (16) 40.

Wolff, Cynthia Griffin. "Lily Bart and the Drama of Femininity." *American Literary History* 6.1 (1994): 71–87.

Yeazell, Ruth Bernard. "The Conspicuous Wasting of Lily Bart." *ELH*, 59 (1992): 713–34.

ETHAN FROME (1911)

CONTEMPORARY REVIEWS

Cooper, Frederic Taber. "*Ethan Frome*." *Bookman*, November 1911, 312.

"Current Fiction: *Ethan Frome*" *Nation*, October 26, 1911, 396–97.

"*Ethan Frome*." *Bookman* [England], January 1912, 216.

"*Ethan Frome*." *Outlook*, October 21, 1911, 405.

"*Ethan Frome*." *Saturday Review* [England], November 18, 1911, 650.

"Three Lives in Supreme Torture: Mrs. Wharton's *Ethan Frome* a Cruel, Compelling, Haunting Story of New England." *New York Times Book Review*, October 8, 1911, 603.

CRITICISM

Ammons, Elizabeth. "Edith Wharton's *Ethan Frome* and the Question of Meaning." *Studies in American Fiction* 7 (1979): 127–40.

Banta, Martha. "The Ghostly Gothic of Wharton's Everyday World." *American Literary Realism* 27 (1994): 1–10.

Bernard, Kenneth. "Imagery and Symbolism in Ethan Frome." *College English* 23 (1961): 178–84.

Blackall, Jean Frantz. "Imaginative Encounter: Edith Wharton and Emily Bronte." *Edith Wharton Review* 9.1 (1992): 9–11, 27.

———. "The Sledding Accident in *Ethan Frome*." *Studies in Short Fiction* 21 (1984): 145–46.

Campbell, Donna M. "Rewriting the 'Rose and Lavender Pages': *Ethan Frome* and Women's Local Color Fiction." *Speaking the Other Self: American Women Writers*. Ed. Jeanne Campbell Reesman. Athens, GA: U of Georgia P, 1997. 263–77.

Dodson, Samuel Fisher. "Frozen Hell: Edith Wharton's Tragic Offering." *Edith Wharton Review* 16.1 (1999): 10–15.

Eggenschwiler, David. "The Ordered Disorder of *Ethan Frome*." *Studies in the Novel* 9 (1977): 237–46.

Farland, Maria Magdalena. "*Ethan Frome* and the 'Springs' of Masculinity." *MFS: Modern Fiction Studies* 42 (1996): 707–29.

Gschwend, Kate. "The Significance of the Sawmill: Technological Determinism in *Ethan Frome*." *Edith Wharton Review* 16.1 (2000): 9–13.

Hays, Peter. "Wharton's Splintered Realism." *Edith Wharton Newsletter* 2.1 (1985): 6.

Hill, Wm. Thomas. "'Man-Like, He Sought to Postpone Certainty': Shadows of Truth and Identity in Edith Wharton's *Ethan Frome*." *Studies in the Humanities* 56 (1995): 63–82.

Hovey, R. B. "*Ethan Frome*: A Controversy about Modernizing It." *American Literary Realism* 19.1 (1986): 4–20.

Killoran, Helen. "Under the Granite Outcroppings of *Ethan Frome*." *Literary Imagination* 2 (2000): 320–34.

Lagerway, Mary D. and Gerald E. Markle. "Edith Wharton's Sick Role." *Sociological Quarterly* 35 (1994): 121–35.

Leder, Priscilla. "Visions of New England: The Anxiety of Jewett's Influence on *Ethan Frome*." *Jewett and Her Contemporaries: Reshaping the Canon*. Ed. Karen L. Kilcup and Thomas S. Edwards. Gainesville, FL: UP of Florida, 1999. 167–81.

Marshall, Scott. "Edith Wharton, Kate Spencer, and *Ethan Frome*." *Edith Wharton Review* 10.1 (1993): 20–21.

Murad, Orlene. "Edith Wharton and *Ethan Frome*." *Modern Language Studies* 13.3 (1983): 90–103.

Nesbitt, William. "Ethan Frome, Necrologic, and Psychological Violence." *Journal of Evolutionary Psychology* 20.3–4 (1999): 161–69.

Nettels, Elsa. "Thwarted Escapes: *Ethan Frome* and Jean Stafford's 'A Country Love Story.'" *Edith Wharton Review* 11.2 (1994): 6–8, 15.

Nevius, Blake. "*Ethan Frome* and the Themes of Edith Wharton's Fiction." *New England Quarterly* 24 (1951): 197–207.

Rose, Alan Henry. "'Such Depths of Sad Initiation': Edith Wharton and New England." *New England Quarterly* 50 (1977): 423–39.

Singley, Carol J. "Calvinist Tortures in Edith Wharton's *Ethan Frome*." *The Calvinist Roots of the Modern Era*. Ed. Aliki Barnstone, Michael Tomasek Manson, and Carol J. Singley. Hanover, NH: UP of New England, 1997. 162–80.

Smith, Christopher, ed. *Readings on Ethan Frome*. San Diego: Greenhaven, 2000.

Springer, Marlene. *Ethan Frome: A Nightmare of Need*. New York: Twayne, 1993.

Travis, Jennifer. "Pain and Recompense: The Trouble with *Ethan Frome*." *Arizona Quarterly* 53.3 (1997): 37–64.

SUMMER (1917)

CONTEMPORARY REVIEWS

Eliot, T. S. "*Summer*." *The Egoist* [England], January 1919, 10.

Gilam, Lawrence. "The Book of the Month: Mrs. Wharton Reverts to Shaw." *North American Review*, August 1917, 304–07.

H[ackett], F[rancis]. "Loading the Dice." *New Republic*, July 14, 1917, 311–12.

Macy, John. "Edith Wharton." *Dial*, August 30, 1917, 161–62.

"Mrs. Wharton's Story of New England: *Summer* a Pleasing Romance of Village Life." *New York Times Book Review*, July 8, 1917, 253.

"New Novels: *Summer*." *Times Literary Supplement* [England], September 27, 1917. 464.

"Plots and People." *Nation*, August 2, 1917, 124–25.

CRITICISM

Blackall, Jean Frantz. "Charity at the Window: Narrative Technique in Edith Wharton's Summer." *Edith Wharton: New Critical Essays*. Ed. Alfred Bendixen and Annette Zilversmit. New York: Garland, 1992. 115–26.

Burleson, Mollie L. "Edith Wharton's *Summer:* Through the Glass Darkly." *Studies in Weird Fiction* 13 (1993): 19–21.

Crowley, John W. "The Unmastered Streak: Feminist Themes in Wharton's *Summer*." *American Literary Realism* 15.1 (1982): 86–96.

Elbert, Monika M. "Bourgeois Sexuality and the Gothic Plot in Wharton and Hawthorne." *Hawthorne and Women: Engendering and Expanding the Hawthorne Tradition*. Ed. John L. Idol, Jr. and Melinda M. Ponder. Amherst: U of Massachusetts P, 1999. 258–70.

———. "The Politics of Maternality in *Summer*." *Edith Wharton Review* 7.2 (1990): 4–9, 24.

Gilbert, Sandra M. "Life's Empty Pack: Notes toward a Literary Daughteronomy." *Critical Inquiry* 11.3 (1985): 355–84.

Grafton, Kathy. "Degradation and Forbidden Love in Edith Wharton's *Summer*." *Twentieth Century Literature* 41.4 (1995): 350–66.

Hays, Peter L. "Signs in *Summer*: Words and Metaphors." *Papers on Language and Literature* 25.1 (1989): 114–19.

Hummel, William E. "My 'Dull-Witted Enemy': Symbolic Violence and Abject Maleness in Edith Wharton's *Summer*." *Studies in American Fiction* 24.2 (1996): 215–36.

Hutchinson, Stuart. "Unpackaging Edith Wharton: *Ethan Frome* and *Summer*." *Cambridge Quarterly* 27.3 (1998): 219–32.

Makowsky, Veronica and Lynn Z. Bloom. "Edith Wharton's Tentative Embrace of Charity: Class and Character in *Summer*." *American Literary Realism* 32.3 (2000): 220–33.

Morante, Linda. "The Desolation of Charity Royall: Imagery in Edith Wharton's *Summer*." *Colby Library Quarterly* 18.4 (1982): 241–48.

Pfeiffer, Kathleen. "*Summer* and Its Critics' Discomfort." *Women's Studies* 20.2 (1991): 141–52.

Rose, Christine "*Summer:* The Double Sense of Wharton's Title." *ANQ: A Quarterly Journal of Short Articles, Notes, and Reviews* 3:1 (1990): 16–19.

Skillern, Rhonda. "Becoming a 'Good Girl': Law, Language, and Ritual in Edith Wharton's *Summer*." *The Cambridge Companion to Edith Wharton*. Ed. Millicent Bell. New York: Cambridge UP, 1995. 117–36.

Walker, Nancy A. "'Seduced and Abandoned': Convention and Reality in Edith Wharton's *Summer*." *Studies in American Fiction* 11.1 (1983): 107–14.

Werlock, Abby H. P. "Whitman, Wharton, and the Sexuality in *Summer*." *Speaking the Other Self: American Women Writers*. Ed. Jeanne Campbell Reesman. Athens: U of Georgia P, 1997. 246–62.

Wershoven, Carol. "The Divided Conflict of Edith Wharton's *Summer*." *Colby Library Quarterly* 21.1 (1985): 5–10.

White, Barbara A. "Edith Wharton's *Summer* and 'Women's Fiction'." *Essays in Literature* 11.2 (1984): 223–35.

Wolff, Cynthia Griffin. "Cold Ethan and 'Hot Ethan.'" *College Literature* 14.3 (1987): 230–45.

THE AGE OF INNOCENCE (1920)

CONTEMPORARY REVIEWS

"*The Age of Innocence*." *Times Literary Supplement* [England], November 25, 1920, 775.

Canby, Henry Seidel. "Our America." New York *Evening Post*, November 6, 1920, 3.

M[ansfield], K[atherine]. "Family Portraits." *Athenaeum* [England], December 10, 1920, 810–11.

Parrington, Vernon L., Jr. "Our Literary Aristocrat." *Pacific Review*, June 2, 1921, 157–60.

Perry, Katherine. "Were the Seventies Sinless?" *Publisher's Weekly*, October 16, 1920, 1195–96.

Phelps, William Lyon. "As Mrs. Wharton Sees Us." *New York Times Book Review*, October 17, 1920, 1, 11.

[Van Doren, Carl]. "An Elder America." *Nation*, November 3, 1920, 510–11.

CRITICISM

Aaron, Daniel. "Three Old Women." *Queen's Quarterly* 102.3 (1995): 633–39.

Ammons, Elizabeth. "Cool Diana and the Blood-Red Muse: Edith Wharton on Innocence and Art." *American Novelists Revisited: Essays in Feminist Criticism*. Ed. Fritz Fleischmann. Boston: Hall, 1982. 209–24.

Asya, Ferda. "Resolutions of Guilt: Cultural Values Reconsidered in *Custom of the Country* and *The Age of Innocence*." *Edith Wharton Review* 14.2 (1997): 15–20.

Blackall, Jean Frantz. "The Intrusive Voice: Telegrams in *The House of Mirth* and *The Age of Innocence*." *Women's Studies* 20.2 (1991): 163–68.

Bloom, Harold, ed. *Edith Wharton's The Age of Innocence*. Broomall, PA: Chelsea House, 1999.

Bremer, Sidney H. "American Dreams and American Cities in Three Post–World War I Novels." *South Atlantic Quarterly* 79 (1980): 274–85.

Cahir, Linda Costanzo. "The Perils of Politeness in a New Age: Edith Wharton, Martin Scorsese and *The Age of Innocence*." *Edith Wharton Review* 10:2 (1993): 12–14, 19.

Davis, Joy L. "The Ritual of Dining in Edith Wharton's *The Age of Innocence*." *Midwest Quarterly* 34 (1993): 465–81.

Davis, Linette. "Vulgarity and Red Blood in *The Age of Innocence*." *The Journal of the Midwest Modern Language Association* 20.2 (1987): 1–8.

Doyle, Charles C. "Emblems of Innocence: Imagery Patterns in Wharton's *The Age of Innocence*." *Xavier University Studies* 10.2 (1971): 19–25.

Eby, Clare Virginia. "Silencing Women in Edith Wharton's *The Age of Innocence*." *Colby Quarterly* 28.2 (1992): 93–104.

Falk, Cynthia G. "'The Intolerable Ugliness of New York': Architecture and Society in Edith Wharton's *The Age of Innocence*." *American Studies* 42.2 (2001): 19–44.

Fracasso, Evelyn E. "The Transparent Eyes of May Welland in Wharton's *The Age of Innocence*." *Modern Language Studies* 21.4 (1991): 43–48.

Fryer, Judith. "Purity and Power in *The Age of Innocence*." *American Literary Realism* 17.2 (1984): 153–68.

Gargano, James W. "Tableaux of Renunciation: Wharton's Use of *The Shaughran* in *The Age of Innocence*." *Studies in American Fiction* 15.1 (1987): 1–11.

Godfrey, David A. "'The full and elaborate vocabulary of evasion': The Language of Cowardice in Edith Wharton's Old New York." *Midwest Quarterly* 30.1 (1988): 27–44.

Grenier, Richard. "Society & Edith Wharton." *Commentary* Dec. 1993: 48–52.

Hadley, Kathy Miller. "Ironic Structure and Untold Stories in *The Age of Innocence*." *Studies in the Novel* 23.2 (1991): 262–72.

Hopkins, Viola. "The Ordering Style of *The Age of Innocence*." *American Literature* 30 (1958): 345–57.

Kekes, John. "The Great Guide of Human Life." *Philosophy and Literature* 8 (1984): 236–49.

Lee, Robert A. "Watching Manners: Martin Scorsese's *The Age of Innocence*, Edith Wharton's *The Age of Innocence*." *The Classic Novel: From Page to Screen*. Ed. Robert Giddings and Erica Sheen. New York: St. Martin's, 2000. 163–78.

Martin, Robert K. "Age of Innocence: Edith Wharton, Henry James, and Nathaniel Hawthorne." *Henry James Review* 21.1 (2000): 56–62.

Morgan, Gwendolyn. "The Unsung Heroine: A Study of May Welland in *The Age of Innocence*." *Heroines of Popular Culture*. Ed. Pat Browne. Bowling Green, OH: Popular, 1987. 32–40.

Murphy, John J. "The Satiric Structure of Wharton's *The Age of Innocence*." *Markham Review* 2 (1970): 1–4.

Nathan, Rhoda. "Ward McAllister: Beau Nash of *The Age of Innocence*." *College Literature* 14 (1987): 276–84.

Orlando, Emily J. "Rereading Wharton's 'Poor Archer': A Mr. 'Might-Have-Been' in *The Age of Innocence.*" *American Literary Realism* 30.2 (1998): 56–77.

Peucker, Brigitte. "Rival Arts? Filming *The Age of Innocence.*" *Edith Wharton Review* 13.1 (1996): 19–22.

Pimple, Kenneth D. "Edith Wharton's 'Inscrutable Totem Terrors': Ethnography and *The Age of Innocence.*" *Southern Folklore* 51.2 (1994): 137–52.

Price, Alan. "The Composition of Edith Wharton's *The Age of Innocence.*" *Yale University Library Gazette* 55 (1980): 22–30.

Robinson, James A. "Psychological Determinism in *The Age of Innocence.*" *Markham Review* 5 (1975): 1–5.

Saunders, Judith P. "Becoming the Mask: Edith Wharton's Ingenues." *Massachusetts Studies in English* 8.4 (1982): 33–39.

Scheick, William J. "Cupid without Bow and Arrow: *The Age of Innocence* and *The Golden Bough.*" *Edith Wharton Newsletter* 2.1 (1985): 2–5.

Strout, Cushing. "Complementary Portraits: James's *Lady* and Wharton's *Age.*" *The Hudson Review* 35 (1982): 405–15.

Tintner, Adeline R. "Jamesian Structures in *The Age of Innocence* and Related Stories." *Twentieth Century Literature* 26 (1980): 332–47.

Wagner, Linda W. "A Note on Wharton's Use of *Faust.*" *Edith Wharton Newsletter* 3.1 (1986): 1, 8.

Wagner-Martin, Linda. *The Age of Innocence: A Novel of Ironic Nostalgia.* New York: Twayne, 1996.

Wershoven, Carol. "America's Child Brides: The Price of a Bad Bargain." *Portraits of Marriage in Literature.* Ed. Anne C. Hargrove and Maurine Magliocco. Macomb, IL: Essays in Literature, 1984. 151–57.

Wolff, Cynthia Griffin. "*The Age of Innocence:* Wharton's 'Portrait of a Gentleman.' " *Southern Review* 12 (1976): 640–58.

RELATED SECONDARY SOURCES

Bakhtin, M. M. *The Bakhtin Reader: Selected Writings of Bakhtin, Medvedev and Voloshinov.* Ed. Pam Morris. London and New York: E. Arnold, 1994.

Brantlinger, Patrick. *Crusoe's Footprints: Cultural Studies in Britain and America.* New York and London: Routledge, 1990.

Eagleton, Terry. *The Idea of Culture.* Oxford: Blackwell, 2000.

Foucault, Michel. *The Foucault Reader.* Ed. Paul Rabinow. New York: Pantheon Books, 1984.

Kaplan, Amy. *The Social Construction of American Realism.* Chicago: U of Chicago P, 1988.

Karlsen, Carol F. *The Devil in the Shape of a Woman: Witchcraft in Colonial New England.* New York: W.W. Norton, 1987.

Marx, Karl and Friedrich Engels. *The Marx-Engels Reader.* New York: Norton, 1972.

Papinchak, Robert Allen. "Testing the Water." *Writer*, November 2001, 26–30.

Smith-Rosenberg, Carroll. "The Female World of Love and Ritual." *Signs* 1 (1975): 1–29.

Strasser, Susan. *Never Done: A History of American Housework*. New York: Pantheon Books, 1982.

Sutherland, Daniel E. "Modernizing Domestic Service." *American Home Life, 1880–1930: A Social History of Spaces and Services*. Ed. Jessica H. Foy and Thomas J. Schlereth. Knoxville: U of Tennessee P, 1992.

Index

About the Author

MELISSA McFARLAND PENNELL is Professor of English at the University of Massachusetts, Lowell, where she coordinates its American Studies Program. She is the author of the *Student Companion to Nathaniel Hawthorne* (Greenwood, 1999) as well as numerous articles on a variety of American writers.